GunDigest
SHOOTER'S GUIDE TO THE
1911

by Robert K. Campbell

Published by

Gun Digest® Books, an imprint of F+W Media, Inc.
Krause Publications • 700 East State Street • Iola, WI 54990-0001
715-445-2214 • 888-457-2873
www.krausebooks.com

To order books or other products call toll-free 1-800-258-0929
or visit us online at www.krausebooks.com, www.gundigeststore.com
or www.Shop.Collect.com

ISBN-13: 978-1-4402-1434-9
ISBN-10: 1-4402-1434-4

Cover Design by Tom Nelsen
Designed by Paul Birling
Edited by Dan Shideler

Printed in United States of America

DEDICATION / ACKNOWLEDGMENTS

First, thank the Lord for what talent I have earned in life and the opportunity to share my experiences with some of the most wonderful people in the world, my readers.

To my children – Robert Alan, Matthew Henry and Bobbie Ann – who are always a challenge or inspiration;

To my wonderful daughters in law: Jennifer, a wonderful teacher and mother and always a constant for her family; and Emily, veteran, citizen warrior and mother;

To my grandchildren: Skye, Ryan and Amber;

And to Carol, who is not especially interested in the shooting sports but is always interested in my success.

As I have been blessed, I hope you, the reader, may be also.

Robert Campbell
South Carolina
Summer 2010

CONTENTS

INTRODUCTION

andguns have played an important role in personal defense, warfare and law enforcement for hundreds of years. The first handguns were simple iron tubes filled with gunpowder ignited by a match. Progress followed first with the flintlock, the cap lock and then the revolver. While a handgun is far less accurate and powerful than a rifle, the light weight and handy size of the handgun make it portable, comfortable to carry and available at a moment's notice.

The handgun is a defensive weapon designed to allow a defender to take control of a situation. The element of surprise in the inherent ability to conceal a handgun has saved many lives. However, only an exceptional handgun may be used as an offensive tool. The 1911 pistol is among a very few handguns that have been used successfully in this manner in warfare. The first offensive use of American handguns came when, first, the single-shot cavalry pistol

There are many idioms in handguns, including, top to bottom, the double action revolver, the safe action Glock and the 1911. The author maintains that there is no combat handgun that is as efficient as the 1911 pistol.

The 1911 was used by mounted cavalry in the Punitive Expedition against Pancho Villa of 1916-1917. Earlier U.S. horse soldiers used the M1873 Single Action Army.

replaced the saber as a cavalry weapon, a role that was later assumed by the revolver. The first large-scale use of the handgun as a sidearm suitable for tactical use began during the Mexican-American War, when the first Colt revolvers proved their mettle in the hands of Americans on horseback. Colt handguns continued to play a part in cavalry charges for 70 years. The Colt revolvers were handy, light, hard hitting, quickly deployable and reliable. No other firearm of the day could match the reputation and effectiveness of the Colt.

The occasional brilliant military use of the pistol is always interesting, but the primary role of the handgun is personal defense. The handgun is a weapon of opportunity that may be carried at all times in anticipation of trouble. Normally, it requires planning and forethought to arm oneself with a long gun. The handgun is a secondary firearm to the rifle in hunting. In competition the handgun competes in events designed to test the mettle of both the handgun and the handgunner. In this arena men and women test their determination, build defensive skills, or simply be all they can be. The self defense aspect is there but sometimes competition is undertaken for its own sake. I am not a doctrinaire on connecting competition to defensive skills. Sport shooting is a good thing. Many of these shooters are outstanding athletes. The 1911 has proven by far and away the most popular and capable of all competitive handguns.

Handguns are fascinating functionally and operationally. Historically handguns have been used to pre-serve the Republic. Simple pride of ownership is reason enough for owning the handgun, giving it a value beyond the practical. My handgun is the 1911. The term 1911 once meant the Colt Army gun but now the term encompasses dozens of makers and numerous variations of the 1911 theme. There is no handgun that suits me as well as the 1911. I have been taken to task as to this choice more than once but no matter how the argument is planned or how skillfully the opponent measures his skill at linguistic jousting, he cannot persuade me to feel any differently from how I feel at this moment. Every year that goes by reinforces my faith in the 1911 pistol and in fact it seems that more and better 1911s are yet to come.

Here is the world's most reliable handgun in action.

Note the blinding speed of operation with the 1911.

The 1911 demands practice. This shooter is wringing out the Kimber .45.

I did not arbitrarily choose the 1911. I did not choose the 1911 because it is a good looking gun or because it was expected of me. I recognized the 1911 for what it is. You simply cannot undermine the persuasive evidence in favor of the 1911. If a Smith and Wesson Model 10 .38 Special revolver had been the *ne plus ultra* of handguns I would have kept my old heavy barrel Military and Police. But it wasn't. The Browning High Power wasn't, either, and the low-bid polymer frame guns are not. The 1911 offered the best combination of fighting pistol attributes of anything I have tested. The term "synergy" comes to mind. Synergy is simply the interaction between elements or forces in a manner that makes the combination of these elements more effective than the individual elements operating separately. While I favor the 1911, I have not avoided firing every other type of handgun. I have gone through case lots of ammunition in testing all types of firearms. I do not believe I wasted the ammunition because I learned a great deal about handgun construction and performance.

Handgun geometry is rather simple. The grip has to be comfortable and the controls in ready reach of the digits. The grip should be angled to present the sights toward the target. Pretty simple, but there is little natural point in most handguns. I discovered the 1911 early in my quest but just the same I continued to test other handguns. After 40 years of experimentation I have come to the conclusion that nothing equals the 1911 in the important particulars. Few handguns even approach the deadly efficiency of the 1911 in trained hands.

With the 1911 the best at what it does, we are led to ask what a handgun should do. The handgun is a personal defense weapon pure and simple. A threat is not enough and the mere presence of a handgun is not enough. The handgun must be brought into action quickly and strike a powerful blow with some degree of accuracy. Speed and power are not negotiable but accuracy requirements are dependent upon the mission. I have seen few 1911s that are not accurate enough to save your life even at a long 50 yards. When you are under the terrifying oppression of fear, a 1911 is a great equalizer.

The 1911 features an ideal blend of weight and balance. The cartridge is the most powerful we are likely to be able to control well in a 40-ounce handgun and does well in handguns appreciably lighter than that. The bore axis or the height of the middle of the bore above the hand is low enough that muzzle flip is limited. There is little leverage for the muzzle to rise. The controls are in the ideal location for rapid and sure manipulation.

This young woman is practicing night fire with the SIG GSR.

The Springfield Super Tuned is carried in a Nick Matthews holster. This is a good kit.

The trigger press is straight to the rear. The single action trigger is among the great advantages of the 1911 handgun; it's well suited for service use and may be tuned to a very crisp letoff. Durability of the 1911 is unquestioned. The 1911 may be broken or mishandled but it will outlast all but the most dedicated competition shooters. The pistol will stand tons of abuse and continue to operate. I have seen pistols with cracked frames and a broken barrel bushing continue to function.

The modern 1911 is a far different pistol than the one introduced in 1911 to the Army and available commercially in 1912. Just the same a trooper who served in Mexico would instantly recognize the modern 1911 pistol. The 1911 is an enigma. A contemporary of the Ford Model T the 1911 has outlived its competition. The pistol is a milestone of engineering expertise. The pistol is as accurate as anyone can hold in its best examples. The 1911 fits most hands well with a natural feel that seems inspired. Let me expound a little. The grip you affirm with the 1911 handgun allows you to take control of the handgun, aim it correctly and recover the pistol from recoil. The barrel should line up with the forearm and

help propagate the locked wrist. The 1911 meets these requirements. Remember, once you have acquired the grip in the holster you have to live with it throughout the firing sequence. There is nothing that feels like the 1911 and no grip as comfortable to the human hand.

Over the years I have interviewed many gunfight survivors. Those who used the .38 Special, the .357 Magnum or a 9mm will relate the tactics they used and tell you what they did to survive. "I did this and prevailed" or "I managed to survive" are the common quotes. Those who use the 1911 will tell you that the gun saved their lives. They used the pistol competently but the awesome efficiency of the 1911 stood them well. Trainers tell us that shooters often perform at a fraction of their "range capacity" when they are engaged in a life or death incident. I believe that trained shooters retain far more of their learned capacity during a critical incident when they have trained with the 1911. A rough trigger and a grip that doesn't fit well are easily overcome on the range with practice and dedication, and you are lured into false confidence. You may feel you are good enough for any defensive need. But are you?

This is the author's personal and often-carried Series 70 Commander and Milt Sparks holster.

The 1911 is simply a different breed. I have little patience with detractors of the 1911. They do not understand the equations involved and often have their own agenda contrary to logic. The 1911 is not a he-man's gun nor is it possessed of arcane properties. It is a good gun that men or women of average physical and mental ability may use well. In trained hands the 1911 is a fighting handgun without equal. Do not let anyone convince you another modern handgun is the fast track to proficiency. The 1911 is the jet stream.

A factor that many of us give much weight is the fact that 1911 is an American design used by American soldiers for many years and still in service. Compared to the modern low-bid polymer frame pistol, the 1911 represents individuality. You may customize the 1911, personalize it or paint it camouflage. It is still a 1911 – and it's the finest fighting handgun ever built.

BACKGROUND OF THE 1911

Chapter 1:

It has been said that the War Between the States was the first great pistol war. In addition to a variety of now-forgotten revolvers such as Pettingills and Forehand and Wadsworths, cavalry troopers had the six-shot Colt Navy or preferably the Colt Army revolver. Many cavalrymen carried five or six revolvers if they could afford this personal battery. Fast-moving actions demanded a repeating firearm and one that could be used from horseback. While the Spencer was more accurate and hit harder than any handgun, this repeating rifle was difficult to use from the mounted position.

The Colt revolver was the ideal one-hand fighting pistol. The earlier horse pistol allowed a trooper to express his will just past saber range. The Colt revolver extended his range well past 50 yards. I have fired reproductions of the Colt 1860 Army .44 revolver. I have never fired an original Colt, so I cannot comment on the difference in quality. The Dixie Gun

More than any other conflict in American history, the Civil War demonstrated the tactical importance of the military handgun.

The Colt 1860 was a great combat handgun in its day.

11

The Single Action Army is still a popular type. This is a USFA Rodeo.

Works steel frame example I have been testing in doing historical research has been very interesting, often producing a five-shot group of one inch at 15 yards when properly loaded. I have managed to work up loads of nearly 900 fps, although this is stressful to a revolver with the basic .36 caliber frame. The .44 caliber Army hit hard. The soft lead ball expanded in flesh, particularly if it hit bone, and produced excellent wound ballistics. The caliber was effective against large animals at short range. Period reports praise the Colt Army. It was exceedingly powerful.

Earlier Colt revolvers were far less effective and less reliable. The famous Colt Navy revolver was a .36 caliber. The .36 Colt was often effective at short range if the soft lead ball expanded. The effect was similar to a modern .38 Special loaded with hollow point ammunition. At longer ranges a loss of velocity resulted in less expansion. The .36 conical ball was less effective. The Colt was accurate enough to strike an Indian war pony at 100 yards but not always powerful enough to drop the pony or the rider. The .44 Walker and Dragoon revolvers were answers to this problem. The big Colts were far too large and bulky for easy carry but they were awesome weapons of war.

I believe that the Colt revolver made westward expansion possible. Prior to the introduction of the Colt revolver, a man armed with a single shot muzzle loader was at the mercy of two or more Indians or bandits. The Colt revolver made a thinking man a match for several adversaries. The value of the Colt revolver was well proven during the Mexican war, although few of the new large caliber Walker revolvers actually made it to the

By 1905, Browning had something going on with the .45 automatic.

front lines. It was common for Texas Rangers to carry two Colt revolvers and sometimes a pair of large caliber horse pistols in addition to their rifle. They were well armed indeed.

After the War Between the States, much development was underway in the field of cartridge firing handguns. The advantages of a cartridge that contained the bullet, primer and powder in one package were obvious. There were many proprietary cartridges and handguns. At the time, if you purchased a Remington you purchased Remington ammunition and the same was true of the Colt. It was the awesome effectiveness of the .45 Colt cartridge and the utility of the .44-40 Winchester cartridge that created a market for a universal service cartridge. Cartridges such as the .44 Remington and the

Merwin and Hulbert rounds died off. The Army service pistol introduced in 1873 became a standard for peace officers, soldiers and outlaws. The Colt Single Action Army was a gate loading single action that proved rugged and reliable on the frontier. The greatest advantage of the SAA was its cartridge. The .45 Colt cartridge was offered in different power levels over the years and began life with a drawn copper cartridge, but suffice to say it was more powerful than any other common loading on the frontier. 250 grains at 900 feet per second is the often quoted figure and my testing with modern black powder loads confirms this.

The .45 Colt produces excellent wound ballistics. Bullet expansion does not matter; the .45 takes its effect from its caliber and mass. The .45 Colt cartridge proved the measure of man and beast. While the crude sights of the SAA were a limiting factor, the Colt SAA, like the earlier revolvers, was capable of striking an Indian war pony at 100 yards in trained hands, the standard I have used in testing 19th century martial firearms. The Colt continued to be a favorite of law enforcement well into the 1940s. The Single Action Army is light for the caliber, handy, and packs real power. In the real world carry you may pack a 4-3/4-inch barrel SAA .45 about as easily as a 4-inch barrel .38 caliber double action revolver.

With a nod of respect to the double action revolver, I understand why old western types continued to deploy the .45. I think that a skilled person is well armed with the SAA .45. It is lighter than comparable double action big bore revolvers and the plow handled grip frame is more comfortable to fire with heavy loads. Interestingly, during this time, the second favorite cartridge of the SAA man was the .44-40 WCF, usually for use in the Winchester carbine, making a fine combination. This

The .45 Colt, left, may be said to have inspired the .45 ACP, right.

is one of the first incidences of specific cartridges for military and civilian users being marketed and becoming popular.

About 1890, the Army made a terrible mistake in handgun selection. We may only wonder what they were thinking. The Colt Model 1892 was among the first of the modern swing out cylinder double action trigger revolvers. While the swing out cylinder and double action trigger are desirable for combat use, the Colt 1892 was a relatively fragile pistol. The action used was not dissimilar to that of the Colt Model 1877 Lightning, a handgun not noted for reliability. While there were various detail improvements during its production life, the Colt 1892 was never a reliable revolver and prone

Left to right—9mm Luger, .38 Special, .44-40 Winchester, .44 Special, .45 Colt and .45 ACP. The author feels that the .45 ACP is by far the most useful.

At the time of the Spanish-American war, the official U.S. Army handgun was the M1873 Single Action Army. Teddy Roosevelt, however, carried a Colt M1889 Double Action Navy .38.

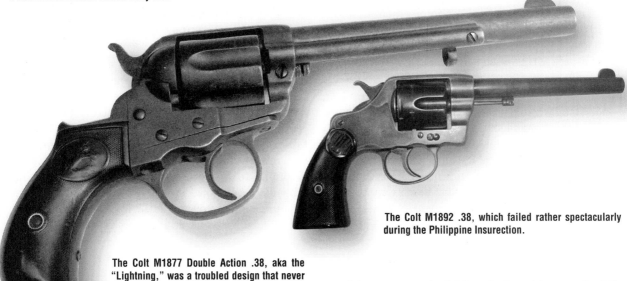

The Colt M1892 .38, which failed rather spectacularly during the Philippine Insurection.

The Colt M1877 Double Action .38, aka the "Lightning," was a troubled design that never gained military acceptance.

to breakage. Equally as damning, the Colt chambered a pipsqueak cartridge. The .38 Colt fired a 152-grain bullet at 750 fps. This cartridge was inadequate for use in combat against men, much less war horses, and it was useless for foraging.

The Army apparently felt that as a badge of office or to direct troops, the Colt .38 was as good as any other handgun. The situation came to a head when our troops were sent to the Philippines to deal with the Philippine Insurrection first and later to do battle with the Moros. Historical research points out that the pistol was a failure in the battlefield. The Colt .38 was appallingly ineffective. My judgment is not harsh, and I came to this conclusion from reading shocking and frightening field reports.

I have researched historical archives and while the prospect of wading through these archives is tiring, it is very important. Much of the research deals with the great men of the past and the sometimes inadequate arms they were saddled with. A quote from Sergeant Matt McGhee of the Rough Riders tells us the Colt .38 was "worthless" even though the Colonel – that Colonel being Theodore Roosevelt – carried the "damn Navy .38." McGhee also had harsh words for the side loading gate of the Krag rifle, another problematic weapon. If anyone doubts the pistol was an important weapon, the after action reports of the period show many pistol actions.

In the Philippines, US forces ended slavery, built hospitals roads and schools, and generally attempted to civilize the island. Muslim inhabitants, the Moros, attacked our forces. Ending the slave trade was a major affront to the Moro leaders. There were many suicide

Teddy Roosevelt at the summit of San Juan Hill.

Webb Hayes

General Leonard Wood, Roosevelt's superior officer.

Allen J Greer

Paul Straub

fighters who fought until killed and never retreated. The battles were often horrendous. After action reports are not difficult to study, and give great insight into pistol battles. Here are a few reports from Cuba and the Philippines:

In Cuba: Private William Profit saw a nice looking pearl-handled machete he wished to retrieve from the battlefield when he was attacked. Private Profit reported, "I was glad to have that old .45 [the Colt SAA]. Just a couple of shots and he went down for good."

In the Philippines: Allen J. Greer charged the enemy with his pistol, killing one and wounding two, capturing three more on July 2, 1901;

Lt. Colonel William Grove charged seven enemy, killing or capturing all, while using a pistol; and

Paul Straub in 1899 was awarded a medal for his actions using "pistol fire."

Webb Hayes, son of former President Rutherford B. Hayes, carried a double action Colt .45 [probably an early New Service] during his time in the Philippines. General Leonard Wood carried a Smith and Wesson .44 caliber double action revolver. Many soldiers were glad to have the Colt .45 when the pistol was rushed to the Philippines after reports of the failure of the Colt .38.

Why was there so much action with the pistol? We were an occupying force in the Philippines, and rear area troops were always armed with a pistol when it was not convenient to carry a long gun.

Rear areas were a place of ambush. The Indians attempted to ambush supply lines and so did the Moros. In one incident reported by historian David S Woodman,

"A *juramentado* [a male Moro warrior who specifically targeted Christians] at Zamboango, hit in seven different places by revolver shots, nevertheless reached an American officer and sliced off one of his legs."

The first really successful military autoloader, the 7.63mm Mauser C96.

The Colt M1905, the immediate ancestor of the 1911.

U.S. Army Chief of Ordnance Gen. William Crozier, who authorized the testing of a new pistol to replace the Colt .38 and .45 revolvers.

There were really two Philippine wars, the first against the Philippine residents who wished independence for the Philippines. This conflict was a result of McKinley's annexation of the Philippines, but it was settled early on with minimal bloodshed. The Filipinos became our allies. The second war, the one against the Moros, was a different matter altogether. Moros could not tolerate non-Moros and attacked at every opportunity. They were hard to stop. The Winchester 97 12 gauge pump shotgun was the preferred weapon by many reports but the .45 revolver and the Springfield .30-06, when introduced, made a great difference. The 1911 saw its first action in the Philippines at Bud Bagask in 1913. But we are getting ahead of the story.

Beginning with the Mauser 1896, gifted inventors introduced modern self-loading handguns to the military scene. The United States was still armed with a gate loading single action revolver that, while rugged and hard hitting, was little advanced from Civil War revolvers when compared to the Mauser pistol. The Luger also made a great impression when introduced a few years after the Mauser. In light of the effectiveness of the .45

and the weak showing of the .38, the Army knew exactly what they wanted: a self-loading handgun that fired a cartridge as similar as possible to the .45 Colt. The Army test program lasted over five years, more if you count experiments with the issue of 1,000 German Lugers in .30 Luger beginning about 1903 and later a smaller number in 9mm Luger caliber. The evolution of the Colt pistols was important. The Colt 1900 in .38 ACP was the first step. John Moses Browning designed a workable and reliable self-loading pistol chambered for a small bore cartridge. The following years saw the elimination of dual barrel links in favor of a single link and an improved safety demanded by the US Cavalry. The Cavalry was a tremendously influential department in those days and demanded a slide lock safety and grip safety, among other features. The slide lock safety operated upon the sear and the grip safety blocked the trigger. These were important safety features for men who fought on horseback. If dropped, the grip safety sprung into the safe position and the Colt would not fire. Other requirements centered on speed. The pistol had to be easily reloaded from horseback and had to be reliable above all else.

Savage and Luger, among others, submitted .45-caliber entries in the Army trial, generally similar to the .32 and .30 versions shown here.

A number of competitors challenged Colt but in the end none came close to the reliability of the original 1911. The final model of what came to be known as the 1911 was tested in March of 1911. The pistol would have to fire 6,000 rounds without a stoppage. The gun would be immersed in mud and sand during various stages. The pistol was dunked in a bucket of water in order to cool down when it became too hot to hold from firing. The Colt 1911 passed with flying colors, according to the test report.

The original 1911 was very similar to the modern 1911. The pistol weighed 40 ounces, was 8.25 inches long and 5.25 inches tall. The magazine held seven rounds and the sights were regulated for 230-grain ball ammunition, firing a little high at 25 yards and regulated for 50 yard hits. The 1911 pistol was adopted by the United States Army and was on its way to becoming a legend. The men who designed the 1911 observed and interpreted. The 1911 was a shared vision of what a fighting pistol should be. Browning, Colt's engineers and the U. S. Army produced a pistol that was easy to use well but hit hard – a velvet-covered brick, one might say. But no handgun is proven until it is blooded.

EARLY ACTIONS

Chapter Two:

The 1911 was proven within months of its adoption. We may only imagine the first impression of troops issued the new Army .45. The pistol not only fed itself but it unloaded itself as each spent case was ejected on firing. The 1911 cocked itself and allowed the individual soldier to concentrate upon marksmanship rather than manipulation.

The 1911 arrived just at a cusp of firearms development. The Colt 1895 machinegun was in wide use and the airplane was used for scouting. Soon the 1911 would see action in a theater that in many ways was the worst ever faced by U. S. troops. the war in the Philippines. The Moro uprising was an Islamic jihad at its worst. The Moros were slave traders and pirates of known ferocity. In this cauldron of blood and death, the 1911 was born.

This is the pistol that began the legacy- an original and well used Colt 1918, .45 ACP.

Frank Luke, the Arizona Balloon Buster, who fought it out on the ground with his 1911 after being shot down by the Germans.

Pancho Villa, who gave "Black Jack" Pershing the slip. March 9, 1916, Villa makes a surprise attack on Columbus, New Mexico. Villa's foolhardy incursion results in retaliation on March 14 when General John Pershing enters Mexico with a "Punitive Expedition" to hunt for Villa. Pershing's expedition remains in Mexico until February 1917.

Pancho Villa and his Villistas. Villa kept his men south of the border to avoid a direct confrontation with the U.S. Army forces.

Gen. "Black Jack" Pershing, a force to be reckoned with.

Maj. Robert L. Howse

Mexico

The Colt came into its own during the Mexican Punitive Expedition (1916-17) against Pancho Villa and led by General Pershing. Pershing was an intelligent man who was among the last Army commanders who fought the Indian. He learned Indian sign and spoken language and took great care to ably represent his country. He was an effective commander against Moros in the Philippines. The General suffered the heartbreaking loss of his wife and three daughters in a house fire just before his expedition to Mexico, but he finished the task at hand. The pistol his troops used, the 1911, had been blooded in the Philippines but along with radio and air communication, was first used heavily in Mexico. Forms of communication and aircraft changed many times but the 1911 remained.

As early as 1913 the United States was ready to engage Mexico to combat political and military unrest. In 1916 Pancho Villa's bandits attacked Columbus New Mexico. This force of 1,000 bandits was stopped by the US Army but twenty four Americans died. The Army invaded Mexico to punish Villa, hence the term "punitive expedition." Among the great actions of the war was the last American cavalry charge. Major Robert L. Howze commanded the second squadron, Provisional, of the 11th United States Cavalry. While on patrol Howze's men were attacked at Ojo Azules by Villa's bandits. Against all odds Howze's men made a charge and 42 Villaistas were

WWI "No Man's Land," the ultimate proving ground for any military handgun.

German barrage balloon of the type so successfully perforated by Frank Luke.

Both of these are reproductions – a 1918 Colt and a 1918 trench knife.

Pvt. John Kelly, USMC.

killed with no American casualties. The majority of the fighting was done with .45 automatic pistols. During the First World War other actions occurred along the Mexican border, often spurred by German agents. One such action took place at Nogales in 1918. Even after the war, fighting took place at La Grulla, Texas, in August 1918 and in El Paso in 1919. The 1911 had been blooded in Mexico but the greater challenge was in Europe.

World War I

When Americans arrived in Europe in 1917, the Germans targeted American divisions in hopes that the United States would have no stomach for such a war and leave. The Germans found they could not advance nearly as closely to the Americans as they had to Allied forces without coming under punishing accurate rifle fire. The Springfield and Enfield rifles were the great weapons of this war, but the 1911 proved its worth time and again. Field reports of the day provide brief, tantalizing glimpses of the 1911's pivotal role: Marine Lt. Overton's last charge took place with a .45 in one hand and a cane in the other. Private John Kelly, USMC, gave a whooping war cry as the young hero from Chicago threw a grenade into a German machine gun nest, then shot a German with his 1911. Frank Luke, the Arizona Balloon Buster, was shot down and fought to the last, engaging German troops at 50 yards with his 1911 before being killed on the ground.

Cpl. Alvin York

The Meuse-Argonne offensive, was the biggest operation and victory by American Forces in World War I. It was during the opening of this operation, on October 8, 1918 that Corporal (later Sergeant) Alvin York made his famous capture of 132 German prisoners.

U.S. Troops in the Haitian "Banana Wars," c.1915

Sgt. Herman Hanneken

Cpl. William Button

By far the best known American hero of World War I was Sgt. Alvin York. A corporal at the time of his exploits, York was a Christian man of unquestioned principle. His exploits are worthy of the Medal of Honor he received, but other marksmen have accomplished similar feats. York was engaged with a German unit that included machine gun nests. He killed at least 25 Germans that day and captured 132. At one point his .30-06 rifle had become too hot to fire and was put aside. York was charged by a German detachment with bayonets fixed that had managed to sneak behind him. York fired his 1911 at the last man first, so that the lead man would not stop to fire at York. He dropped seven men with seven shots.

Haiti

Haiti was a particularly nasty hellhole for the hard-bitten Marine veterans trying to hunt down ruthless bandits during the "Banana Wars" of 1915-1934. Sgt. Herman Hanneken and Corporal William Button found their way into the camp of a bandit leader. They worked with a local gendarme who pretended to be a traitor. Hanneken wore a pair of concealed 1911s. Penetrating to the center of the camp, Hanneken slammed two .45s into the leader's chest. Button cut down the bodyguards with his BAR. Not long after, Sgt. Albert Taubert took out the bandit Batraville with a 1911. The .45 saw heavy use in Haiti.

Lt. Col. Robert Cole

Corpsman Robert E Bush

Sgt. Darrell Cole

U.S. Troops at the Douve River bridgehead, June 1944.

The "Hot Rocks" at Iwo Jima.

World War II

The second world war was the greatest conflict in which the United States has ever been involved, and it was here that the 1911 really came into its own. Though it's tempting to pause here at length, a few examples must suffice.

Lt. Colonel Robert Cole led forces in France when he found himself in a pinned down position. He drew his .45 and instigated a charge that carried the day, establishing a bridgehead on the Douve River.

Sgt. Darrell Cole was in action at Iwo Jima when he used hand grenades and the 1911 to take out enemy pillboxes. Robert Bush was a corpsman on Okinawa. He was administering plasma to a soldier when the Japa-

nese, at least six in number, charged Bush. He fired his .45 until it was empty and also found and used a .30 carbine to kill at least six Japanese. He lost an eye but he and his charge survived.

Among the hardest-fought actions involving a single soldier in World War II took place in Heckhuscheid, Germany in 1945. Corporal Edward Bennett's unit was held down by enemy fire. Bennett crept into a house in which Germans were barricaded. He killed a sentry with his knife and then killed three with carbine fire. Another was clubbed to death. He then drew his 1911 and killed three more. He was awarded the Medal of Honor for "stalwart combat ability and fearless initiative.'"

The Japanese were not the only danger in the Pa-

Heckhuscheid, Germany, scene of Cpl. Edward Bennett's one-man war.

Cpl. Edward Bennett

Japanese Mitsubishi A6m Zero.

This WW II .45 has seen a great deal of use. GI's used thousands of these pistols on the battlefield.

B24 Liberator of the type flown by 2nd. Lt. Owen Baggett.

2nd. Lt. Owen Baggett, who actually shot down a japanese Zero with a 1911.

cific. A headhunter attacked a sleeping airman in one incident. A comrade fired twice with a .30 caliber carbine with no effect, as the native bore down with a long knife. Lt. Walt Hagan dropped the headhunter with a single round of 230-grain ball from his 1911.

The following report is so incredible that it sounds suspect, but all of my independent research accounts for the veracity of this incident. Second Lt. Owen Baggett was shot down in the Pacific theater of operations. As was often the case the Japanese proceeded to machine-gun survivors as they hung by their parachute. (It was necessary to feather the propeller and fly slowly in this gruesome operation, which also increased the rate of fire of the cowl mounted 7.7mm guns. The slower the prop's revolution, the greater the rate of fire.) Baggett's arm was grazed on the first pass. Zero pilots often flew with the canopy open at slow speed, and Baggett took aim with his .45 and fired four shots into the Mitsubishi's cockpit. The Zero crashed. Baggett was captured and the Japanese informed him that the crashed Zero held a pilot with a .45 caliber hole in his head. (Baggett survived the war, by the way.) A similar incident occurred in the final days of the European war. An American Piper Cub observation plane confronted its opposite number, a German Storch, over Allied lines. The Ameri-

The 1911, below, has progressed greatly. The upper pistol is arguably one of the best of the 1911s, the Les Baer Monolith.

Whatever the 1911 once did, it could do today. Top photo, Bushmaster AR 15 and Springfield LW Operator. Below, Springfield 1903A3 and Colt 1918.

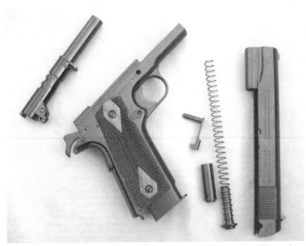

The 1911 is easily field stripped for routine maintenance. The author believes that a 1911 destined for the battlefield should be simple today as well and uncomplicated by FLGRs and the like.

The 1911 continued to serve well in Vietnam and serves in other battles every day.

can pilots unloaded on the Storch with their .45s, causing the plane to land.

These stories are often questioned by modern writers but I wonder why. Anyone who questions the fighting ability of the American soldier and the .45 automatic needs to tell it to the Marines. But he won't like the response. The American fighting man, armed with a good handgun like the 1911, can do the impossible.

A CARTRIDGE OF INTEREST

Chapter 3:

General S.V. Benet, U.S. Army Chief of Ordnance and father of the .45 Colt cartridge, who specified a 45-caliber centerfire way back in 1873.

The development of the 1911 pistol would not have so dramatic without the .45 Automatic Colt Pistol cartridge. The 1911 would have been just another pistol if offered in a small bore cartridge, although a very good pistol. The .45 ACP is among a few handgun cartridges scientifically planned and designed with anti-personnel performance in mind. Many pistols were designed simply for small size and light weight; with the .45 ACP, practical and mechanical properties were foremost.

The .45 ACP is a great cartridge not only on the anti-personnel score but also on a ballistic efficiency scale. Relatively modest charges

When you use high quality, standard pressure loads, wear and tear is of little consequence with the 1911 .45.

The Model 1873 Single Action Army in .45 Colt, the first cartridge revolver adopted by the U. S. Army.

Gen. John T. Thompson, head of the Army pistol trials and designer of the Thompson submachine gun.

of fast burning powder will propel a .451" bullet to high velocity with modest pressure. In properly configured handguns such as the Kimber Gold Match, the 1911 will produce superb accuracy. Lesser 1911s will prove adequate and modestly priced handguns often produce good accuracy. In a properly formulated personal defense loading such as the Black Hills 230-grain JHP, muzzle signature is subdued. Only a few sparks are evident on firing. An accuracy load such as the Black Hills 230-grain RNL may be as accurate as any combination of powder and lead are capable of.

The cartridge has been drafted into competition and target use. The .45 ACP maintains sufficient accuracy to 50 yards to give excellent results in target competition. The .45 ACP will do well in the hunting field at 35 yards or so. Remember, the .45 ACP was intended to be powerful enough to drop a war horse at moderate range. There is no unchecked theory or guesswork inherent in the design. The .45 ACP is not a great hunting cartridge like the .44 Magnum but will do the business on deer or wild boar at close ranges with good loads. (The Hornady 230-grain XTP +P is one example.) The many advantages of the cartridge are not immediately obvious without a working knowledge of ballistics.

The typical GI .45 with ball ammunition is a very efficient handgun. This is a reliable combination, accurate enough for the task, and a combination with a guaranteed propensity to perform well after long, hard

use. The 1911 does not lend itself to catastrophic failure. It gives you warning when it becomes worn. A Kimber Gold Combat with Black Hills jacketed hollow point ammunition is a great personal defense combination, but a GI .45 with Winchester service ball is formidable as well. A Colt Gold Cup with a handload featuring the Oregon Trail 200-grain SWC at 800 fps will cut a single ragged hole at 25 yards. The 1911 .45 is well mannered and useful, among one of the most versatile handguns ever made. There are cartridges of similar power, such as the .44 Special and the .45 Colt, but they do not couple their power with the self-loading action.

The grandfather of the .45 ACP cartridge was Steven Benet, U.S. Army Chief of Ordnance in 1873. When the Single Action Army revolver was being developed, Benet looked over the hodgepodge of .44 and .45 caliber cartridges in both rimfire and centerfire variations and demanded a centerfire .45 caliber cartridge. All then in production were lacking in one way or another. Realizing the importance of the revolver in action against aboriginal tribes and enemy cavalry, Benet wanted our troops to be well armed with an effective revolver. The .45 Colt cartridge was the result. The .45 Colt performed so well for so long against so many adversaries it became a model of performance. While world view and standards of esteem may change, the non-stop issues of life do not. The cartridge offered performance unlikely to be exceeded by a controllable handgun. Even today, many prefer a heavily loaded .45 Colt to the .44 Magnum. I am one of these. Benet's vision is alive and well today.

When John Moses Browning began to develop self loading pistols, he first designed pocket pistols. The .25 Automatic Colt Pistol, the .32 ACP and the .380 ACP are still popular. The .38 ACP is roughly equal to the 9mm

Whether used with ball ammo, left, or 230- or 185-grain JHP bullets from Hornady, the .45 ACP is a formidable cartridge.

Luger. None were efficient service cartridges. Colonel John T. Thompson (of later Thompson submachine gun fame) was instrumental in working to design a self-loading cartridge that approximated the power of the .45 Colt cartridge. Thompson also set on the Ordnance board that approved the 1911 pistol. Thompson was also instrumental in unprecedented wartime delivery of goods during the Spanish American War and a genius of manufacture and Ordnance during World War I.

There was experimentation with cartridge length (settling upon a .900"-long cartridge case) and extractor groove diameter but the .45 ACP was available in its modern form in 1905. The .45 ACP cartridge is more efficient than the .45 Colt, but slightly less powerful. The standard operating pressure of the .45 ACP is 18,000 pounds per square inch. At this pressure the .45 ACP

will jolt a 230-grain bullet at 830 fps, while the .45 Colt will send a 250-grain bullet out of the muzzle at 800 fps at only 12,000 psi. But the .45 ACP uses less powder to achieve the same velocity and offers subdued muzzle flash. I would rather look at a cartridge on its own merits than engage in comparison, but we will note that the 9mm Luger, .357 SIG and .40 Smith and Wesson operate at well over 30,000 pounds per square inch pressure.

The .45 ACP's .451" bullet is well balanced, with plenty of bearing surface to ensure proper engagement with the rifling. Practically any bullet weight from 152 to 260 grains will give good accuracy with proper load practice. Despite improvements and modifications to the cartridge, when most of us think .45 ACP we think of the original 230-grain ball loading. This loading has a tremendous reputation for effectiveness. I have researched shooting results for more than 30 years. The process has been a pursuit full of pain and labor. Affording a close view of cartridge effectiveness isn't easy. You begin with newspaper and police reports.

According to my research, the .45 is not infallible but represents a good choice for personal defense. An important distinction must be made between personal observation and studying after action reports. When a cop tells you he has seen something, he means he arrived just after the action was over or when the people were still running around, not necessarily something he saw over his own sights. When you arrive at a scene and the victim is still mobile after being perforated by small caliber bullets, that is a significant outcome you use to form some type of opinion. When you arrive and a body is silent with a single wound you have respect for the cartridge. (Most often you cannot tell the difference between calibers by the entrance hole with one exception: the full power .357 Magnum often produces an entrance wound resembling an exit wound.)

Just a few of the loads the .45 ACP uses well, left to right, 165-grain Cor Bon, 200-grain Oregon Trail handload, 230-grain Winchester FBI load, 230-grain Oregon Trail handload, 230-grain Gold Dot, 230-grain Cor Bon Performance Match, and 260-grain Buck Ammo.

With proper loads the .45 is effective against vehicle glass.

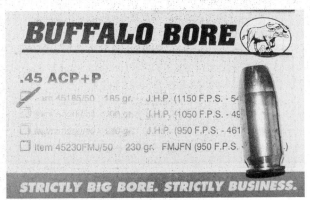

Buffalo Bore is synonymous with performance.

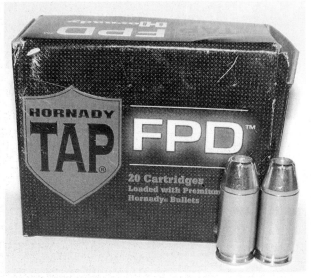

Hornady TAP loads have given excellent results in every test program.

The .45 1911 pistol supports the case head, keeping overly enthusiastic handloaders out of trouble most of the time. The round at right was fired in a Glock.

All cartridges have lethality. A body perforated by small bore bullets will not live long. A .22 caliber bullet possesses sufficient penetration to reach vital organs, but the immediate stop is not guaranteed. Lethality is irrelevant to the issue. The attacker must be stopped as soon as possible. A small bore bullet that completely penetrates the body may produce a killing wound but only after the person that was shot bleeds out. In the interim he may kill or injure innocent persons. A .45 in the arterial region is ideal but there is some evidence that a .45 to the shoulder, hips or other heavy bone will produce a rapid stop. Gaining a critical insight into wound ballistics requires some grappling with reality. The .45 ACP is a very consistent caliber. I would be surprised to see any .45 ACP load perform with the ferocity of a .357 Magnum but I would also be surprised to see it fail in the dismal manner the common small bores often do. There are cartridges more powerful than the .45 ACP, but they are difficult to control. They require considerable effort to master but they will never be as controllable as the .45 ACP. Those who cannot adapt to the self-loader may be ballistically secure in the .45 Colt but not as well prepared for action against multiple assailants. The big bore revolvers are also slower to present from the holster.

There have been various published studies that contradict the historical reputation of the big bore handguns. I have specifically studied the flaws in these studies, the chief one being that multiple hits are not factored out. Obviously in any such database, multiple hits make the small bores look better. There will be many more failures and multiple hits needed with the small bore cartridges. I do not think discussing these studies at length is profitable for the reader who is interested in facts. Suffice it to say that the best indicator of cartridge effectiveness, at least in a self-defense role, is its ability to produce one-shot stops. In this regard the .45 ACP is more than adequate.

Controlled Feed

A great advantage of the 1911 pistol is controlled feed. The cartridge is controlled from the time it is loaded in the magazine until it is ejected from the handgun. The cartridge is inserted in the feed lips of

The .45 offers plenty of velocity for spectacular test programs and real expansion.

the magazine. The magazine spring acts against the follower to maintain control of the cartridge. The feed lips hold the cartridge secure until the cocking block at the bottom of the slide catches the case rim and sends it toward the feed ramp. The bullet nose bumps into the feed ramp. The cartridge is stopped for a split second. At this point the cartridge case head is snugged into the extractor and against the breech face. The bullet then continues into the chamber. After the pistol fires the extractor brings the cartridge case out of the chamber and the ejector gives the cartridge a kick out of the ejection port. The controlled feed advantage of the 1911 results in a pistol that may be fired from any angle, even upside down, and it will perform normally as long as the proper secure grip is maintained. This is why a person who understands the advantages of the 1911 is not likely to wish to polish a feed ramp to enhance feeding. Too many modern handguns of the non 1911 type feature a relieved feed ramp that does not fully support the case head. I am not willing to modify the 1911 feed ramp and lose this controlled feed advantage.

Back to the cartridge: all ammunition makers must show a rational basis for their claims. Jacketed hollow point bullets must have advantages aside from wound ballistics. The expanding bullet will limit overpenetration and ricochet. A round nose bullet is ricochet city on a hard surface, but that's irrelevant in a combat environment. An expanding bullet will usually flatten and deform on a hard surface.

The .45 ACP has a balance of performance that is not a delicate one. A lightweight high velocity bullet or a slow heavy bullet may each give good results. I have performed comparative testing and alloyed these results with practical experience. This practical experience includes a dramatic failure of a popular 200-grain JHP that was the darling of the popular press in the day. This load dramatically underpenetrated, expanding to one inch and stopping in less than four inches of tough shoulder bone and muscle. I went back to 230-grain hardball after this incident. Interestingly, the Police Marksman's Association study showed that 230-grain loads of all stripes were considerably more effective than the 185-grain JHP. I respect the PMA study while taking its results as a suggestion rather than anything else but the PMA study opened its books to interested parties and the results actually made sense and reflected my own historical research. The PMA study came first and spurred my own research.

The Springfield GI .45 and Black Hills hollow points are a natural combination.

A requirement of personal defense ammunition that must never be compromised is penetration. If the adversary is firing with his arms outstretched toward you, the bullet may be required to penetrate the thick arm bones or heavy clothing to reach the vital blood bearing organs. When an adversary attempts to take your life you need an effective counter response, one that will not be put off by clothing or other intervening materials. The bullet must have adequate penetration and should expand to one and one half the original diameter of the bullet. This means a .45 ACP bullet should expand from .451" to .680".

There is more to the ammunition selection process than ballistic performance, however. I also check my personal defense ammunition in an exhaustive program. I soak a representative sample of the loads in oil, water and solvent. It must fire after being soaked all night. I check the integrity of the loading by chambering a single cartridge ten or twelve times. If the bullet is bumped back into the cartridge case, then cartridge case mouth seal is not adequate for personal defense. Carefully evaluate your chosen load. If the load is killed by water, oil, or solvent immersion, then it is a practice load only. At present the personal defense loads offered by Black Hills, CorBon, Hornady, Speer and Winchester are at the top of the heap in my testing, but they do not have a monopoly on quality. I simply have tested them thoroughly.

Handloading the .45 ACP

The .45 ACP is a joy to load. For economy you must handload to enjoy your hobby and to build skill and proficiency. The .45 ACP is a low pressure, straight-walled cartridge case that responds well to a careful handloader. Handloading does not require a great expenditure of funds to begin, but you need to obtain good quality equipment to enjoy the hobby. RCBS offers several beginner level kits that get the job done and offer real utility. I have used the RCBS Rockchucker press with excellent results for many years. An RCBS startup kit solves a lot of problems. Depending on the level of sustained toil you can endure, hundreds of handloads can be produced in the space of one evening. I have worked up a number of loads using economical cast bullets that give excellent economy and good accuracy. You can load for competition and accuracy or you can load a suitable bullet for hunting thin-skinned game.

The .45 ACP is decisive on coyote and the big cats at moderate range and may be used to take deer sized game to about 35 yards, given proper shot placement. In short, the .45 ACP cartridge is a cartridge of great interest. It is easily the most versatile of self-loading handgun cartridges and a thoroughly reliable cartridge in all its particulars.

HUMAN ENGINEERING

Chapter 4:

The 1911 was designed for serious business but it can be one of the all-time fun pistols as well.

We can compare handguns in many ways, but most comparisons are subjective. Some pistols are beautifully wrought and worth owning as an object with value far beyond the utilitarian. The Les Baer Monolith is among these.

Human engineering is an excellent predictor of performance. A pistol with good human engineering will encourage good shooter performance. The 1911 offers excellent human engineering. I have become used to the pistol and use it well, so you may argue I am simply familiar with the breed. But as a professional I often test other hand-

When running a .45 on demanding combat courses, the human engineering shows that nothing else handles like a 1911.

When you draw the pistol, the 1911 naturally lines up for excellent results on the firing range.

This teenager's first shots from a centerfire handgun were fired with the Commander .45. She did not flinch and enjoyed the shooting session.

The original flat mainspring housing is much easier to work with when you are using a beavertail grip safety.

gun types. I test all handguns objectively, but subjectively I often feel as if I am riding a Honda to the biker's meet in Sturgis when I test any other handgun. Some are close to the 1911 in hand fit, often by design. They are advertised not as having good hand fit but as having a grip similar to the 1911. Think about that one.

Some handguns may have one good feature or the other but none equals the 1911 in the overall package. The 1911 has had many competitors. Some of these had but a brief currency while others have managed to hang on. I fire them occasionally on a combat course and feel as if the pistol is limping along like a three legged dog. It isn't simply me; it's you, too, if you honestly give the 1911 its due. Nothing does it like the 1911 in trained hands. Even a ragged old GI gun, beautiful as a wart, will impress you on a combat course.

The 1911 offers excellent hand fit. The hand melts along the handle. The pistol feels comfortable in all adult hands. Trigger reach is comfortable, with the first pad of the finger landing on the trigger face in the ideal firing position. The 1911 does not overly stretch average size hands. The dynamics of trigger compression are seldom well understood when shooters address a handgun type. Fast and proven sight alignment depends upon a proper grip being taken as quickly as possible. The 1911 features a well shaped handle that allows rapid hand placement. The trigger offers straight to the rear trigger compression. A properly executed draw affords good hand placement and leads into the proper stance and the resulting proper sight picture. It is all interconnected.

The 1911's geometry lends itself well to fast work. Pressing a five pound trigger isn't a strain when the pistol weighs 40 ounces. Learning to use a double action first shot pistol is far more difficult. With the double action pistol the trigger finger begins above the trigger and moves downward and to the rear in an arc. The trigger action breaks the sear and the piece fires and then the hammer is cocked for a deliberate single action press. You must understand both trigger actions. This is far from ideal, but as Colonel Cooper often said, the double action first shot pistol is a good answer to a nonexistent problem.

The 1911's slide lock safety lies naturally under the thumb. When the pistol is handled, the safety is in the ideal position for manipulation by the strong side thumb. It is amazing that practically every design since the 1911 has made it not less difficult, but more difficult, to manipulate the safety. The slide lock is easily used when manipulated as designed with the shooter's thumb. Only the use of modern magazines with overly tight magazine springs will make the slide lock safety more difficult to manipulate. The magazine release is easily activated by the shooter's thumb. A person with

The author's long-serving Commander .45 is a good fit, with the short trigger and arched mainspring housing.

short digits may require a little shifting in the hand to reach the magazine release but most of us have little difficulty in activating the 1911 magazine release. This "Browning Type" magazine release is now universal among self loading pistols. Few competing designs exist. The Heckler & Koch is among a few alternate designs that work well.

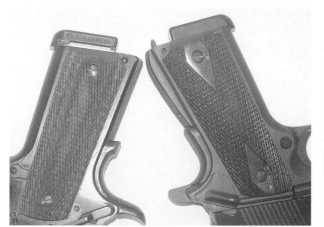

The flat mainspring housing, left, compared to the arched housing, right. Either works for most of us but the original flat housing seems most popular.

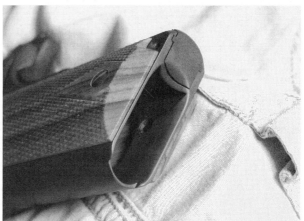

Hilton Yam has carefully beveled the magazine well of this 1911 for better handling. It is not difficult to carefully tweak the 1911 for better hand fit.

The 1911 is a good candidate for fast-paced action shooting. Nothing else hangs on the hand like the 1911.

This shooter finds the 1911 a good fit and a better fit than anything else she has tried. Why look further?

Christen Smith is making brass with a SIG GSR. She appreciates the balance and hand fit of the 1911.

The 1911's beavertail grip safety is a non-issue in human engineering. If you grasp the pistol, you press the grip safety. John Browning had a great mind and he simply designed a pistol in the proper manner. It fits most hands well and the controls are placed in easy reach of the digits of the hand. Whether a mark of genius or simply competent design, the features of the 1911 are a marvel of human engineering.

Comparison in hand fit and size

Handgun	Grip Circumference	Grip Width	Trigger Reach
Beretta 92	5-7/8"	1-5/8"	2-5/8"
Colt 1911	5"	1-1/8"	2-1/2 "

Government Model Specifications

Overall length	8.5"
Barrel length	5.0"
Front strap height	2.6"
Back strap height	3.2"
Weight unloaded	38 oz.
Maximum width	1.5"
Maximum grip thickness	1.4"
Grip circumference	5.5"
Trigger span or trigger reach	2.5"

It is remarkable that as we have added advanced sights, an ambidextrous safety and a custom beavertail safety, the human engineering of the 1911 is not adversely affected. In fact, modern improvements have enhanced the advantages of the 1911. The larger slide lock safeties fall under the thumb readily and offer ease of manipulation. The Ed Brown design in particular is a good design. The high upswept beavertail safety offers an advantage in handling as well. There are those who occasionally miss depressing the safety correctly or who use the high thumbs grip, which gets the palm off the grip safety. A modern beavertail safety such as the classic Ed Brown solves these problems. Springfield Armory uses the ambidextrous safety pioneered by Armand Swenson as a faithful reproduction. The modern Kimber design also works well. These enhancements aid in properly deploying the 1911 pistol. The magazine guide is a competition aid not strictly needed in a defensive pistol. After all we will seldom see a running gun battle. But I own several pistols with these guides. The Smith and Alexander type is particularly pleasing to use; manipulation and smoothness are much enhanced. Range work is easier with the magazine guide and so is administrative handling.

The geometry of the 1911 is such that not only is it handy as issued, but a minimum of modification greatly increases the ergonomics of the pistol. This is a handgun that was designed to fit the hand, not engineered for efficiency in hopes that the hand would adapt. The location of the controls and hand fit are ideal. The bore axis is low, limiting recoil. In short, the 1911 is a great design with no flies on it. There isn't much room for improvement in its basic engineering. You may spoil yourself with a set of Ahrends grips or add a beavertail safety, but the pistol is still a purebred 1911.

IMPROVED COLT PISTOLS

Chapter 5:

Evolution and gradual improvement in mechanical devices are inevitable. The shape of things to come was there in 1911. A year before the 1911 pistol trials a biplane was tested with a jet engine. The electric starter was in development. Double action and double action only trigger mechanisms were on the drawing board or in use. Radios and aerial reconnaissance were coming into use.

Certain dramatic improvements have been made to the 1911 but the most beneficial features, including handfit, trigger compression and a

U.S. Troops spent the winter of 1917 - 1918 training with French Army veterans.

This Colt Series 70 is a first-class fighting pistol even today. This was Colt's first improved 1911.

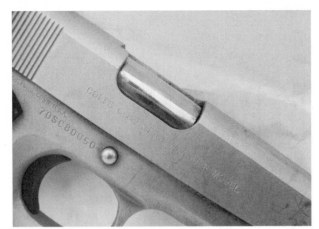

The Combat Commander was introduced with the Series 70 line. Note GI type slide window.

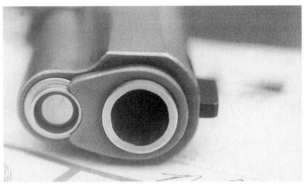

Gunsmith improvements include a national match bushing and later, the full-length guide rod.

This is the Colt Delta Elite in 10mm. While an interesting pistol, many did not regard the 10mm as suitable for the 1911 frame.

low bore axis, are intact. The barrel link barrel bushing and the basic fitting are the same. Detail changes and improvements have been beneficial. The first improved version of the 1911 was the 1911 A1. It is the 1911A1 we refer to as the 1911 today and there are no original 1911s in production, in my opinion.

There were a number of changes in the 1911A1. These changes were approved in May of 1924 and were incorporated in production by June 15, 1926. They included improved sights, specifically a wider front sight; a longer hammer spur and grip safety; an arched mainspring housing; a shorter trigger; and relief cuts in the frame to allow the trigger finger to reach the trigger more easily.

A pertinent observation is that the 1911A1, circa 1930, might be brought up to modern standards with sufficient time and money. Also I should note at this time that while Colt's 1918 replica pistols are excellent examples of the gun maker's art, they are not true 1911s but rather 1911A1 types, in my opinion. In fit finish and overall construction, they are modern Colts.

The impetus for improvement of the 1911 came from wartime experience. When death came howling out of Europe in 1914, the 1911 was in the thick of it,

This is a first class custom 1911 from Hilton Yam, based on the classic Series 70.

first with our British allies and then with our soldiers in 1917. After the war the 1911A1 improvements were incorporated. The Colt remained unchanged as far as military use but then no new GI pistols were delivered after 1945. Commercial Colts were changed again in 1970. We knew what the 1911 was and what it would do and didn't expect more. Anyone wishing to fit better sights or to tighten the Colt up took it to a custom pistolsmith. Some purchased the National Match pistol. Market pressure was exerted in the 1960s, however, as 1911 fans were tired of spending good money to tighten the pistol up. They wished to be able to purchase an accurate 1911 off of the shelf. At the time a GI pistol could be had for a modest cost and the Government Model cost less than $125 new. Commercial pistols were supplied with a nice blue finish but otherwise offered little demonstrable advantage over the GI pistol. An improved Government Model would enhance sales and redeem Colt's prestige.

The 1911 was also accepted by large numbers of defense shooters and Colonel Cooper and his advocacy of the 1911 were well known. Serious defensive shooters

This Commander has a spare Bar-Sto barrel. This barrel improved the Colt more than the Series 70 tightening program.

demanded a superior pistol. Colt introduced the Series 70 pistols to great expectations. There was no improvement in the sights, but the trigger action was often superior to GI Colt .45s. The big news was a special three-

The Colt Defender is arguable among the best concealed carry handguns ever fielded.

The author often carries his Commander in this K & D concealment holster, which is suitable for either inside-the-waist or outside-the-waist wear.

fingered collett bushing that gripped the barrel tightly and promoted accuracy. My experience indicates that over time the collett bushing cuts small grooves in the barrel and the pistol becomes more accurate with use. The Series 70 became a popular pistol and maintained a type of cult status well into the 1990s. The Series 70 pistols featured good commercial blue and were well fitted, but they were much like the previous commercial pistols in that they didn't particularly care for hollow point ammunition.

Also, the three fingered bushing proved to be problematical in general use. Owners did not fully understand the bushing and often tried to pry it off the barrel during disassembly. The bushing fingers sometimes broke. A lack of cleaning contributed to barrel bushing problems. I once had a collett bushing lose one of its fingers, which didn't tie the gun up, but others soon broke, too, and tied the pistol up. There was no room for the new style bushing on the Commander. While tightened to an extent, the Commander was never as accurate as the Government Model in the Series 70 runs. During the Series 70 run Colt introduced the

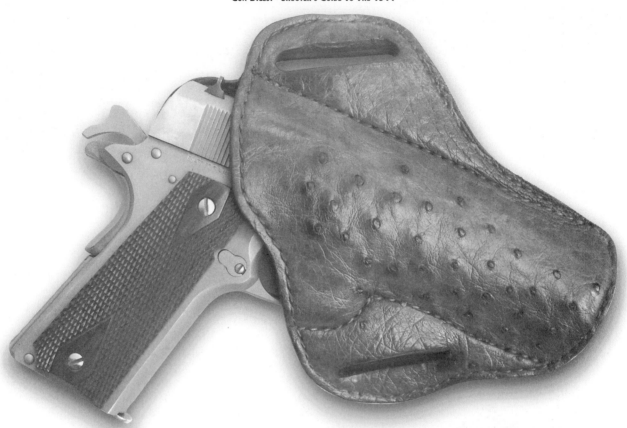

Sometimes you need flash. This Series 80 stainless Super .38 is carried in a Rocking W Ostrich skin holster.

Combat Commander, a steel frame Commander. Some shooters felt that a steel frame Commander was pointless and the 3/4 of an inch inch lopped off the barrel cost the Combat Commander the use of the collett bushing. Just the same, these are among the most popular and well balanced Colt pistols ever produced. Today, the Colt Commander is a steel frame pistol and the LW Commander is an aluminum frame pistol.

The legendary Series 70 is a fine Colt but not a mythical totem to be ransomed at high price at the gun show. I would strongly prefer a new commercial Colt over an older Colt of uncertain storage and originality. But to each his own. Some of the finest custom pistols in the world are built upon the Series 70. A custom pistol built on a Series 70 will command a greater resale value than practically any other Colt.

The next Colt, the Series 80, was a very important one in the scheme of things. This included the 1991A1 and the Enhanced Model as well as the first stainless steel Colt 1911 pistols. Much of this was in response to market pressure from Springfield, Randall and others. But the firing pin block or drop safety was an answer to SIG. The SIG P 220 series had become a successful pistol in police sales. An important selling feature was the positive firing point block or drop safety. The success of

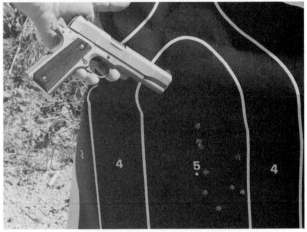

This late model Series 80 is a great shooter and very reliable.

the SIG and criticisms of the 1911's single action design led to the Colt firing pin block. The firing pin block is the defining feature of the Series 80 in comparison to the Series 70. The Series 80 also features larger sights, although they are not as highly developed as later types. The Series 80 also features a larger slide window and a barrel bushing that, while conventional, is well fitted.

The Series 80 is at least as accurate as the best Series 70 pistols and the difference between the Commander and Government Model pistols in accuracy is far less pronounced in the Series 80 pistols. Series 80 Commanders are almost always more accurate than earlier

This Series 70 is fitted with Ahrends Tactical grips. This is a great defense pistol.

Commander pistols. The firing pin block has been controversial. It adds parts to the pistol and there is a real possibility of failure, particularly if the pistol is tampered with. My advice should be well taken. If you prefer a pistol without the Colt firing pin block, purchase a Springfield or Kimber. Do not remove a safety device from a Colt! The Colt firing pin block operates by means of a plunger that holds the firing pin locked in place. When the trigger is pressed completely to the rear, the plunger is released and the firing pin is released in order to fire the pistol. The firing pin block may be short circuited if you are not careful. As an example, when making the pistol ready to keep by the bed at night most of us lower the hammer on a loaded chamber. If we depress the trigger we have released the block. We lower the hammer on a loaded chamber. There is a good chance we will move the firing pin forward and it will remain there. The firing pin block works fine for cocked and locked carry, but be certain to release the trigger before lowering the hammer for hammer down carry or home ready.

Another new Colt is the 1991A1. I am not certain we can call the 1991A1 an improved Colt. This is actually a stripped down pistol designed to compete with the Springfield Armory GI pistol. The 1991 A1 is comparable to the Springfield Mil Spec. The 1991 A 1 is designed to compete with other GI pistols but it does so at the cost of using synthetic parts such as the trigger and mainspring housing. While they work well enough, the

1991A1 is not the Colt that gives us the most pride of ownership. The Enhanced Model Colt is another matter. This pistol incorporates a number of features once limited to custom pistols. A cutout under the trigger guard aids in hand fit and feel and there is a rib on the slide similar to that found on the Gold Cup pistol. Like all Series 80 pistols the Enhanced Model feeds all hollow point ammunition and incorporates the firing pin lock.

Now replaced in the Colt lineup by the XSE, the Enhanced Model was a good Colt. The XSE features true high visibility sights and some versions feature forward cocking serrations. The XSE is also a good Colt and a fine example of the gunmaker's art. Just the same, when I fire the pistol I somehow think I should expect more from Colt. While a good solid gun there is little if any advantage over the Springfield, and the Kimber pistols usually are more accurate. However, the last Series 80 I tested had a crisp trigger and the usual Colt attention to detail, and it printed two-inch groups at 20 yards with Winchester and Fiocchi ball and handloads. I am now awaiting a Colt Combat Elite. The grand old company has its moments.

Special note on Gold Cup pistols: I am more interested in shooting than collecting but a few notes on the Colt Gold Cup are in order. The original National Match pistols were standard weight Colts delivered with quality fixed sights and later the Stevens adjustable sight. They could be used hard and they were as reliable and robust as any Colt. They were fitted better than most

The Series 80, fitted in this illustration with Paladin grips, is a good all-around 1911.

and delivered with match grade barrels or at the least match grade fit. Later, the Gold Cup pistols featured fully adjustable sights and a long target trigger.

Much confusion centers around Gold Cup recoil springs. When you look at the part number of a vintage Gold Cup recoil spring and a Government Model recoil spring, the part number is the same. The Gold Cup achieved function by cutting the weight of the hammer spring. Think about it and experiment. Rack the slide of a 1911 with the hammer down, then rack the slide with the hammer cocked. The greater resistance of the hammer makes for a certain component in recoil. By using a lighter hammer spring, target loads in the 185-grain at 750 fps range could be used. The problem came when misinformed shooters decided to fire hardball loads in the Gold Cup. They replaced the Gold Cup recoil spring with a Government Model recoil spring, which was the same as the Gold Cup. They proceeded to batter their pistols to death.

The situation became worse in 1957 when Colt lightened the slide by two ounces in order to make it even easier to convince the pistol to function with light target type loadings. The balance of the pistol was adversely affected. These pistols were even more likely to be beaten to death by heavy loads. The Series 70 Gold Cup eventu-ally returned to the standard weight slide. Today the Gold Cup is delivered with two recoil springs, one for light loads and one for standard hardball type loads.

The Gold Cup is a wonderful target pistol but the spring situation must be understood for best results. If you are going to use heavy loads, replace both the hammer spring and possibly the recoil spring. (1957- to 1970-era National Match pistols would need an 18.5-lb. recoil spring rather than a 16-lb. standard in order to make up for the light slide. W C Wolff Company provide such a spring.)

The Gold Cup remains one of the more accurate 1911 handguns in the world. Recently I tested my personal box-stock Gold Cup against some of the best modern 1911 pistols from several makers now in the ascendant, and the Gold Cup not only held its own but it outperformed all production pistols pitted against it. In the past, there was a definite difference in accuracy between Colt Government Models and the Gold Cup. Despite the improvement in Government Model pistols, the Gold Cup remains the accuracy champ. I would not have it any other way. The improved 1911 has come a long way, and while there are other pistols available, the Colt Gold Cup is still the pistol to beat for accuracy. Colt can still do it right.

THE GREAT 1911 WARS

Chapter 6:

Those who are spoiled by the great number of 1911 handguns available today find it surprising that when I was a young man, Colt was the only show. Other than GI pistols such as Remington and Ithaca built to Colt standards there was nothing worth having. The Spanish ironmongery was not suited for hard use and did not always work out of the box when new. The Star pistols were the best of the lot, and while modified considerably in their trigger action from the original 1911 and lacking a grip safety, they were adequate performers for the money. They were not up to the standard set by Colt, however. The license-built Norwegian and Argentine pistols were seldom seen in the states.

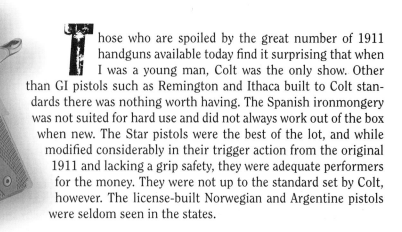

The Kimber Pro Carry is a very popular modern 1911.

The Taurus 1911 has come into its own as a good seller with a reputation for reliability.

This is the first widely distributed stainless steel 1911, the Randall. This one has just been given a bath.

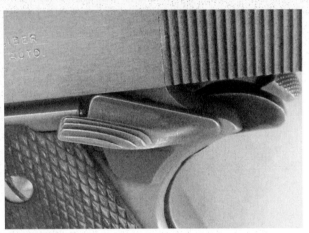

The Randall featured an improved slide lock safety with greater area.

The Randall introduced a special barrel with a slight bell for accuracy and a standard full-length guide rod.

During the 1960s and 1970s Colonel Cooper's promotion of the 1911 led to a greater demand than Colt could fill. GI pistols became difficult to find. Those that were left in circulation were well worn and others were put under the knife by gun butchers. It was all a learning process. While the Colts ran well with a bit of judicious gunsmithing, the Spanish copies lacked heat treating and were not worth customizing. There was room for another maker of 1911 handguns.

Companies began to offer quality frames and slides on the 1911 pattern for those who desired to build their own, and these frames became the basis for several now-defunct handgun companies. Caspian is the standout among frame suppliers and has been the basis of several good quality custom handguns I have put together. Cas-pian frames and slides are among the best for custom use and are offered in a wide variety from GI types to highly developed tactical versions. Today shooters pay big money for factory pistols built on Caspian frames.

The market that existed for finished 1911s was a large one partly due to the fact that 1911 shooters are a different breed. They are not content with a single example of the pistol but will own as many as finances and marital harmony allow. Once they have the bug it isn't unusual for a 1911 shooter to acquire a half dozen good pistols in short order. Some eventually gravitate to the one great custom or factory gun of a lifetime, but most of us will use and shoot many examples on the way. Makers began to test the water with 1911 handguns. In those days all of the non-Colts were "off brand" pistols.

Some of these were very rough, others were well made of good material. The Vega and the original Detonics are rare today but they showed the buying public that someone could make a 1911 other than Colt.

A benchmark of sorts was the Randall. The Randall introduced a full-length guide rod and stainless steel frame and slide as a standard item. The Randall also featured an enlarged slide lock safety and improved sights. The Randall Combat model featured a rib down the top of the slide years before the Colt Enhanced Model. The Randall pistol was a very interesting handgun. Among the Randall rarities was a true reverse image left-handed pistol. The bar was raised. Colt responded with improved versions of the 1911 but the die was cast. Colt codified many of the improvements made in the Randall, but the buyer was now aware of other operations. As is often the case, some of Colt's competitors were intended as an improvement over the Colt while others were designed to be made more cheaply. But none survived. A number of companies producing inferior products went through several renditions before thankfully closing the doors for good.

Colt has one advantage: no other maker has a history to compare with Colt. This 1918 is not necessarily a commemorative but simply a reintroduction.

The Firestorm 1911, top, and the RIA Tactical, bottom, are both produced in the Philippines.

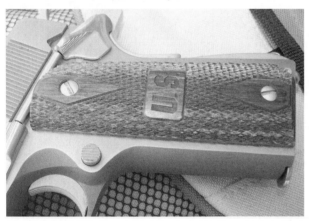

The Springfield GI features among the most attractive grips ever fitted to a 1911 pistol.

Arriving on the scene a few years after the others was Springfield Armory, easily the most successful of the Colt competitors. They began by offering a good solid GI-type 1911 at a fair price in 1985. Springfield's GI pistol quickly earned the respect and appreciation of shooters. An experienced engineer at one of the big three ammunition companies told me that Springfield had the best barrel-to-frame fit he had ever seen, and he had seen it all. Springfield has continued to adhere to that standard. I currently own a half dozen Springfield 1911 pistols, from the GI pistol to the Tactical Response Pistol and including my favorite Springfield of all, the Super Tuned. As for fit, the gap between the feed ramps

in the non-ramped barrel pistols is the uniform 1/32" we find desirable. The slide to frame fit is excellent as well.

Springfield still offers GI pistols but also offers the Mil Spec line. The Mil Spec features a lowered ejection port and improved sights. Springfield has gone on to an accomplishment that would have been unthinkable a generation before.: the Springfield Professional Model 1911 .45 has been selected by the FBI as their standard SWAT pistol. The Professional underwent grueling testing and may be the single most proven 1911 handgun of all time. Many young shooters grew up with Springfield and consider the maker an old line company. Producing a quality product has paid off for the company and for the public.

If Springfield was a breath of fresh air, Kimber blew in like a California zephyr. The original Kimber pistol, introduced in 1995, set the world on its ear. There is no basic or GI Kimber. The Custom pistol was offered with good quality sights, extended controls, and most of all, excellent fit and finish. The Kimber Custom II as issued today features custom sights, a lowered ejection port, an extended slide lock safety, a beavertail grip safety, and smooth trigger compression. Barrel fit is excellent and the pistol will feed any commercial ammunition. The frame and slide are produced on the high end of 1911 dimensions to ensure a tight fit. The three point pedestal lockup for the barrel is well executed.

The Springfield, top, and Para, bottom, are comparable handguns with good features and performance.

The Kimber pistol remains the single most consistent-quality 1911, in my estimation, and is reminiscent of the SIG P series production at its best. The 1911 is a more complicated pistol than a modern SIG or Glock and there is more that has to be right for the pistol to perform well. Kimber has introduced special models including the successful Gold Combat and Gold Match versions, as well as the Tactical and Warrior versions of the 1911. The Custom II is good enough for LAPD SWAT and should be good enough for us, too. Kimber, Springfield and Colt remain at the top in 1911 performance unless you wish to spend a lot more money and move to an Ed Brown, Les Baer or Wilson Combat pistol. (The situation may change if Rock River Arms resumes 1911 production.) There are other contenders but these pistols are the most proven. There is a certain subjectivity of analysis and one pistol may appeal more than the other. A universal impairment I see among shooters, and not just young shooters, is a difficulty in judging quality. We all have different viewpoints. But some pistols seem superficial and many are mediocre. I am not saying they are a calamity waiting to occur; they simply are not going to last as long as the quality pistols nor will they deliver the same performance. Their performance is not exciting.

If you are able to find a Rock River Arms 1911 for sale, obtain it. This is a remarkable pistol.

Some pistols have good features that the original 1911 did not. As an example, the Rock River Arms 1911 pistols feature a thickened frame just in the spot that is known to crack in the case of high round-count 1911s. As of this writing RRA handgun production is curtailed as the company attempts to meet the demand for their AR-15 type rifles. I am hoping they will come back with the 1911 but who knows?. The pistols cost about twice what a Springfield Loaded Model will set you back, but they are flawless performers.

51

Kimber's Eclipse is among the most popular of modern 1911 handguns.

The SIG Granite Series Rail gun has proven a popular choice with 1911 shooters.

Today, makers bemoan the number of competitors they face while remarking upon the seemingly insatiable demand for good 1911 handguns. A new 1911 is quickly snapped up and the ability to put together a 1911 is not beyond the reach of better companies. Caspian and Essex supply frames and any number of companies offer parts that are good and cheap and excellent and expensive, depending upon your taste or budget. The quality of the materials that go into the pistol are important. As an example, both Smith and Wesson and SIGARMS offer good quality 1911 handguns. Smith and Wesson has experience in producing 1911 frames and they put together a credible 1911 handgun. They went with the external extractor design some find more modern and more desirable than the original.

The SIGARMS Granite Series Rail gun is changed slightly from the 1911 format in order to more closely resemble other SIG products. SIG chose first-class aftermarket parts and put the pistol together in their own custom shop. The SIG is a good example of a factory custom pistol with first class parts that we could not easily build for a similar price. But others have offered a pistol that is basically a kit gun with low-bid parts. I tested a fairly expensive pistol that I expected a lot from – I'll not mention its name here. The magazine release

dumped the magazine on the first shot. It was almost funny. The magazine release was a cheap cast part, not even a GI type.

Caveat emptor applies to the modern 1911. The explosion of 1911 makers and the ensuing trade war has been mostly a good thing for consumers, however. To the credit of 1911 shooters, we are willing to pay for quality. While the Kimber Custom II and Springfield Loaded Model are very good pistols, the Kimber Gold Match and Springfield Tactical Response Pistol are exceptional firearms. You have to clear conceptual space in your mind and grasp the implications of such handguns. You can purchase an off-the-shelf handgun that your father would have had to pay several thousand dollars in upgrades for to approach in performance. Modern CNC processes and tight controls results in superior pistols. Looking back and reconstructing the surrounding situation decades ago, it appears as if the appetite for top-end 1911 handguns in personal defense and competition has created a huge market. Make something excellent enough and someone will recognize the product for what it is and desire to own one or two samples of it.

The 1911 market is big enough to have raised both Kimber and Springfield to their current position. Each

This is the Springfield Loaded Model, often deemed the best buy among all mid-range 1911 handguns.

has wrestled to learn hard lessons concerning handgun manufacture. The market is volatile enough that some makers have dropped out. Not surprisingly, a number of makers recognized the 1911 market and made an entry. Among the most innovative has been Para Ordnance, now known simply as Para. Para began with high capacity magazine frames for the 1911 and than moved to complete handguns. They also introduced the Light Double Action Trigger. Their latest achievement is the Power Extractor, a new style of extractor that has approximately 50% more bite on the case than the original. I cannot help but observe that the modern Para LDA pistol with its ramped barrel, high capacity magazine and new power extractor is a far cry from a WWI 1911 – but it is still a 1911. Para also makes good single-stack 1911s. They are improved pistols but more traditional in appearance. They feature a ramped barrel and the improved extractor.

It was a simple matter for Taurus to introduce an affordable, working 1911. After all, the design work was completed in 1911! The PT1911 has proven popular and remains one of the better choices in an affordable 1911. There have also been inroads by new makers from the Philippines, at least makers with a new name. The Rock Island Armory pistols and the High Standard 1911 handguns are Armscor pistols at an entry level price. They are manufactured using cast frames and slides, which brings us to another discussion. At this time it would be appropriate to discuss the different manufacturing techniques in building a 1911. That inexpensive pistol may not be as attractive once you understand casting, but then you may not be firing ten thousand rounds this year. Proofed, broken in and kept in the home for an emergency, the cast frame 1911 will serve forever.

Investment Casting

Casting is simplicity itself. Molten steel is poured into a mold. The steel hardens and the mold is broken way. The molds are usually wax. After the part is broken from the mold, final machining and hardening is done. Cast parts are less expensive to produce than forged parts and expense is the bottom line. Cast parts serve the bottom line well. The only process less expensive than casting is the production of polymer frames.

There are drawbacks with casting. Density is less than desirable when compared to forged parts and sometimes the grain structure is practically nonexistent. Porosity is evident in the metal surface, although some cast frames look better than others. I have personally enjoyed generally useful results with cast frames such as the Rock Island Armory types. They seem durable enough. I do not push the envelope but for what they cost the cast frame 1911s are quite attractive.

Metal Injection Molding

MIM is an economical method of producing parts. Metal powders are mixed with polymer binders and run through injection molding machines. Several steps are

The Para 7.45 Series offers the PXT extractor and other good features. A good choice from a solid company.

taken to remove the binders and compress the material. When properly executed the parts are nearly as strong as forged parts. There have been recalls of MIM parts with voids in the metal that resulted in breakage. That is the primary drawback of MIM. MIM is here to stay, however, and seems suitable for peripheral parts with low stress. Do I prefer forgings? Of course I do – but I do not wish to pay two grand for a basic 1911, either.

Forging

By far the most desirable and the most expensive means of manufacture is forging. 1911s are expensive pistols to forge and machine, and forging itself is an expensive process. Forgings are hammer forged for the most part and sometimes there are several steps in forming the part. Yes, forging parts is the old blacksmith method, with modern CNC machinery and power hammers taking the place of the brain and brawn of the blacksmith.

Preferences

It is difficult to criticize a process that makes a good quality handgun affordable. Investment casting and MIM allow an affordable pistol. Some makers used forged frames and slides but cast internals. Looking back at past experience, most of the problems I have encountered revolved around poorly made or fitted internal parts rather than a cast frame. One now-defunct maker was renowned for using good frames but lousy cast-off GI parts and whatever could be obtained cheaply. You have to carefully inspect each pistol and take each on its own merits. I prefer the orthodox manner of manufacture and that is forging, but I am willing to suspend judgment until I test each handgun for myself.

The bottom line is this: the 1911 trade wars have given us a buyer's market. We are blessed with many choices.

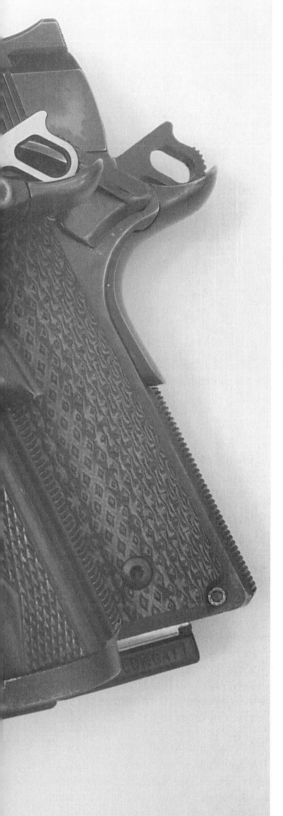

COCKED AND LOCKED

Chapter 7:

We have discussed the 1911's history and particulars. At this point we need to discuss the pistol's manual of arms.

Each handgun has its own requirements. Some require the use of a decocker to lower the hammer, others use a striker fired mechanism. The 1911 is a single action pistol that offers a simple means of operation. We begin with an unloaded pistol with the slide down on an empty chamber. We may lock the slide to the rear using the slide lock before loading, or we may simply insert a loaded magazine into the magazine well. If the slide is locked to the rear, we lower the slide by releasing the slide lock and letting the slide run forward, or using the alternate method we rack the slide and load the pistol. With either formula we now have a pistol in our hands with a

This SW1911 is shown with the hammer to the rear and the safety on, cocked and locked.

Cocked and locked is the way to go. What is so hard to understand?

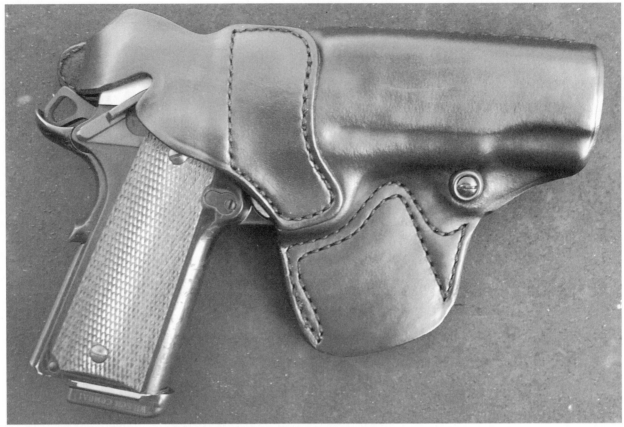

The DeSantis HRT holster features a thumb snap that rides between the hammer and the firing pin, a feature many prefer.

This Springfield is riding cocked and locked in a Barber holster. No conflict here.

cocked hammer. To make the pistol safe we apply the slide lock safety. To fire we simply thumb the safety off and press the trigger. When the pistol is carried with the hammer back and the safety on, this is known as cocked and locked carry.

Sooner or later any discussion of the 1911 turns to cocked and locked carry. The appearance of a pistol with the hammer back and the safety on seems rakish to some and dangerous to others. If you cannot get over an aversion to cocked and locked carry, then you may need to choose another action type. If you do not feel comfortable with a self-loading pistol with a round in the chamber, simple readiness demands you consider a revolver. If your head is on straight and you understand mechanics, you will realize that cocked and locked carry is both mechanically safe and tactically advantageous. When the 1911 is ready to fire, the hammer is cocked against the pressure of the mainspring. The trigger must be pressed in order to fire the pistol. The trigger is pressed against the sear. The sear trips and the hammer is released. The hammer falls. The grip safety does not block the hammer or sear, only the trigger. Once the grip safety is fully depressed (most modern 1911 types release the trigger at about half of the travel of the grip safety) the trigger may be pressed to release the hammer.

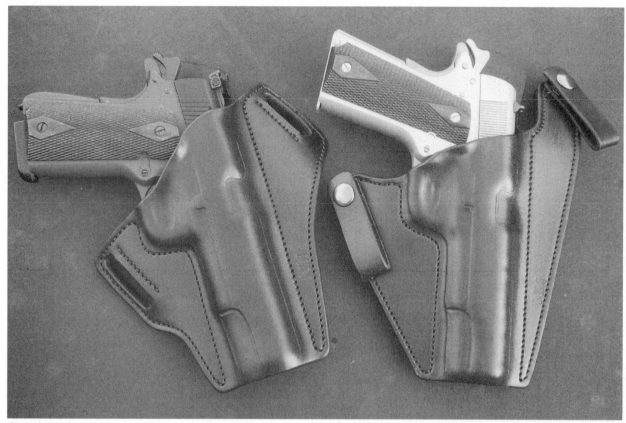

These holsters, an IWB and an OWB, are from Nick Matthews. He incorporates a sweat guard that also prevents the safety from rubbing off. This is good kit.

Carrying a 1911 hammer-down on a loaded chamber is a waste of time and tactical efficiency. When it comes to safety in a single action pistol, the slide lock safety is the answer. When the safety is applied the inner part of the safety locks solidly into the sear and bears against it. The safety also locks into the hammer. The hammer cannot drop unless the safety is released. When the safety is released the pistol may be fired. By using a single action handgun with a straight-to-the-rear trigger compression we are able to produce a handgun with excellent practical accuracy. There is no handgun faster for an accurate first shot than the 1911. The 1911 was designed to be deadly against multiple adversaries at close range, and no other system works as well in this regard.

Some designers have attempted to mimic the 1911 with various takes on the 1911 safety, but there is no handgun with the combination of low bore axis and excellent hand fit that allows such a rapid engagement of the target. Handguns with a long double action (double action is defined as a trigger that both cocks and drops the hammer, whereas the single action trigger only drops the hammer, hence, one function, hence single action) first shot are not nearly as tactically efficient. The double action is severely handicapped in action. The double action only trigger that is partially prepped

The little Springfield features an ambi safety, properly carried cocked and locked.

when at rest is not as crisp and controllable as the 1911. I believe that any self-loading handgun that does not feature a positive manual safety abrogates major advantages of the self-loading pistol.

We are not here, however, to compare the 1911 to lesser types but to concentrate on its advantages. Cocked and locked carry is among the main advantages of the 1911 handgun. Cocked and locked carry is safe, but you must know what you are about. You cannot carry a cocked and locked handgun thrust into the waistband

This LW Operator features the very efficient Springfield Armory ambidextrous safety.

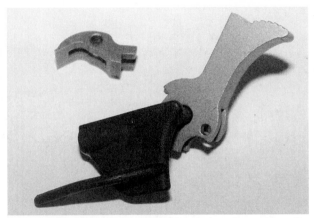

Once you understand how cocked and locked carries works on the mechanical side, you understand the efficiency of the design.

without a holster. The safety will rub off and while the grip safety is a secondary safety, this is tempting fate. A 1911 or any other handgun should always be carried in a properly designed holster. You run the risk of losing the handgun, or of it falling into your pants leg, or of it becoming impossible to draw when you need it the most if you do not employ a holster. Many shooters prefer a thumbreak holster when deploying a 1911 handgun. They prefer the safety strap between the firing pin and hammer of the 1911. This is a safe and time-proven advantage, one that I prefer for uniformed carry. The concealed carry holsters I prefer seldom have a thumb break. While the person who practices relentlessly with a thumbreak holster will become pretty quick with diligent practice I prefer a properly molded open top holster, either a strong side belt scabbard or an inside the waistband design for concealed carry.

I carry my 1911s cocked and locked. When I draw, I take the safety off as my hands meet in a two-hand hold. It is not necessary to disengage the safety while the handgun is in the holster. It is preferable to disengage the safety after the gun is drawn. Few other handguns offer this advantage. A handgun with a slide-mounted safety is much more difficult to quickly manipulate. In the case of the Beretta and similar designs, it is mandatory to disengage the safety while the handgun is holstered in order to achieve proper leverage to quickly disengage it. In comparison the 1911 safety may be disengaged the moment before firing with little appreciable difference in speed. The safety may be quickly re-engaged. The frame mounted safety falls under the thumb quickly and smoothly. In short, on a mechanical and tactical basis the cocked and locked feature of the 1911 is both commendable and practical, and it's a key part of the mechanical advantage that makes the 1911 such a superior fighting handgun.

1911 Conditions of Readiness

There are three acceptable conditions of readiness for the 1911:

Condition One, cocked and locked, which we have discussed;

Condition Two, which is hammer down on a loaded chamber. This is not suitable for on-body carry but will serve well for home ready. Using the hammer-down mode, the pistol may be placed on a nightstand or thrust under the mattress or, better still, be carried in the Diamond Products Night Sentry, an excellent accessory for the tactically minded home owner; and finally

Condition Three, which is hammer down, chamber empty. This is the military carry and a carry also once demanded by some agencies that allowed the 1911 to be carried by plainclothes personnel. Do not think for a moment that soldiers carried their pistols chamber empty close to the combat zone. I have read a directive from the Marine Corps Commandant, circa 1927, that not only specifically ordered cocked and locked carry, but also noted that on mail escort details the full flap holster then in use should be folded back to allow a more rapid draw. Chamber empty requires two hands to make the pistol ready. Just the same, more than a few gunhandlers go this route. A friend practices often with his 1911 and keeps it at home ready chamber empty. He loads it for range trips and is never confused concerning the condition of readiness. I have seen quite a few plainclothes officers issued the modern Glock also carrying chamber empty. This is the only safe carry with the Glock when it is simply thrust into the waistband without a holster. If you do not use a holster then condition three is indicated.

Cocked and locked carry is efficient. The other carry modes are far less efficient for on-body carry.

ALTERNATE ACTION TYPES

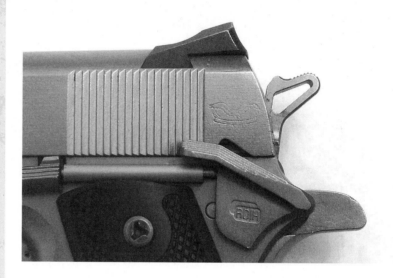

Chapter 8:

Despite the obvious advantages of cocked and locked carry, there have been a number of attempts to convert the 1911 to a different action type. Some have been more successful than others. While operators may recognize the advantage of single action handguns, administrators and legislators generally do not and most often police administrators will not approve a single action pistol. While many administrators are good at shuffling papers, when it comes to tactics they are less competent. It is true that the situation is better today and there are agencies that issue the 1911 and many more that approve the 1911 on a case by case basis if officers are able to quality with the type. While you may demonstrate the superiority of the 1911, many administrators are too ignorant of firearms function to recognize the 1911's superiority. For this reason, and others, the double action double action only and safe fast action pistols were developed. The goal was to retain the good features of the 1911 in the greatest majority while making the action more acceptable to civil authorities.

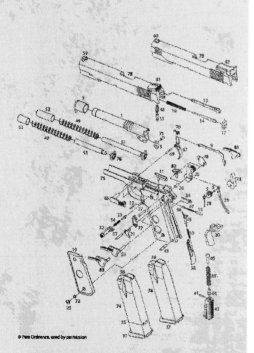

The Para Ordnance LDA maintains the main advantages of the 1911 while also making the pistol more attractive to many shooters.

With the SFS the hammer is down but cocked and locked at the same time.

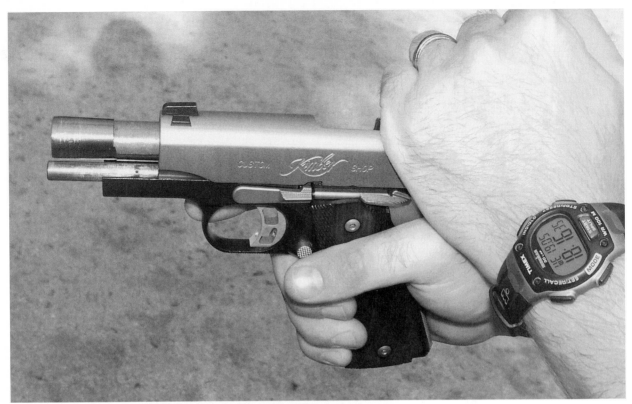

Racking the slide to make it ready is not acceptable in a personal defense situation.

A side note in history is the Caravelle squeeze-cocking conversion unit for the 1911 that was marketed circa 1970-1980. I have never personally examined an example, but the Caravelle conversion spurred development of the Heckler and Koch P7 squeeze cocking single action pistol. With the Caravelle conversion, a lever on the back strap was pressed and the hammer of the 1911 was cocked via a linkage (properly termed a drawbar).

Another attempt at converting the 1911 was the Seecamp double action trigger conversion. Double action simply means that the trigger does double duty or performs two actions. The double action trigger both cocks and releases the hammer. The Seecamp conversion features an enlarged trigger guard and a curved trigger. The trigger was hooked to a drawbar that cocked and dropped the 1911 hammer. After the first shot, the pistol reverted to single action fire. The Seecamp conversion was relatively expensive.

Colt introduced a factory version with their double action first shot Double Eagle pistol. There are those who view the Double Eagle as a monstrosity. I favor the handling of the standard 1911 but as double action pistols go the Double Eagle handled as well as many. The problem is in design. A true double action places the trigger finger above the trigger guard and the trigger arcs down and to the rear to press the trigger. A converted double action pistol is a different piece altogeth-

er and not as useful. The original Double Eagle proved fragile in use, with the double action trigger giving considerable problems. The components were held in place by plastic grip panels and the piece was difficult to field strip and reassemble as a result of this complication. In later production, with some improvements, the pistol performed better. I have fired two late-model 10mm Double Eagle pistols extensively with good results. They were each reliable and accurate. Still, this is not a pistol we should seek out, obtain, and deploy if we have a choice. It is a curiosity more than anything else.

Today there are two practical alternatives to the single action 1911. One is available in a new production pistol while the second option may be used to convert any single action 1911. The Para Ordnance Light Double Action trigger is a true double action only. The trigger is pressed and the trigger both cocks and fires the pistol. The pistol fires and the recoiling slide does not cock the hammer. The hammer rides down with the slide, and a subsequent trigger press fires the piece again.

There have been other more or less novel iterations of the 1911 action but this is the most practical we have tested. With practice, good combat shooting may be done. Todd Jarrett, a noted competition shooter, has fired the LDA in matches with good results. Contrary to claims, the average shooter will not use the LDA as well as they may use a good single action 1911. However, he will use the LDA better than any other handgun type save a true single action 1911. And those who clutch the light single action trigger of the 1911 – and there are a few of these shooters – will often excel with the LDA. If I could not have the single action 1911 authorized for duty use I would be more than happy to deploy the high quality Para Ordnance LDA pistol. The LDA press is light and short. It is consistent and may be learned with a minimum of acclimation. It has proven reliable and durable.

Although the LDA action is carried hammer down, I strongly recommend always carrying an LDA on safe. The advantages of on-safety carry are many. The LDA has been around long enough for me to recommend the action type to those who cannot accept cocked and locked carry. There may even be advantages. When the piece is at home ready, you need not carefully lower the hammer to hammer down ready. The LDA hammer is always down and the piece is always ready to fire with a press of the trigger. You never lower the hammer manually. The LDA seems to have hit the ground running with no problems from its inception.

The second choice may be retrofitted to any single action 1911. The Safety Fast Shooting System or SFS was developed in Europe as an alternative to cocked and locked carry. The SFS, now offered by Cylinder and Slide Shop Inc., actually is cocked and locked – it just doesn't look like it. The SFS uses an internal hammer ring. When you load and cock the SFS-equipped handgun, you press the external hammer forward against the internal hammer ring. The hammer catches on the downside and the safety clicks on. A bar rises that stays between the hammer and the firing pin. When you release the safety, the external hammer is released to the full cock position. It is a little odd to see the hammer fly to full cock position but you will get used to it. There is no difference in speed between the SFS and a standard single action trigger.

A tactical drawback is that the thumb safety may not be placed on during movement. If you are shooting and moving with a standard 1911, you simply place the safety on. With the SFS, you must lower the hammer- but you do not go to a double action trigger press as is the case when decocking a double action first shot pistol.

The SFS is a brilliant solution to the problem of public and administrative perception of cocked and locked carry. It is not prohibitively expensive. The SFS is devalued as an ambidextrous unit. The right hand

The 1911 is cocked and locked; the Glock is arguably only 5.5 pounds from firing. It is that cocked hammer that meets resistance!

safety component for left handed shooters is synthetic and broke off at around 10,000 rounds in my test pistol. There were no spares at the time and none seem to be forthcoming. The SFS equipped pistol as delivered exhibited a very clean three and one half pound trigger action. The SFS does not affect the trigger action; this is simply how my pistol was delivered. Today the pistol has over 20,000 rounds on it and I have had it refinished twice and blown it up once. The trigger action has settled into two and one half pounds and the SFS has never failed. The SFS is very interesting. If for some reason you wish to carry the 1911 but hammer down carry is mandated by your agency, the SFS may be added to an existing pistol. The price is reasonable and the product seems durable enough. I am not pleased with the synthetic ambidextrous safety lever, however, as the lever came off of my personal SFS conversion and there are no replacement parts.

In closing, when it comes to alternative action types for the 1911, there is only one choice in factory pistols and that is the Para Ordnance LDA. This is a modern reliable action that will get good pistols into the hands of those who really need them. I strongly prefer the original single action pistol but there are many good shooters using the Light Double Action trigger system.

MODEL OF 1911.U.S.ARM

10-

PERFOR

1911 Tr

❑02 - Lo

Oversized, requ
installation. Ov
fixed and must

www.10-8Per

No liability is ex
for damage or injury w
improper installation

A CONSENSUS GUN

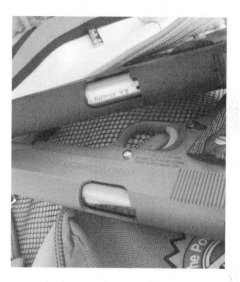

Chapter 9:

The term "consensus" means a general agreement. As applied to the 1911 the term means the general agreement reached by the great men of the old California Leather Slaps, where all types of handguns were matched against the other. While there were vicars and and crusaders in abundance, Jeff Cooper was the archbishop. I was not there but I have read widely on the subject.

Men who were there penned reports. The competition was open. Colt Single Action Army revolvers competed against Walther P38s, Smith and Wesson revolvers, Colt Python revolvers, the Browning High Power and the 1911. The 1911 showed its superiority but there are good things about other handguns as well. After using GI Colts in competi-

The primary difference in the Springfield Mil Spec slide is the larger slide window.

With the correct combination of parts it isn't difficult to build a consensus pistol that will do anything you wish to do in personal defense. However, it is easier to buy one factory made with just enough to get the job done.

The Springfield Mil Spec is arguably the greatest of the factory ready consensus pistols and a fine handgun by all accounts.

tion, the men shooting against Smith and Wesson K38s and Colt Pythons found that the 1911 needed better sights. Some modified the target sighted Colt Gold Cup to handle hardball; others fitted Smith and Wesson adjustable revolver sights to the 1911.

The 1911 also needed a speed safety. In those days they simply pinned the grip safety shut if the shooter had a problem hitting the grip safety on the draw. The consensus was further that the 1911 needed a trigger job and good sights to be all that it could be. A GI pistol with a good crisp trigger that fed SWC bullets was as rare as a hairy egg.

Over a period of time, gunsmiths perfected packages or a series of improvements and offered these to shooters as a matter of course. The result by the 1970s was a pistol codified as the consensus pistol. The sights, trigger and speed safety were added, and if you cared to use Super Vel hollow points you had the pistol throated. Knowing what I know about the 1911s controlled feed system I am not hoping to polish my feed ramp, but it was done often and often done badly during this time.

The consensus gun has good features and a considerable argument may be made that this is the ideal handgun for personal defense. If you think that a full length guide rod is an overcomplication or that advanced sights

This 10-8 (Hilton Yam) pistol features larger sights and other improvements: very much a capable handgun.

are not needed at combat distance the consensus pistol is for you. The sights and speed safety make a significant difference in shooting for a skilled shooter. A smooth, reliable trigger at five pounds is ideal for use by most shooters including myself. GI Colts and the general run of commercial pistols exhibited a trigger compression of six to eight pounds when new. Some were on the rough side. Many shooters went to bullseye-type three pound triggers but considerable experience led to an

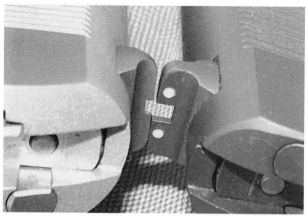

The Mil Spec, right, features larger sights than the GI pistol, left.

The 1911 was designed to use flush fit magazines. This Metalform magazine is ideal for most uses.

agreement on the five pound trigger. A five pound trigger compression is controllable and smooth. It is not so light that you will clutch it during rapid fire.

The consensus gun is a tractable, fast handling handgun with what is needed and nothing more. Most of the consensus guns were built from GI pistols but once we had the Series 70 pistols we had a base gun that produced much better results. Add sights and a speed safety to the Series 70 and you had a combat pistol that could hold its own with any modern pistol given a good hand behind the sights. Today we have factory pistols that are reasonably close to the original consensus .45. The Springfield Mil Spec pistol is perhaps the best example of a ready-to-go consensus pistol – but it is not perfect. My personal Mil Spec features a trigger compression that I have tuned to five pounds although it was delivered with a smooth but heavy six pound trigger compression. I have also added a 10-8 National Match rear sight. This is a sight that features a brilliantly fast U notch that gets you on target quickly. You could start with a Springfield GI and end up with a similar pistol, but you would have to replace the short front sight to match a taller rear sight such as the 10-8.

In preparation for this book I put together a rather special handgun that I believe is an inexpensive version of the consensus pistol. I obtained a new High Standard 1911 pistol. Since the trigger compression was thoroughly modern, breaking at a smooth four and one quarter pounds, I did not have to address the trigger. The slide lock safety is not as small as that of the GI but neither is it a true extended version. It was left as is. The original grips were replaced with Herrett D 45 grips, among the best buys on 1911 grips to be had. I also fitted Trijicon night sights. These sights give the pistol a true 24-hour utility and offer superior daylight sight picture as well. The result is a reliable and efficient but inexpensive handgun that will place five rounds of Winchester hardball into three and one half inches at 75 feet. This handgun will save your life if properly wielded.

The consensus gun is important as this was the first standard by which modified 1911 handguns were judged. It may be said that the Randall Combat model was a factory version of the consensus pistol. Today the Armscor Tactical versions of the Rock Island Armory pistol are consensus pistols. I place the Kimber Custom II at the top of the list in a modern consensus pistol. The Kimber has features that place it above the rest in many regards, but these features are also the ones that give a shooter the most advantage and the Custom II is only a little more expensive for a lot more pistol than some of the others.

I think that the consensus pistol is a good starting point and a good personal defense pistol. Before spending a ton of cash on a high-end 1911 take a hard look at the consensus pistol. This may be all the .45 you need.

GI .45

Chapter 10:

A friend of mine marvels at the continuing popularity of GI (General Issue) 1911 pistols. Examples of 1911 handguns produced during World War II are still in service with our armed forces. The GI .45 continues to be a commercial success, and not all GI pistols are cut rate imports. The Springfield GI is a great seller for the company and a good pistol. A number of Colt special editions of the GI .45 are relatively expensive but remain popular. For example, the Colt Black Army retails for $1000.

WWII-era military police, their Harleys, and their 1911s.

The Springfield GI stainless version is among the most desirable of GI .45s.

This is a good comparison. The RIA Tactical, above, sports good sights and an extended ambidextrous safety. The High Standard, bottom, is strictly GI.

I understand its historical significance but with pistols with more features available what is the appeal of the GI .45? First of all, the pistols are the very same configuration as used by our troops in two world wars and many other adventures. (If you own a real GI .45 in good condition you are a lucky individual – the rest of us have to get by with a reproduction!) When you use the GI .45 you are saluting the soldiers and Marines who used the type. The modern GI pistols features better fit and finish and most of all better heat treating than the original, at least in the case of the Colt and Springfield. The cast-frame Philippine pistols are a reasonable choice. The GI pistol is what it is: the 1911 in its basic plain vanilla form. The sights are original and perhaps embryonic but they are precise if properly lined up. These sights are usually set to shoot a little high at 25 yards and practically dead on to 50 yards. Most

Note the rough casting marks on this High Standard. Just the same, the pistol works fine.

will group five rounds of Winchester hardball into five inches at 25 yards or a little better.

Many shooters find the GI pistol's performance more than adequate for their needs. I do not wish to be a wart

Sometimes we do not let the GI pistol remain stock. This RIA pistol has been to Wilson Combat. Note the Wilson Combat stocks and night sights. And it is a .38 Super.

Not all GI .45s are 5-inch guns. This is a 3.5-inch barrel RIA .45.

Beware cheap cast parts! This actually came out of a thousand dollar 1911.

on the nose of progress, but for what is really needed in a personal defense pistol the GI .45 will serve well. The loosest modern GI .45 will cut one ragged hole for seven rounds at seven yards. The GI .45 is looser than high end guns and more likely to continue to function if dropped in sand, mud or grass.

A number of very experienced shooters regard the GI .45 as the high point of 1911 efficiency. Their arguments are well thought out. These men speak with the edge of truth in their voice. Those with less visual acu-

ity will need high visibility sights but the GI sights can be hooked on web gear or a belt and the slide racked to clear a malfunction, something that cannot be done with low snag sights. GI pistols can be used in one hand malfunction drills.

GI pistols never feature a match or adjustable trigger. Adjustable triggers are considered a liability by tactically minded shooters as the set screw may become loose and the pistol will refuse to fire. GI pistols do not have the added complication of a full length guide rod, either. The GI pistol can be field stripped with only the fingers. The simplicity of the GI pistol is appealing. The modern GI pistol will feed more reliably than World War II pistols. I have mentioned the controlled feed system of the 1911. The 1911 controls the travel of the cartridge from the time it is stripped from the magazine until the empty case is ejected. The magazine holds the cartridge in place. the cocking block moves the cartridge case out of the magazine and into the feed ramp. The nose of the bullet stops for a millisecond on the feed ramp. This snugs the cartridge case into the extractor. The bullet nose continues into the feed ramp and into the chamber. The pistol fires. The extractor removes the

At close range a GI .45 like the short barrel RIA is a capable defense piece.

when ejecting a dud cartridge. A fully loaded cartridge will sometimes hang up. There are shooters who prefer the original appearance on a historical scale and that is fine, but for general use the enlarged ejection port is superior and has no drawbacks.

As for precision, I recently tested a brace of GI pistols for accuracy. As may be expected, some were more accurate than others but all were accurate enough for personal defense. I tested the pistols with five shot groups at 25 yards.

Model	Load	Group@ 25 Yards
Rock Island Armory GI .45	Black Hills 230 gr. FMJ	4.0"
High Standard 1911A1	Black Hills 200 gr. SWC	4.5"
Rock Island Armory 4"	GI Winchester 185 gr. Silvertip	4.6"
Springfield GI	Black Hills 230 gr. FMJ	3.5"
Springfield Stainless GI	Winchester 230 gr. ball	4.5"
RIA .38 Super Gov't Model	Fiocchi 129 gr. Ball	3.45"
Argentine FMAP	Fiocchi 230 gr. FMJ	5.65"
Colt 1918 "Black Army"	Black Hills 185 grain JHP	2.75"

cartridge case from the chamber and at the end of slide travel the ejector bumps the case out of the extractor. While you no longer have to modify 1911 feed ramps to feed ammunition with hollow nose bullets – and modern ammunition is better designed than ever before – the controlled feed of the GI .45 is appreciated.

The GI pistol enthusiast will prefer flush fit magazines rather than magazines with a bumper pad because John Moses Browning designed it that way. True GI pistols do not incorporate a firing pin block into the design. The Springfield version features a lightweight firing pin and heavy firing pin spring for added safety. Most GI pistols still feature the original small slide window. The Springfield Mil Spec and the Rock Island pistols have the larger ejection port. A word of warning: the original port is fine for ejecting cases but may be a bit dicey

As you can see, the GI .45 is accurate enough for personal defense even in the new short GI pistols and with inexpensive ball ammunition. The GI pistol will get you through the night. If you have an old GI frame and wish to fit quality internal parts to it, you have something to work with. The Rock Island and High Standard pistols are acceptable, the GI Springfield a great pistol.

There may be more expensive pistols and pistols with more features, but never discount the GI .45.

SERVICE GUNS

Chapter 11:

Events have convinced me that police need a more reliable and powerful handgun than ever before. So does our military. The expanding use of the 1911 in both circles is a renaissance of sorts. For much of the time since the 1911 pistol's introduction, good men and women have treasured the 1911, and many have carried it against regulation. I wish some people could better appreciate the many choices they have. My friend Trevor was obliged to part with a month's pay for his Colt .45 automatic when he served as a member of the Rhodesian SAS but there was simply no other choice. The Colt was the obvious service pistol if you wanted to survive.

WWI recruiting poster featuring U.S. Marine with a Model 1911 pistol. Don't monkey with this fellow!

The SIG GSR, complete with 10–8 and Wilson Combat additions, is a fine service pistol.

73

The Springfield TRP is brilliantly fast on target and controllable in rapid fire.

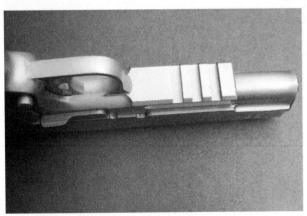

If you prefer a rail, take a look at the SIG GSR.

The 1911 is in use by a number of SERT, SWAT and emergency services teams. Tacoma, Washington, and San Diego, California, authorize the 1911 as a private purchase. In many jurisdictions officers vote with their personal funds and not only purchase the pistol of choice but train on their own time and their own dime. Most shell out over a thousand dollars for the pistol, leather, and support gear. Since the system is proven this is a good investment in officer safety.

A modern 1911 handgun must sport good sights and well designed controls but also feature excellent reliability along with incidentals such as a highly corrosion resistant finish to be competitive in this market. The pistol must be readily available and have good factory support. While there are quite a few cottage industries producing 1911 handguns, I tend to recommend Colt, Kimber, Para Ordnance and Springfield as service pistols for several reasons. There is usually some type of competition or qualification exercise for police pistols. In any fair contest the control and shootability as well as the handling qualities of the 9111 are second to none.

All automatic pistols function basically in the same manner. There is a reciprocating slide, a magazine in the handle, and a trigger action. The devil is in the details. The main advantage of the 1911 is in the straight-to-the-rear trigger action. The trigger does one thing: it drops the hammer. In contrast, the more complicated double action pistol's trigger both cocks and drops the hammer. This is the root of the term double action. A double action trigger requires that the trigger finger begin its travel above the trigger and that the trigger finger sweeps down in an arc to press the trigger. The much more tractable single action pistol requires that you press the trigger straight to the rear.

The TRP always gives good results in combat drills.

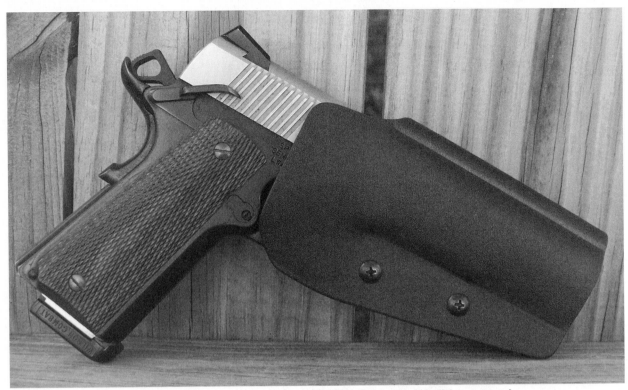

The Springfield LW Loaded Model often rides in the Dale Fricke Gideon Elite Kydex holster, good kit all the way around.

The double action trigger is more difficult to manage due to two factors: the length of travel and the greater weight of force needed to press the trigger. After the first shot is fired in either type the slide recoils and cocks and loads the pistols. Double action first shot action types require that you master two trigger actions as subsequent shots after the first shot are single action. The double action only pistol fires each shot with the long heavy pull. The DAO trigger usually lies in position between the single action and double action type trigger, and is not particularly easy to learn. Many of the double action only pistols are hopeless as far as accuracy potential past 15 yards. (The Para LDA is an exception, but requires more acclimation than the single action 1911 handgun.) The perceived advantage of these pistols is liability and administrative: the technical outweighs the tactical. I do not see this as an advantage, but see the systems as unacceptable for tactical use. Only the Light Double Action from Para may be shot well to my standards.

Let's consider terminology. I consider a pistol a double action only if the trigger both lifts the hammer and fires the pistol. A striker fired pistol with a prepped striker is called a double action only but is it really? This takes a stretch of the imagination but the safe action Glock is technically a double action only by a stretch of the term. A service pistol must have safety features in order to have a certain level of protection for personnel and the public, but a pistol that is difficult to fire ac-

Among the best service pistols ounce for ounce is the Springfield LW Operator.

curately doesn't seem like a pistol with a safety feature. Poorly designed slide mounted safeties and long DAO triggers are a triumph of the technical over the tactical. The trend is to make pistols easier to fire, hence the absence of a manual safety, but more difficult to control, hence the heavy trigger action. Conversely the 1911 features a short, crisp trigger action. The 1911 features a positive slide lock safety that is not difficult to learn to control well but that is very positive in use. The safety falls under the thumb in a natural position and in no way impedes speed to an accurate first shot.

One of the essential elements of the service pistol is complete reliability with every service load. This RRA pistol has that reliability in spades.

The 1911 also features the additional safety of a grip safety. Unless this grip safety is fully depressed the pistol will not fire. Modern 1911 handguns usually feature a positive firing pin block. This firing pin lock keeps the firing pin stationary until released, either by pressing the grip safety or by completely pressing the trigger to the rear. Some 1911 handguns, including the FBI's HRT pistols, use a lightweight firing pin and heavy duty firing pin spring to achieve an approximately equal level of drop safety.

Public Issues

While the acknowledgment of the 1911 as an excellent fighting pistol is not difficult, acceptance of the 1911 as a duty pistol is another matter. The Glock will fire with a 5.5 pound trigger press but has no manual safety. The public perception is different, however, because the public must deal with a hammer that is reared back, cocked and locked, with the 1911. "Out of sight, out of mind" applies. The 1911's cocked hammer gets attention. But cocked and locked is the proper carry model. A modern duty holster with a retention strap that runs between the firing pin and the hammer is recommended for uniformed holster use. Many agencies require a thumbbreak holster at all times, even in plain-clothes and off duty. This is a reasonable requirement. These holsters offer an even higher degree of safety. An administrator I once worked with felt that the automatic pistol in general and the 1911 in particular was "dangerous as a coiled rattlesnake." He was perfectly happy to allow officers to carry .357 Magnum and .44 Magnum revolvers, and he approved the problematic and inaccurate Smith and Wesson Model 59 9mm. Only conscientious demonstration will win over the hearts and minds of administrators. Be persistent honest and professional and you may have the 1911, a tactical piece with real advantages, approved for service use.

The point is often made that the 1911 is the most efficient of handguns in trained hands. It will win every competition of any note. But the 1911 has proven well suited to average trained shooters as well, a point that advocates of the 1911 often fail to adequately represent. Those who have difficulty managing a long double action trigger respond well to the 1911. Those with small hands find the 1911 a godsend. Training and knowledge are most important. Trigger press, sight picture, sight alignment and follow-through count but the straight-to-the-rear trigger compression allows good shooting and excellent control. I have trained 17-year-old female shooters with the 1911 .45. They have done well because no one told them they had physical limitations! Even in a compressed time frame we were able to achieve good results. These results were not what I would expect from the graduate of a reputable training academy but they are better than I would have expected with any other handgun given the training time.

The 1911 is comfortable to fire because the grip frame is well designed. It is fast into action because the controls are a model of human engineering. A rapid presentation from the holster is not often needed but when needed the 1911 offers a smooth positive draw, with practice. A rapid follow-up shot is possible because of the low bore axis and inherent controllability of the type. Yet the piece may be made safe instantly with a flick of the safety.

The pistol should be carried and kept at ready on safe until the decision to fire has been made. *Not when you think you will fire, but when you are about to fire.* No other service pistol offers so positive and handy a safety. There is no excuse for walking around with the finger in register or with a pistol off safe. The 1911 has practical handling advantages as a service pistol. As an example, one of the most common in-service accidental discharges involves shoving a pistol into the holster. The common fault is a handgun becoming tangled in the safety strap and the strap actuating the trigger. If the trigger finger is on the trigger during holstering – a terrible but not unheard-of mistake – the pistol will fire. The Glock, revolvers and most DAO pistols are subject to this type of AD. A cocked and locked 1911 will not fire if the trigger contacts the holster strap. If the grip safety is not depressed, the pistol will not fire even if the safety is off. Sure, this is a failsafe against foolish gunhandling but it is a failsafe just the same. Gunhandling is most important but the dual safety features of the 1911 are a real advantage.

When the 1911 is fired, the rapid trigger reset and smooth compression are not the only advantages. The pistol sits lower in the hand than any other service pistol. This low bore axis simply means the centerline of the bore is relatively close to the hand. The grip angle allows a locked wrist at all times and avoidance of the "H" grip

The LW frame service pistols are controllable with practice, as this young solider demonstrates.

or offsetting grip that trainers attempt to avoid. As another advantage, the 1911 can be modified to individual hand size. Removable mainspring housings and trigger options were available with the 1911 long before the modern removable back strap of polymer frame pistols. The flat housing and long trigger work best for shooters with large hands, while the arched housing and short trigger are best for average shooters and speed shooting in my experience. It is difficult to obtain a proper beavertail safety with the arched trigger housing.

Unlike many self-loaders, the 1911 invites practice. There is only so much you can achieve with a DAO pistol. Few shooters fire the 1911 to its true potential. But the challenge is there and we can give it our best efforts. The 1911 is also low maintenance. Among the few items requiring replacement are the recoil spring and in high round count pistols, the extractor. With the modern external extractor pistols from Smith and Wesson and the Para Ordnance Power Extractor, the extractors may never need replacement. Hand fitting skills are not really needed. Disassembly and clearing are simple enough. It takes a few seconds longer to break the 1911 down for maintenance, but when have you needed to speed-disassemble a service pistol?

The main advantage of the pistol is handling but the cartridge is very important. There are other .45 service pistols. The Glock M21 is reliable and accurate enough for service, but the grip frame is too large for most hands. The SIG P 220 is a very accurate and reliable handgun but the high bore axis and long double action trigger press limit its usefulness. As for the cartridge, I have not shot drugged goats and don't believe anyone else has but I have done quite a few tests of the 1911, taken game, and studied its effect. No amount of revisionist history or blurry thinking will change the laws of physics. The combination of frontal diameter, bullet weight and velocity make the .45 ACP an effective service cartridge. The .45 is a low pressure cartridge with a clean powder burn and excellent accuracy potential.

Quality handguns are not inexpensive. Polymer frame handguns are a low-bid wonder. The bean counters love them. For the individual officer in a department that follows the big boy rule ("carry what you are able to qualify with"), the 1911 is a credible choice. Many say the 1911 is not for everyone but I disagree. Anyone who is able to handle a police service pistol at all should be able to handle the 1911. Give the 1911 an honest try. You may find an outstanding service pistol and a lifelong companion.

Best Choices

As we examine theory, application and tradition we realize that the 1911 pistol's primary calling is as a service pistol. Whether for police or military service the 1911 is the outstanding service pistol of two centuries. With this conclusion firmly in mind, we have to choose the attributes of a good service pistol. There are many considerations in a service pistol but the primary considerations are reliability and caliber.

The 1911 pistol with steel frame and 5-inch barrel is the archetypical .45 caliber service pistol. The GI pistol and the consensus pistols are examples of basic service pistols. Today we have service pistols built to a higher standard. These handguns have features that are integrated into the design rather than added on as an afterthought. These handguns features advanced sights, forward cocking serrations in some editions, and even rails for mounting combat lights. The strengthened frame of the Rock River Arms pistols is just one example of a worthwhile improvement. The Novak sights found on a Springfield Loaded Model is another example. (As of this date there have been over 2,000,000 Novak Lo Mount sights produced.) A service pistol is a 1911 designed for the most demanding use and to give the user an advantage. The handguns are similar in some regards and share features such as Novak sights and the full length guide rod. But the main advantage of the service pistols is that we are able to obtain a pistol that is ready for hard use out of the box, without any type of modification.

What do I demand of a service pistol? The pistol must be reliable and simple to maintain. The trigger must be smooth but not so light as to promote accidental discharge or clutching. The sights must be useful in all conditions and the grips must offer good adhesion. I have isolated a number of excellent 1911 handguns that I feel are among the best service pistols ever produced. Let's take a look at them.

Kimber Custom II

The Kimber Custom II has enjoyed wide acceptance in law enforcement. A modified Custom II is in service with the Marine Corps and Kimber has the inside track in military procurement. I would be more than pleased to see the U.S. military adopt the Kimber Custom II and cashier the second rate 9mm pistol now in service. Our young warriors can handle the Kimber pistol. With a level of sustained toil you can master the Kimber Custom II and be as well armed as possible with a handgun. There are those who are both eloquent and hot tempered in favor of this or that polymer frame handgun, but I can equal their decibel power when I must. The Kimber Custom II is a great service pistol.

Of course we require proof of performance. I recently tested a brand new Kimber against my aging and well used but still completely reliable Custom II. The pistol showed no bind or hesitation in fit. While not made for precision but neither a loose plinker, the Custom II is well fitted. The only reason anyone would be poorly armed with this pistol is because of a lack of practice. As expected, the Kimber came out of the box running. There have been no failures to feed, chamber fire or eject with this pistol or any other Kimber we have tested. Accuracy is well above average. The Kimber line features a positive firing pin block or drop safety that is activated by the grip safety. There is no interference with the trigger action. I like this system very much, more so than the Colt Series 80 type.

Accuracy @ 25 Yards

Load	Group
Black Hills 185-gr. JHP	3.4"
Winchester 230-gr. Personal Defense	2.5"
Fiocchi 200-gr. JHP (old stock)	2.75"

Kimber Pro Carry

The Pro Carry is a popular police handgun and as such must be covered. The Pro Carry is a new variety, a 4-inch barrel 1911 with an aluminum frame. The piece is as light as the polymer pistols but more durable. Along with the Springfield Champion and the Para Ordnance Tac Four, 4-inch 1911s are gaining acceptance among those conscious of the dead weight on their hip. I find the Pro Carry well fitted and well balanced. In combat drills the Kimber is faster from leather than the Government Model, and lively in the hand. While the lightweight pistol suffers in combat drills compared to the steel frame pistols, this is a trade off. The gunload and the first few shots are what counts. I have followed the career of the Pro Carry closely, and it gets a clean bill of health.

Accuracy @ 25 Yards

Load	Group
Zero 230-gr. JHP	4.0"
Winchester 230-gr. Bonded Core	3.0"
Black Hills 230-grain JHP	2.75"

Springfield Loaded Model

The Loaded Model features Novak sights, a beavertail safety, an ambidextrous safety and, perhaps most importantly for a service pistol, stainless steel construction is an option. The Loaded Model also features a lightweight firing pin and extra power firing pin spring. This is a reputable safety feature that avoids the complication of the firing pin locks used by Colt, Kimber and Para Ordnance. Just the same there is no firing pin block, which may be an issue on the purchase circular. The FBI SWAT pistols do not use a firing pin block and I trust the Springfield system. While I am perhaps not an avatar of open-mindedness when it comes to monkeying with a proven system, I accept the modern firing pin blocks but prefer the Springfield system.

Stainless pistols were once subject to galling and were not as reliable as carbon steel pistols. The cure was a frame softer than the slide or of subtly different alloy. The Springfield shows no evidence of galling and has proven reliable through thousands of rounds of ammunition. The Loaded Model is an efficient and modern service pistol well worth your time.

Accuracy @ 25 Yards

Load	Group
Winchester 230-grain ball	3.65"
Black Hills 200-gr. SWC	2.0"
Fiocchi 230-gr. XTP	2.8"

Springfield Champion

The Champion has been around for some time and has earned a good reputation. While some were offered in a GI format, the present 4-inch barrel Champion features Novak sights and a speed safety. The 4-inch coned barrel offers good lockup. There is little perceptible play in the barrel and the piece overall is impressive. There are Loaded Model versions available with ambidextrous safety levers and stainless construction.

I have fired several with good results and the Champion tested was no exception. However, the accuracy potential was disappointing. Perhaps I did not find the proper combination or I had a bad day. My son did fire the pistol with more accuracy than I. The Champion pistol was reliable and handled well. The trigger was smooth enough at five pounds. While I performed adequately in accuracy testing and was well satisfied with combat drills, something was amiss in the equation. (The LW Operator has demonstrated much better accuracy and our old Champion Super Tuned is a phenomenon.)

Accuracy @ 25 Yards

Load	Group
Black Hills 185-grain JHP	4.0"
Winchester 185-grain Silvertip	4.1"
Hornady 230-grain JHP +P	3.65"

Para 7.45 PXT

The Para SSP or Single Stack Pistol is a service pistol with good features. The Para Power Extractor (PXT) features excellent extraction potential. We have tested an SSP with matte finish but gravitated to the handsome and more expensive Sterling edition illustrated. While the Sterling with its stainless with blacked-out round top slide may be window-dressing, the 7.45 shoots well. The trigger was properly set with each part fitted to suit my idiosyncracies as the pistol shot very well in my hands. In combat drills the piece was not up to the Kimber or Springfield, but the difference was slight. Perhaps the lower profile of the sights was at play. Just the same, the pistol ran at about 90% of the potential of the other 5-inch service pistols. In slow fire accuracy potential, the pistol really shone. While the matte finish SSP is less expensive and perhaps attractive in a proletarian manner, it performed well. We preferred the Sterling edition. The 7.45 is a good service pistol.

Accuracy @ 25 Yards

Load	Group
Black Hills 200-gr. SWC	2.5"
Winchester USA 230-gr. FMJ	3.8"
CorBon 185-gr. JHP	2.8"

SIG Granite Series Rail

SIG's 1911 is billed as a service pistol rather than a high-end pistol. It does not have some of the high-end features such as the ambidextrous safety and forward cocking serrations. This is a dirt-tough performer with much to recommend it. The GSR is heavier than the average 5-inch barrel 1911 due to the addition of a frame rail for adding a combat light. Nothing wrong with that; the addition of a rail mounted light is something that experienced officers and home defense shooters find attractive. The SIG may not be as lively in the hand as a lighter 1911 but it is very solid in the hand.

Our pistol has been fitted with the 10-8 combat sights and this improves performance to a considerable degree. The U notch sights are especially well suited to aging eyes. How much accuracy is enhanced is an open question but the mechanical accuracy of the GSR has been high from the first shot. This is a rugged handgun that we have come to trust. I replaced the rather blah factory grips with a set of tactical grips from Wilson Combat. Adhesion is excellent. The GSR is clearly a front runner as the most effective of service pistols. Of particular note is the pistol's relatively mild recoil with +P loads.

Accuracy @ 25 Yards

Load	Group
Cor Bon 200-gr. JHP	2.95"
Black Hills 230-gr. JHP	2.50"
Wolf 230-gr. Ball	3.75"

ALUMINUM FRAME 1911 PISTOLS

Chapter 12:

Oh my aching back! After carrying a steel frame handgun for a day or more, the weight may induce a situation similar to diaper drag on the trousers and feel like a pile driver on my back. I do not wish to save a few ounces at the expense of my life but I do wish to carry the lightest effective gear possible. You have to understand aluminum frame handguns to use them properly. When I deploy a LW frame 1911 I do so with confidence because I have

The 1911 is the most controllable of big bore handguns, and this was proven in wartime.

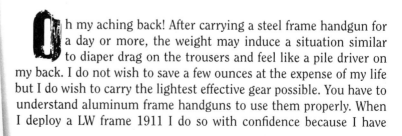

The author has carried the Colt Commander (left) for many years but these days the Kimber CDP is his top choice.

This military intelligence officer and NRA certified trainer finds the Kimber CDP good enough to ride with.

proofed the pistol, followed proper procedure, and practiced. I often deploy a Springfield Loaded Model with LW frame and the comfort level is pleasing. Weight reduction is on the order of 25%. I will not tell you that an aluminum frame pistol is as durable as a steel frame handgun or that the handguns are as easy to use as well as a steel frame pistol but the tradeoffs are reasonable. If you are practical and serious concerning personal defense, you may have come to the same conclusions I have. Lightweight 1911s make sense.

Practical aluminum frame pistols were introduced just after World War II. Aircraft aluminum technology evolved rapidly and the technology transferred well to handguns. In less than a decade, aluminum made the jump from an expensive showcase such as the Stout Scarab automobile to the Colt Commander pistol. The Colt Commander featured a shortened slide and barrel of 4-1/4 inches. The aluminum frame reduced weight to 28 ounces. The Commander made it possible to be well armed with a degree of comfort. Recoil is more evident

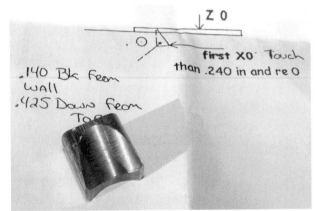

Sometimes the frame is hopelessly damaged in the LW 1911. This EGW frame insert is a lifesaver in those situations.

than with the Government Model but not uncomfortable with the proper shooting grip and stance and not uncontrollable with proper practice. A rule of thumb is that the aluminum frame pistol requires about 25%

CorBon PowRBall feeds like hardball and will not gouge the feed ramp. This is a good diet for aluminum frame pistols.

more practice to achieve a high degree of proficiency. The pistol will never be as controllable as a steel frame handgun in skilled hands, but speed and accuracy to the most important first shot are equal. You must understand these rules.

Many comment that the recoil of a LW .45 sneaks up on you. The first few magazines are not a challenge but after a box of ammunition you are rubbing your wrists. Be certain practice sessions are well spent. Only standard pressure loads should be used. +P loads are too much for good control in a LW .45. The Winchester 230-grain Bonded Core or the 230-grain Personal Defense load are good choices for the Commander and Defender size .45s. The Bonded Core load is noticeably hotter than most but not quite in +P range.

The main complaint with the LW .45 has been damaged feed ramps. The cartridge should be at the proper 1.250" overall length for best feed reliability but makers don't always produce ideal ammunition. The service life of an aluminum frame pistol is many thousands of rounds of ammunition, but once the feed ramp is gouged or damaged wear proceeds rapidly. At one time ammunition companies produced bullet shapes that required the feed ramp of the 1911 to be polished for good

When reassembling the pistol be careful when you snap the slide lock in place with the aluminum frame pistol.

feed reliability. Original design specification called for a 1/32 inch gap between the barrel and frame portions of the ramp. Some bullet nose shapes took a gouge out of the feed ramp. You might be able to dress the feed ramp to an extent but a new frame was needed in some cases. Evolution Gun Works offers a steel frame insert that can repair a damaged frame if you own such a pis-

The DGL Badger Backup is very comfortable with the Colt Defender. You can do things with LW frames not possible or comfortable with steel frames.

tol. The repair is not for amateurs but requires a skilled machinist. Today frames seem to be of better material and the ammunition situation is much better.

An exception to the rule against +P loads in the LW .45 is the CorBon PowRBall load. Since the 165-grain load is lightweight, momentum is less, and the round nose always feeds but expands well in test medium. If I were to deploy an original Commander and did not wish to carry hardball, I would load PowRBall. This is a good product.

A solution to the frame wear problem is simply to use a ramped barrel in every aluminum frame handgun. Even today, ramped barrels are not universal in aluminum frame handguns. There are no concerns about feed ramp damage with this design. With a little care you may avoid the disasters that occur with LW 1911 pistols. As an example, special care is needed when disassembling and reassembling the LW .45. If you detail

The 5-inch pistol is this much longer than the Commander and offers a better chance of a hit due to the longer sight radius.

strip the pistol, the frame may be damaged by prying the safety away from it. Any time one part is steel and another aluminum, the aluminum part is subject to damage. The plunger tube is another troublesome item. When you field strip the pistol, avoid snapping the slide

This shooter is doing his best with the Kimber Tactical Model, a LW frame 3-inch pistol. His best was very good.

A good argument for LW efficiency is found in the form of the Kimber Tactical model. With every advantage of a full size custom pistol, the Tactical Model is a great shooter.

lock into the plunger tube as the tube may wallow in the frame. This is difficult to repair. Be careful in pressing the part back into place. Ten-thumbed handling will trash your aluminum frame handgun.

There are other concerns with aluminum frame handguns, mostly pertaining to the short slide variants. If you use the pistol heavily it is a good idea to change the recoil spring more often than with a Government Model .45. Rather than changing the recoil spring every 3,000 rounds of full power ammunition I would recommend that the recoil spring of a Commander be changed every 2,000 rounds and every 1,500 rounds for a 3-inch barrel variant. This simple expedient will keep you out of trouble as far as malfunctions go and also increase the service life of the pistol by protecting it from battering.

Among my favorite light 1911 carry guns and the smallest handgun I normally carry is a Colt Defender. This pistol has proven excellent in service, with several thousand trouble-free rounds. I have fitted Ahrends grip panels to it and normally use Wilson Combat magazines. The pistol is carried in a Milt Sparks Summer Special IWB holster. This is as good as it gets in a 22-ounce defensive handgun.

The lightweight aluminum frame handgun is a great boon to concealed carry handgunners. It has the same power and intrinsic accuracy as its steel frame counterpart but at a considerable weight saving. It requires more practice to learn but if it are used for real, it speaks with authority. You need not sacrifice combat ability for convenience. Aluminum frame handguns are proven effective and here to stay.

COMMANDERS, OFFICERS MODELS AND DEFENDERS

Chapter 13:

f there is a legitimate criticism of the 1911 as a carry gun, it is size and weight. The pistol is thin but long and heavy. Do not let anyone convince you the 1911 is dated. It is simply from another era in which handguns were designed to save your life and were not based on liability concerns. The pistol is designed to be as fast as a good boxer, with a well timed and devastating blow foremost.

These choices are pretty simple. They are all aluminum frame pistols with barrel lengths of (top to bottom) 5, 4 and 3 inches.

Top to bottom, the popular concealed carry barrel lengths – 4.25-inch, 4-inch and 3-inch.

Before the advent of the Commander, you had little choice in a carry piece: either carry a heavy big bore or a light .38 or 9mm. The Commander changed the world.

The Colt Commander is the result of a desire for a lighter and handier 1911. While the story goes the Commander was designed to offer the military a downsized pistol, there had been prototypes of a short .45 kicking around Hartford before World War II. The use of aircraft grade aluminum for the frame allowed a very light and handy concealment piece. The Commander retains the full size grip of the Government Model. This allows comfortable firing and a good sharp draw. Size has much to do with confidence and control. Although it is appreciably lighter than the Government Model, the Commander is a controllable handgun – with practice.

With the Series 70 production run the Combat Commander Colt was introduced. This is simply a steel frame Commander. The Combat Commander is now known as simply the Commander while the aluminum frame Commander is the LW Commander. The steel frame Commander offers excellent balance. The problem with reducing the length of the pistol as far as reliability was the higher slide velocity, which was addressed by spring technology. But then we also had a shorter spring that had to exert more pressure. The shortened slide length

While heavier than some pistols, the steel frame Commander is very controllable and well balanced.

reduces the total reciprocating mass but also alters the way the magazine presents the round to the breech face. In the end, it was a wonder the Commander was so reliable. It's a great pistol.

Choices, choices and more choices: 5-inch LW frame, 4.25-inch steel frame, 4-inch LW frame and 3-inch barrel LW frame.

The Officer's Model was the original short 1911, with a 3.5-inch barrel and grip shortened enough to cut magazine capacity by one round. Today most compact pistols have 3-inch barrels. The Officer's Model demanded considerable revision of the design but the 3-inch pistols even more so. In order to accommodate the sharper barrel tilt in a short slide pistol, the barrel no longer used a barrel bushing. The Commander used a standard bushing, although it was shortened. The Defender features a belled barrel that contacts the slide directly. One of the standard 1911 locking lugs was removed in order to allow the barrel to recoil proportionately more to the rear of the pistol. These design changes were essential in order to produce a functioning short slide handgun.

The 3-inch idiom has proven very popular. The Officer's Model is now out of production and seems unlikely to return. These three idioms – the Government Model, the Commander and the Officer's Model – were once the defining descriptor of 1911 frame and slide sizes. Today Government Model, Commander and Defender are more apt descriptions of the increasingly popular compact and ultra-compact descriptions.

A new and very popular handgun is the 4-inch barrel 1911. Some of the best of the modern 1911s are 4-inch

Go for the gold – this is the Ed Brown Kobra Karry.

Kimber, Spyderco, and easy carry. This is good kit for concealed carry.

guns. These include the Kimber Pro Carry, the Kimber CDP, the Para TAC FOUR and the Springfield Champion. The 4-inch barrel 1911s are more in line in size and weight with the popular service pistols from other makers such as the SIG P226 or Glock Model 23. They are superior service pistols and take much drag off of the uniform belt. They are also ideal concealed carry pistols. They are available in both aluminum frame and steel frame versions in weight ranging from about 26 to 33 ounces. These pistols feature the belled barrel type lockup as they are too short to utilize a barrel bushing properly. In my experience these are very reliable handguns. They clear leather quickly, get on target quickly, and offer excellent hit potential. They also rate high on the smile test, with most raters reacting favorably to the handling and accuracy potential of these handguns.

A LW frame 1911 is not for non-dedicated personnel. The pistol demands attention to detail and proper technique to master. I find the lightweight 4-inch barrel 1911 easier to control than a polymer frame .40 caliber pistol, but there is time and effort in the equation. The difference is that you will be able to reach a high level of competence with the 1911 that may elude shooters using the polymer frame pistols. The 4-inch pistol certainly falls into the 'if I could have only one pistol' category. It is that versatile.

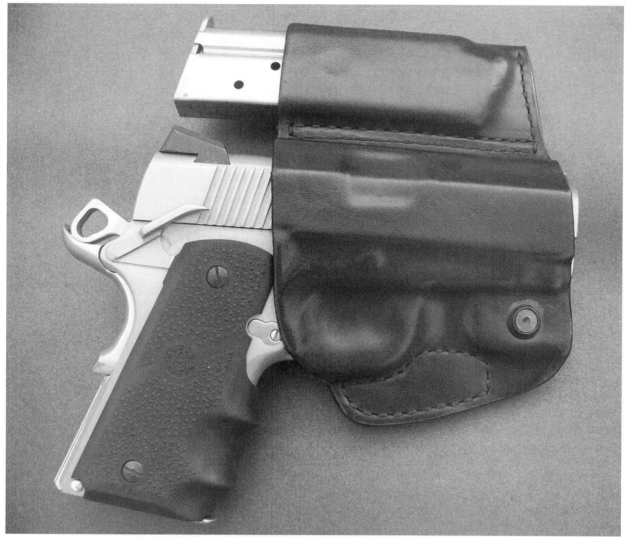

This Springfield LW is carried in a Blackhawk holster. Lots of efficiency but little weight.

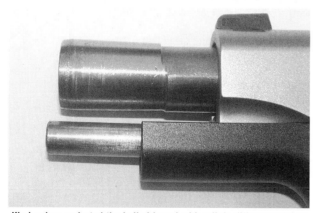

Kimber has perfected the belled barrel with a little different twist on the equation.

At this point you may reasonably ask for a recommendation on which 1911 is best for you. My recommendation is always to begin with a steel frame 5-inch barrel Government Model. I might add that it is best to purchase the best quality handgun you can afford for a good return on performance and future trade-in. If you are beginning with a concealment pistol, then the steel frame Commander is an excellent first choice. I simply do not recommend jumping into a lightweight frame 1911 without considerable experience with the Government Model. A good 4-inch barrel steel frame pistol may be concealed, and with proper selection of a good holster such as the inside the waistband holster illustrated from Milt Sparks, then you will have a good comfortable platform for carrying the pistol. There is more weight but as you begin your shooting career you will appreciate it.

Moving to the lightweight 3-inch barrel pistols such as the Colt Defender is a gradual process. As an example, I began my 1911 journey with the Combat Commander. It was some time before I considered the smaller pistols, and I found many of them not as reliable as the Government Model. Times have changed. The Colt Defender and the compact Kimber pistols are

Today we have 4-inch pistols with night sights and complete reliability – and frame rails as well. The LW Operator is a first-class all-around 1911.

another story. These handguns demand attention to detail but they are reliable, accurate enough for personal defense, and good examples of the gunmaker's art. They are not as useful for all around informal target practice and competition shooting but that is not their design goal. These are first class lightweight personal defense handguns. When you consider the snub nose .38s and double action only 9mm pistols in wide use, the Colt Defender as an example is a wonderful defensive handgun in trained hands.

The short sight radius of the Defender and the Kimber compact pistols may challenge marksmanship. A slight misalignment of the front sight is less noticeable when the sight radius is shorter than average. I recommend that any compact defensive handgun have good sights. Superior sights are an aid in hit probability, perhaps more important in the case of the compacts that with the full size handguns. Fit, feel and a long sight radius may be compromised in the compact pistols, but, just the same, these are first class defensive handguns.

Despite their short grips and short sight radius, the position of their controls is all 1911, and that means very ergonomic. Increased recoil is far from startling if you have began your shooting career on the Government Model. These handguns are a technical accomplishment well worth your praise and attention.

Common 1911 Frame and Slide Sizes

	Gov't Model	Commander	4-inch	Defender
OAL	8.5"	7.75"	7.5"	6.75"
Sight Radius	6.8"	5.95"	5.7"	4.7"
Height	5.25"	5.25"	5.25"	4.75"
Weight	38 oz.	33.0 oz.	28 oz.	22.5 oz.

Note: LW Commander weighs 28 oz.; weight illustrated is for steel frame.

TOP END 1911s

Chapter 14:

I have optimism for man as an effective being. He is ever-advancing and demanding more and better tools. A number of improved or customized 1911 pistols have been tested in the course of researching this work. Some – a vary small percentage – tested my powers of invective. They provided endless moments of pure aggravation. The problem is that not everyone can improve the 1911. It takes more than simply adding parts.

As an example, not many years ago a maker collected together American-made slides and frames and GI parts and offered a cut-rate pistol. It did not work well. Another offered a high-end pistol with the same quality frame and slide but improved sights, but the internals were not well fitted. The new pistol had three times the features and price and a well-known name but worked no better. When you attempt an improvement over a proven handgun it is important to produce a smooth, integrated package. The sights must look as if they have been melted onto the slide, not hammered on.

Christen Smith finds the Les Baer a pure joy to use and fire.

The Les Baer Monolith is a good example of the high-end 1911, perhaps the best example.

I have seen stabs at high-end 1911 handguns that were as beautiful as a wart. Others were nice looking but so unreliable they needed the bum's rush out of town. All high-end pistols are not necessarily something you can bet your life on. I am not embittered or cynical but a number of the pistols I have tested during the past two decades were laden with problems. During the time I have tested these pistols I have had more than a casual interest. I was looking for the real thing for personal use. Many shooters today feel that the only personal defense pistol worthwhile is a GI .45 or Springfield Mil Spec. They have seen staked-on sights fall off and poorly fitted safeties break off. They have seen pistols fail. Part of the answer lies in the success of genuine craftsmen such as Ed Brown and Bill Wilson. Ed Brown and Bill Wilson pistols always work. Others wished to jump on the bandwagon to success but they simply were not qualified. The gun butcher made a revolting reconstruction of many a good 1911. Don't get me wrong: most gunsmiths are considerate and capable. One of these that I hold in high regard is Don Williams of the Action Works. You can expect a wait of 12 to 24 months for a custom pistol from Don Williams but the wait will be worthwhile. Accurate Plating and Weaponry and Robar Industries are other shops with a good name.

Today we have improved or top-end pistols available from the factory. These purpose-designed high-end pistols known as tactical or combat handguns garner a lot attention. They are not simply GI pistols with added parts. They feature function and durability as a baseline. In other words, the pistols are not chosen off an assembly line for upgrading. They begin life with superior fitting. The slide to frame fit or particularly the barrel fit is improved. The pistols shows that a maker is sweating the details. Top-end 1911 handguns that combine accuracy and reliability were once rare. This is no longer the case. I think that it is important to grasp the delineating line between a good service pistol and a top end 1911. For example you can take a Springfield GI and add parts and produce a pistol much like a Loaded Model although this would be an expensive route. You cannot take a Loaded Model and produce a Professional Model. The frame and slide are handled differently at the factory. You can add a Nowlin barrel to the Loaded Model – the Nowlin is specified by the FBI for their SWAT pistol – and you will reap an improvement. But you will not have a true Professional. The Springfield Tactical Response Pistol (TRP) is also a custom shop item. The Kimber Custom II is another good pistol but you cannot take the Custom II and produce a Gold Combat. The cost would be prohibitive in light of the availability of the real thing straight from the factory. Custom Shop guns are often especially fitted at the factory by a process that while indeed special is also affordable.

The Kimber treatment isn't the same for every pistol, and that means custom quality. This is the Aegis.

Let's look at some of the better high-end pistols. There are a number of good service pistols that didn't make high-end status. The Colt XSE, Springfield Loaded Model and Kimber Custom II are service pistols. So is the SIG GSR. Occasionally particularly good examples will push into top-end accuracy but the overall package isn't as capable. As examples of top-end pistols I have chosen several from Kimber, Springfield and Rock River Arms. And then there is Les Baer. These pistols feature good sights, good trigger compression, checkering when appropriate, and excellent fit and finish. Lets take a run to the range with each.

Kimber Gold Combat

It speaks volumes that three examples of the Kimber pistol are included in this shootout. I suppose it says something about the author's preferences as well but then this is what we have on hand. The Kimber Gold Combat is arguably a fine combination of performance. The pistol features luminous iron sights of the Meprolight brand. The pistol features first class adhesion. The front strap is well checkered as is the bottom of the trigger guard, a nice touch. There is a modest magazine guide and my example sports rosewood grip panels. The newer pistols use non-slip micarta. The pistol features the usual beavertail grip safety and ambidextrous safety. The advantage of the Gold Combat is in fitting and overall handling. The improvements over the Custom II are in grip adhesion, a very consistent trigger compression, and in both practical and intrinsic accuracy. The Gold Combat runs with the best custom guns. You may

The Kimber Gold Combat features front strap checkering and attention to detail that is a product of the Kimber Custom Shop.

notice that the example illustrated shows considerable wear on its Kimpro finish. The pistol has been used hard and, I have to admit, even abused. The finish has held up well but in the future I will probably choose stainless steel for my hard use pistols. Absolute accuracy is also good. The pistol has grouped five shots into two inches with quality ammunition such as the Winchester 230-grain Bonded Core on any number of occasions. I seldom shoot this one for groups, however. It is too good a combat pistol.

Springfield Tactical Response Pistol (TRP)

The Springfield features sharper checkering than most, which gives excellent purchase when you are shooting fast-paced drills and when your hands are cold or sweaty. The micarta grips are often universally voted best of the breed. The pistol features a well-fitted match grade barrel. Trigger compression is smooth and the pistol features Novak sights with self luminous inserts. Perhaps the great mechanical advantage over other types is that the TRP uses the Smith and Alexander magazine guide. This fully checkered guide from the Mag Guide people is the standard by which all others are judged. Nothing handles like the Smith and Alexander.

The TRP was delivered with two magazines including one magazine that did not work well, but we have on hand a good supply of Wilson Combat ETM magazines

to cure that problem. The sights were not properly adjusted, but we took care of that as well. There have been absolutely no functional problems with this pistol once the recalcitrant magazine was trashed. Accuracy has been excellent, above average for the type. The single best group we have fired has been a 25-yard 15/16-inch group with the Black Hills 230-grain JHP. Most groups with premium ammunition have been in the two-inch range, but with the best types the pistol shows its heritage. I appreciate the TRP's heightened performance over the Loaded Model and see little need for the Professional Model in my collection.

Springfield's TRP is a spectacular performer in trained hands.

Kimber Eclipse

The Eclipse may not be a high-end pistol in the sense the Gold Combat is but I included this pistol on the basis of performance. The Eclipse does have some of the features of the Gold Combat and plenty of performance. This pistol has been among the single most accurate factory handguns I have ever used. The combination of well checkered grips and front strap checkering gives excellent purchase and the trigger action is a smooth four pounds. The pistol always functions with light and heavy loads and gives excellent all-around accuracy. My example is fitted with the vault-tough Kimber adjustable sight, a huge improvement over adjustable types of the past. I have registered several groups just over one inch with the pistol, the best coming from a handload that jolts the Nosler 185-grain JHP to well over 1000 fps. The single most accurate factory load is no surprise – the Black Hills 200-grain SWC has always given excellent results.

Kimber Tactical

This is the only compact featured among the top end pistols, but its place is well deserved. It is even more important that a compact pistol have good features.

This Kimber Custom Defense Pistol is another example of the work done by the Kimber Custom Shop.

Compacts are more difficult to hang onto when you are firing and the sights are more difficult to keep lined up. As such you need all of the advantage you can get. Many shooters will claim a GI type compact is "good enough for carry." Well, it may be, but if you wish every advantage when carrying a compact .45, this is it. I have a Colt Defender that has served long and well but when the advantages of the Kimber are taken into account, there is really little comparison. You may note that my particular Kimber is among a few in a production run that used an external extractor. What the hell am I doing with this, you may ask? Well, the pistol has proven completely reliable and, like the Gold Combat, it has paid its dues. I have heard some of the external extractor pistols manufactured from 1993-1996 did not come out of the box running. Mine did and it still does. The pistol fits my hand well and the combination of features makes this the single most combat-accurate compact pistol I have ever used. I have carefully benchrested the piece with the Winchester 230-grain FBI load and achieved a three-inch five-shot group at 25 yards.

Rock River Arms

The Rock River 1911 is currently out of production but available in used condition if you are lucky enough – I found a dozen on Guns America this morning. As I write this, RRA is swamped with orders for their AR-15 rifle. Who knows when the pistol will be back in production, but we hope it will be soon. The RRA is delivered with well-executed front strap checkering and excellent fit and finish. My example features Bomar sights and a Novak front post. It is more of a custom pistol than a production pistol, so this account may be colored by handfitting in the case of my own pistol. But all RRA pistols feature a strengthened frame in the area where 1911s tend to crack. My example also features a BarSto barrel while the production RRA features another type. This is personal preference. This is too good of a pistol to let die. As for accuracy, when it comes to this pistol the piece is obviously more accurate than I can hold. I have worked up several handloads that have given good service. The Black Hills 230-grain JHP has delivered groups of 1-1/4 inches on several occasions. The pistol shoots into two inches at 25 yards with practically anything.

Wilson Combat

If the Wilson Combat pistols are not top-end, none is. These handguns are completely made up of Wilson Combat parts. Many makers use Wilson Combat parts and government agencies, including the FBI, have specified Wilson Combat parts in their SWAT team handguns. The handguns are the most expensive mentioned but well worth their price. I have tested several Wilson Combat pistols including a long serving Close Quarters

Another example of Kimber individuality on high end pistols: the Raptor.

Battle pistol. The results have been excellent. The Wilson Combat pistol does not feature a full length guide rod but just the same will group with the best custom handguns and is easily field stripped. The pistol is tight but it does not bind after firing a few hundred dirty handloads. Accuracy is often gilt edged. For example, I have fired several groups of two inches or less with factory ammunition such as the Speer 230-grain Gold Dot, a good defense load. With specifically tailored handloads the Wilson Combat .45 will do even better.

A handgun is only the sum of its parts. The Wilson Combat pistol is made up of very good parts. My impression is that they are built for long term serviceability above all else.

Les Baer

We cannot be equivocal concerning accuracy and quality. The pistol either has them or it does not. The Les Baer pistols have quality and have plenty of accuracy in spades. The only quibble I have with the type is a small one that seems to have been resolved: the original Baer pistols were probably delivered too tight. They required considerable effort to rack the slide and a lengthy break in period. Just the same, the average Les Baer pistol – if "average" can be used to describe this type of handgu – was capable of a three-inch group at 50 yards with quality ammunition. Not 25 but 50 yards. It takes a lot of money and more than a little time and effort to accomplish this type of repeatable accuracy with a custom pistol. Lots of care and experience in fitting the barrel is required. Les Baer knew this and elected to produce his own slides, frames, barrels and small parts. He gained control over every part of the production process. The result is an estimable pistol designed for excellence. Baer's design target is not to sell 50,000 guns a year but to produce a top-end 1911 that will perform to a high standard in the hands of a skilled shooter. My personal Monolith may not be the most practical pistol, but I am enamored of the type.

Note the quality of the forward cocking serrations. This is not found on typical production pistols.

The Monolith features a elongated dust cover. Before you jump on the Monolith bandwagon, realize that the Monolith is not legal for IDPA and certain other types of competition because of its length. It will not fit "in the box," in other words. Holsters are difficult to come by with Rusty Sherrick recommended as one of the few makers who produce such gear. This does not bother me a whit. My Les Baer is used for targets and for pure shooting enjoyment. Period. I see nothing wrong with that at all. I have other handguns for defense; this is one is for pride of ownership. It is also a handgun that challenges the author to perform at his best. And finally I am able to test handgun loads and understand just how accurate these loads and a .45 ACP handgun can be.

I am hoping one day to own one of the short Comanche-type Monolith pistols. I will have to stop robbing the piggy bank for other handguns and let the pennies add up a while longer! The fit finish and performance of the Les Baer pistols leave nothing to be desired. I have stopped short of recommending the type for service because I have not used mine hard. I have fired it a lot but I do not recall when it has been found dirty and it certainly has not been abused. The pistol is quite reliable and should prove as reliable in service as some of the other elevated pistols. The type has simply not been proven in extensive testing as some of the others have. As a blue steel and walnut man I find the Les Baer pistols extraordinarily attractive. As for accuracy, I have a standard handload using the match grade accurate Nosler 185-grain JHP at just over 1,000 fps. The Les Baer pistol will group these into an inch and a little more almost on demand. I have to do my part.

I own pistols that are as accurate with certain loads but few that are as accurate over a wide spectrum of loads as the Les Baer. And the fact is, many handguns that are accurate at shorter range fall apart at 50 yards. The Les Baer is more accurate at 50 yards than most handguns at 25 yards. This is a very appealing handgun.

MEU SOC

A few words on this legendary pistol are warranted. The more I learn about the 1911 the more I respect the design. At times I am in awe. While my personal experience with the 1911 is extensive there are men with much, much more hands-on experience. Many soldiers have seen more action in a day than I saw in over 20 years of police work. That they choose the 1911 above all other handguns is a satisfying reinforcement of my own opinions.

When the 1911 handgun was replaced in official issue in 1981, many of us were appalled. Not that new pistols were not needed; the old GI guns were worn out. But that a foreign design in a minor caliber was adopted was rather surprising. That the choice was based on poor scholarship is an understatement. The Walther P-38 had

Marines practicing with the MEU SOC.

influenced certain types in the military and with the Beretta 92 the military had their highly developed double stack magazine version of the Walther. (The Smith and Wesson Model 39 is basically an American P-38 but was not officially adopted.) The Walther P-38 is a fine pistol and a very influential handgun. But it is neither as powerful nor as robust and reliable as the 1911.

The comments I have heard from veterans about the 1911's replacement cannot be repeated here but suffice it to say that as long as supplies held out, the 1911 was the handgun of choice. It must be noted that none of the 1911 handguns in military inventory had been manufactured later than 1945. It is a moot point that the M9 pistol wasn't tested against new 1911 handguns but against well-worn pistols with different design parameters. The original 1911 had been built under a system that demanded a five-inch 25-yard group and a 10-inch 50 yard group with military ammunition. We can only imagine what a well-worn pistol was capable of!

Almost as soon as the contract for the 9mm NATO pistol was let, the Marines began looking for a few good pistols. And they were 1911 .45s. The Force Recon Element of the Marine Expeditionary Unit began to search for a pistol worthy of the young Marines. A major concern was the fact that this special unit training schedule included firing 50,000 rounds during a training cycle. During the course of writing seven books over a 10-year period I have fired perhaps 100,000 rounds or more in testing a hundred 1911s or so. Concentrated training in select budget teams is for more demanding and tells a lot about handgun durability. A contact in the service

tells me that several operators have exceeded the 50,000 round count deemed necessary for a 1911 rebuild. Some have gone 80,000 rounds. Very few of us will subject a pistol to this type of use.

For example, at present I own and use two 1911 handguns with over 20,000 rounds each fired. The others, over a dozen of them, may bring the total round count for my brace of pistols to 80,000 rounds. Yet, one in-service pistol has fired this many rounds without any problems. Some of the high round-count pistols are on the original extractor ejector and internal parts. The Precision Weapons Section of the USMC schedules rebuilds of the MEU/SOC pistols at 10,000 rounds. This rebuild does not always happen. According to sources close to the PWS, the first MEU SOC pistols were built on GI frames that dated to 1945 or earlier. The frames were re-stamped and rebuilt. According to another source, one frame was isolated and found to have 500,000 rounds on the frame. The long frame life coupled with the 1911 parts durability could not be expected from any other handgun. It simply isn't in the geometry of any other type. Aluminum frame pistols in particular will not survive a fraction of this total.

When rebuilding 1911 pistols, the PWS had considerable leeway in ordering parts. A serialized frame would represent a new pistol, however, so the orders were primarily for slides and parts. Many of the original pistols featured Springfield slides and BarSto barrels. The frame was gutted and a veritable who's who of custom parts were fitted. The Wilson Combat extractor was heavily used. It is a matter of course for these custom

The Springfield Champion Super Tuned. Note the Heinie sights and tactical grips.

Springfield's Super Tuned monogram really means what it says. These are exceptional handguns.

fitted pistols to have the serial number stamped on the barrel and on the right side of the slide and sometimes other locations. This is a departure from the usual Mil Spec demand for complete interchangeability with other handguns. The numbered system is demanded of high-end performance handguns. A well-fitted pistol has less eccentric wear and will last much longer than a general issue handgun. The original pistols used Pachmayr grips for non-slip purchase. The Pachmayr is never a bad choice.

As the program proceeded, some pistols were given a checkered front strap and synthetic grips of micarta or G10. The Simonich Strider grip was used often. At a later date with more armories overloaded with work, purchases were made of commercial 1911 handguns. The Kimber pistol as supplied to LAPD SWAT is one example of a pistol favored by the USMC. This handgun is similar to the Custom II but fitted with night sights and given the checkered front strap treatment. Quite a few new MEU SOC pistols are based on the Kimber. There have been reports of the Springfield Professional, the FBI SWAT pistol, in use by the unit in small numbers.

Springfield Professional

Not long ago I attended an NRA instructor's class. I particularly enjoyed working with a young marine and operator named Shane. Shane qualified with a Springfield Professional. The Springfield Professional is the civilian version of the Federal Bureau of Investigation's Bureau Model. Supplied with a custom grade barrel and careful hand fitting, the Professional is as good as it gets in a factory available handgun. When the FBI tested prospective SWAT pistols, the Springfield Professional passed the test with flying colors and no malfunctions in the firing of 20,000 rounds. This makes the Professional the single most proven 1911 handgun of all time.

There is often a question asked concerning the high-end pistols, particularly the Springfield: is the TRP or the Professional worth twice the tariff of a Loaded Model or three times in the case of the Professional? The TRP is a tight, accurate and capable handgun with features that make it more desirable than the Loaded Model. It is well worth its price. As for the Professional Model, it will take a great shot to isolate the difference between the TRP and the Pro. You will know then you reach that point.

TARGET GRADE 1911s

Chapter 15:

The Gold Cup remains among the most accurate of any modern 1911 pistols.

here is a class of 1911 handguns that are designed to deliver first class accuracy above all else. They are also designed to function with relatively light target loads. While some of these handguns are versatile all-around handguns, the true target grade 1911 as exemplified by the Colt Gold Cup Trophy is a specialized pistol. After WWI 1911 handguns were used in National Match shoots. A pistol capable of grouping five shots into 10 inches at 50 yards was not an effective choice for 50-yard bullseye matches. The Colt National Match pistol was developed by Army gunsmiths and later codified by Colt as a regular production handgun.

The Colt Gold Cup illustrated has been fitted with grips from Deathgrips.com

The Springfield Loaded Model Target is an exceptional 1911 in every way.

The Springfield target sights are first class, vault tough and well suited to accurate fire.

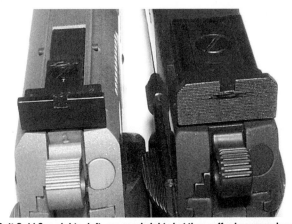

Colt Gold Cup sights, left, are good sights but they suffer in comparison to the Kimber adjustable sights fitted to the Eclipse. Note Eclipse has tritium insert.

Suffice it to say the Gold Cup pistol features a host of improvements that for the most part center upon the trigger action and the fitting of the barrel. Moreover, the Gold Cup is delivered with a standard weight recoil spring. If you wish to use the pistol with standard loads, you must also replace the lighter hammer spring. A great aid is the Wilson Combat Spring Caddy. This neat pouch comes with an assortment of recoil springs that allow the end user to tune his pistol specifically for target loads. I have loaded the Oregon Trail 180-grain SWC as light as 650 fps with good function with the aid of a 10-pound recoil spring. (Standard rating is 16 pounds.) The most accurate factory load in an unmodified Gold Cup is often the Black Hills 200-grain SWC.

However, this load breaks 870 fps. While it will function in any pistol that feeds hardball, this is a bit heavy for target use. A 185- to 200-grain SWC at 750 to 800 fps is preferred. With careful tuning there is no reason that the Gold Cup cannot produce good accuracy with a light bullet at modest velocity.

Today there are match-grade 1911 handguns offered by the major makers. Examples include the Kimber Gold Match and the Springfield Trophy Match. Both are excellent handguns, and both offer well-designed adjustable sights. Adjustable sights and an appropriate post front sight of sufficient height to allow good adjustment are mandatory for a target-grade 1911 handgun. A handgun that I have great confidence in

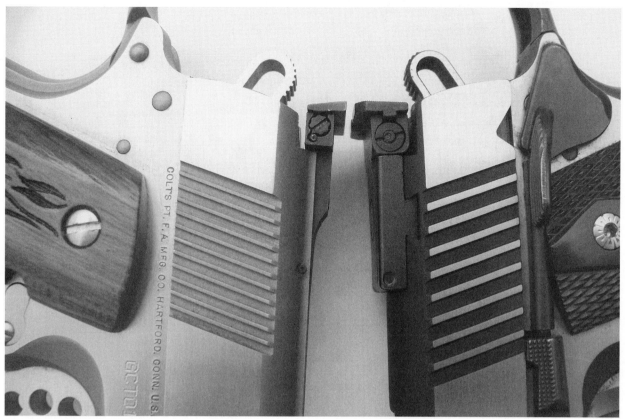

The dovetail attachment of the Kimber, right, is much more rugged than the old style roll pin attachment of the Colt, left.

The Kimber adjustable sight has proven to be rugged enough for hard use, a great improvement over adjustable sights of a generation ago.

Kimber offers first class target grade pistols right off the shelf.

that is less expensive than some target grade pistols is the Kimber Eclipse in the adjustable sight version. The sights are well designed and will not be easily knocked out of whack. The Gold Cup is at a disadvantage as far as rugged sights are concerned. The sights are well designed for target use and the adjustment is good, but the method of attaching the sights to the frame is lacking. The sights are attached by a roll pin that is prone to working loose or even being ejected in high round-count pistols. The pat answer often given is to replace the roll pin with a solid pin; however, this is not always a solution. It is the method of attachment itself that lends the sights to premature loosening. In some cases the sights take flight. A solid pin is better but even a solid pin must be checked for movement. The Kimber pistol uses a sturdy dovetail to hold its sight in place.

These pistols are intended for maximum accuracy. They are delivered with passing fair trigger actions that can be cleaned up to an extent and will deliver even

The Tactical Solutions .22 caliber conversion rivals and in some cases surpasses the accuracy potential of .45 caliber pistols.

The Colt and Kimber use different barrel bushings and even different crown styles. The Kimber also uses a full length guide rod. Either is good to run with.

King's Gun Works barrel bushing is used on Colt Gold Cup.

better accuracy once they have been polished. The adjustable sights offer a bold clear sight picture. With the proper lightweight recoil springs and perhaps a lightweight hammer spring – but be very cautious and understand the balance you are looking for – these handguns may be used with target grade ammunition. Quite a few shooters will simply fire the target-grade pistols with standard factory ammunition and appreciate their accuracy in an informal environment. Reloading cranks like myself will appreciate the availability of adjustable sights that allow zeroing the pistol for a wide range of bullet weights, ranging from 152 to 260 grains.

When it comes to accuracy, BarSto is a legendary name with performance to back up the legend.

Bomar sights are among the very best units ever designed for the 1911.

There are more Gold Cups in private hands that are being enjoyed simply for pride of ownership and for informal shooting that are used in matches. Just the same the Gold Cup remains a first class target grade 1911. Recently I was able to match the Gold Cup up against likely contenders in a test program that challenged not only the author but also the handguns and several experienced raters. My primary load was a wonderfully accurate handload using the Nosler 185-grain JHP at 1050fps. This is not a +P load but a good strong .45 ACP. I also used a load comprising the Oregon Trail 200-grain SWC at 790 fps. These are hotter than target loads, but they work in any 1911. I also used the 230-grain RNJ CorBon Performance Match, an up-and-coming load that proved its worth.

In the end, the stolid Gold Cup proved its mettle. We used experienced shooters in rollover prone, several of whom recorded three-inch groups at a long 50 yards. We posted one remarkable two-inch five-shot 50-yard group. Naturally most of the groups were larger. The only handgun in our modest battery that is more consistently accurate than the Gold Cup is the Les Baer Monolith. For what it is worth, the Nosler bullet load proved the most accurate, with the CorBon match-grade bullet and the Oregon Trail handload running close behind. That is real accuracy. The Colt Gold Cup may well be the most accurate 1911 pistol of all time. When Colt does the Gold Cup, they do it right. This handgun is well worth its price when the primary goal is accuracy. However, with proper spring technology combined with a knowledgeable user, the Gold Cup will serve well as an all-around 1911 .45 for serious use.

Sight Adjustment

There have been charts published that address the proper zeroing of adjustable sights. While straightforward mechanically, adjustable sights are not consistent in the operation. I have used sights that require a minimum of nine clicks to move the point of impact an inch while others do the business in a thrice. That is a lot of difference in mechanical leverage between three and nine clicks. There is a rather simple formula for learning the exact number of clicks needed to move the pistol for windage. If done correctly it does not require a prodigious amount of ammunition. First, be certain you are getting good groups. If you cannot control the piece and you are not getting good groups then your experiment will be a waste of ammunition.

I recently conducted this experiment with the Kimber Eclipse and CorBon Performance Match ammunition. I fired the initial five-shot group then moved the rear sight windage adjustment 10 clicks right. I measured the exact movement of the group by firing another five rounds. (I was getting two inch groups.) I then moved the sights to the left 10 clicks and fired five more rounds. I was dead on again. This type or repeatability and reliability is important. I measured the movement obtained by making 10 clicks and divided by 10. That is the value of a single click, and it will vary among Colt, Kimber, Springfield and Caspian types. Ten clicks and a five-inch change means each click is worth .5 inch; a three-inch movement would mean the clicks are worth .3 inch each. This is a foolproof test that works well with quality equipment.

In this illustration a young shooter is advancing and firing. There is no other handgun that will produce results like the 1911.

1911 ACCURACY

Chapter 16:

When we discuss accuracy, everyone wants to know how accurate this or that handgun is. The true value of accuracy is zero. I know of no pistol that has zero dispersion although some come pretty close at seven yards. I can fire a .45-inch group at 50 yards – if I fire a single shot. Within certain guidelines some pistols are as accurate as any other. One GI pistol is about as good as the other when all is said and done.

It is the luck of the draw whether your Kimber Custom II or Springfield Loaded Model will be the more accurate. Once you begin paying for a Kimber Gold Match or a Springfield Professional, you expect more. The single most important consideration is barrel fit. The fit of the barrel to the slide is far more important than the fit of the frame to the slide, although each must be good and tight for first-rate accuracy. We all want accuracy but we have to understand how much we need and how much we are willing to pay for. We must also consider our skill level.

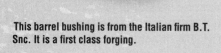

This barrel bushing is from the Italian firm B.T. Snc. It is a first class forging.

Sometimes you have to have fun. An accurate 1911 is a pure joy.

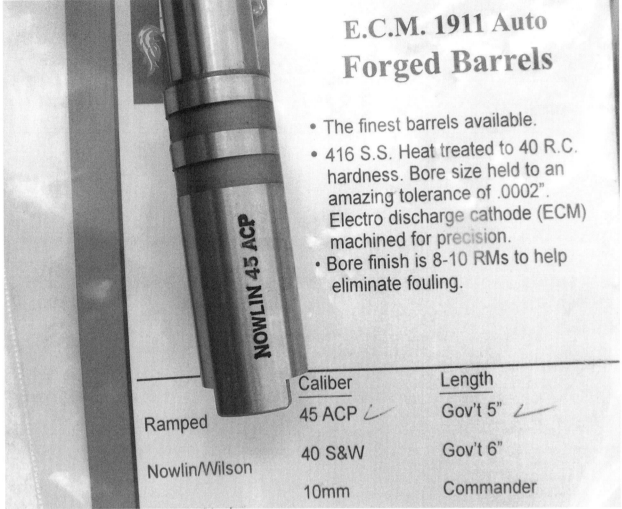

E.C.M. 1911 Auto Forged Barrels

- The finest barrels available.
- 416 S.S. Heat treated to 40 R.C. hardness. Bore size held to an amazing tolerance of .0002". Electro discharge cathode (ECM) machined for precision.
- Bore finish is 8-10 RMs to help eliminate fouling.

	Caliber	Length
Ramped	45 ACP ✓	Gov't 5" ✓
	40 S&W	Gov't 6"
Nowlin/Wilson	10mm	Commander

Nowlin barrels are specified by the FBI for use in their HRT pistols. The Nowlin is a fine choice for anyone wishing to upgrade his or her personal 1911 handgun.

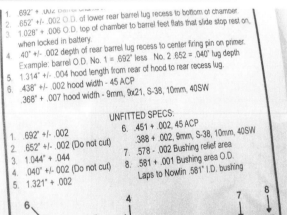

If you fit a 1911 barrel, know what you are doing. These directions are from Nowlin.

A top-end pistol with good features, a light trigger and great accuracy may actually be counterproductive for a beginner. A beginner might be better served learning to master a heavy but smooth trigger action. GI pistols will save your life in a defensive situation but I prefer more accuracy. Since there is no great accuracy demand on average-grade 1911 pistols, makers sometimes resort to the cheapest manufacturing method. With the price point so important these days this is understandable, but the parts should give good service. For example, a popular GI pistol has a two-piece barrel. The front and rear sections are brazed together. The front half meets the rear half at the chamber and barrel lug line. This is a serviceable arrangement that keeps manufacturing costs to a minimum but some feel these barrels are less than ideal. If you are willing to spend the money, a custom-grade barrel will offer considerably better performance. You can order a drop-in barrel from BarSto Precision that will usually work with little fitting in a Series 70 type pistol such as the Springfield Loaded Model or a Colt Government Model.

If you are hoping for maximum accuracy, you can order a gunsmith-fit barrel. If you do not completely understand how the 1911 functions or you do not have

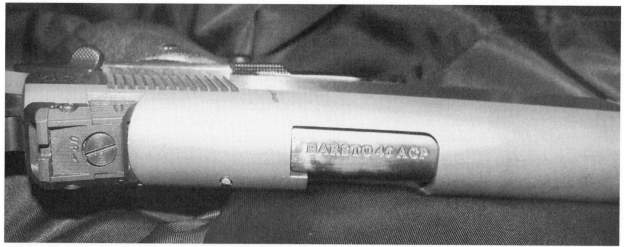

This Caspian slide has been fitted with a BarSto barrel. Good kit all the way.

patience in working with firearms, do not attempt to replace a barrel! Barrel fit is relatively simple but must be understood. When the pistol locks in the same manner time after time we have accuracy. Both the locking lugs and the barrel bushing must be reasonably tight. We have all heard of the archetypical 1911 that rattles when shaken, but the piece may have been accurate enough for general use when the barrel bushing and lugs were well-fitted. The rest of the fit was less critical. There are those who claim that an original 1911 is more accurate than I suggest, and will prove so with a machine rest. Humans are not capable of holding the piece and aiming it consistently, they say, and some claim the GI .45 will place a gunload into two inches at 25 yards. I do not agree.

A quality drop-in barrel almost always increases accuracy but a fitted Match Grade barrel is predictably more accurate. The only 1911 .45s in my battery that consistently approach the highly desirable but often mythical one-inch standard at 25 yards are those with a match-grade barrel. These pistols included a custom shop Kimber, a Rock River pistol with a BarSto barrel, a Springfield with a Nowlin barrel, and the Les Baer. Let's look into what goes into fitting a superb barrel.

First, we must understand the lockup points. These are the locking lugs, the barrel bushing, the barrel hood, and the bottom lugs. A quality barrel will be oversize for a good fit. The barrel hood is larger than the breechface opening. The hood is filed to conform to the breechface with a file and the cut and try method: file and try the fit. Do not get too happy and go too fast and end up with a poor fit. You must have .003" clearance on each side of the hood and the hood must remain parallel to the breechface sidewalls for good fit and function. This means attention to detail. The barrel extension is also oversize and must be measured with a hood gauge (This means Brownells!) and properly shortened. This

is usually done on a lathe. The hood will end up about .003" longer than the hood gauge measurement. Next carefully file the barrel until the hood fits the slide and the barrel lugs slide into the slides with no excess movement, a good tight fit. The rear cut of the BarSto barrel controls upward motion and demands your attention during fitting.

The method I use begins with placing the upper lugs in the slide slots and carefully and slowly tapping the bottom lugs with a brass hammer. Tap toward the muzzle for proper fit. Filing the barrel allows it to move more fully into contact in the locking recess. As you file for fit, be certain your filing strokes are even. Metal will be filed away and evenly removed. You will reach a point where the barrel rests in its locking lugs without springing away from lock position when pressed into place. In short, the barrel is properly fitted and also perfectly centered in the slide. With care and deliberation this will happen. But pay close attention at every step. Problems may come up. The bottom lugs may bind on the slide stop. This is not common but seems to occur most often with the heavier oversize slide stops. The barrel hood must be centered and the bottom lug must not bind on the slide stop but ride smoothly against it and be squared properly.

There has been some confusion concerning the proper length of the link. This is not an arcane art but I am surprised it is not understood more thoroughly. Once the barrel lower lugs are properly fitted and smoothed, with a proper fit to the slide stop, measure the length from the link pivot hole to the area that has been polished. Next, measure the area between the two holes of the swinging link. The measurements must be the same. If not, the link will not be properly fitted. When using a larger-diameter slide stop, this measurement becomes critical, but I have had to use the Chip McCormick oversize slide stop on occasion with off-specification 1911 pistols to ensure function. While not strictly related to barrel fitting, snugging up a top unit on various caliber conversions has required this oversize slide stop. You must understand the relationship between link length and barrel to locking lug to slide stop measurement to produce a functioning custom fit. Once you are done, check for smoothness. Any drag will usually be the lower lug against the slide stop. This is addressed by filing and smoothing.

With a well-fitted match grade barrel, what type of accuracy might we expect? Some handguns are intrinsically more accurate than others. My personal Rock River 1911 has been fitted with a BarSto barrel. The Les Baer Monolith is a high-grade factory pistol. The Springfield Tactical Response pistol is a first-class tactical 1911. I tested the accuracy of each of these pistols with five different proven loads. The results are interesting. I also tested a Springfield GI pistol with which I have added a Nowlin barrel. However, I have not yet addressed the trigger action of the Springfield GI nor have I added high visibility sights. Still, it is what it is and it was available. Perhaps it was a good test subject as this is a pure barrel upgrade. I think that the results are very interesting. I fired all of the shots off of a solid benchrest. I listed the groups fired with the GI pistol both before and after fitting the Nowlin barrel.

Accuracy, Average of Three Five-Shot Groups at 25 Yards					
	RRA	Monolith	TRP	GI	GI/Nowlin
Black Hills 230-gr. RNL	1.25"	1.0"	1.75"	4.5"	2.5"
Black Hills 200-gr. SWC	1.5"	1.25"	2.0"	4.0"	1.9"
Fiocchi 230-gr. XTP	2.0"	1.0"	2.1"	5.0"	2.0"
Winchester 230-gr. Bonded Core	1.5"	.9"	2.0"	3.5"	2.15"
Handload /WW 231/Nolser 185-gr. JHP/950 fps	.9"	1.35"	1.5"	4.25"	2.0"

The results are typical of high-grade pistols and pistols with fitted barrels from a benchrest. In practical terms the more expensive pistols were the most accurate. The Springfield GI showed a great increase in accuracy potential from a carefully hand fitted barrel; however, this is not a true gauge of the advantages to be gained from a Nowlin barrel. I have a special project for the GI pistol. In a proper platform – such as the Springfield Loaded Model – the Nowlin is capable of stellar accuracy. More to come with the GI pistol as sights are added and a bit more work is undertaken.

I also freshened up my old service Colt Commander with a BarSto barrel. I had thought the Commander was pretty accurate as it always did the business and hit what I was aiming for, but then I didn't shoot it very often at 25 yards. I seldom fired groups. Groups are okay for experiments but the true test of a marksman is firing at small targets at known and unknown distances. The Commander is a stalwart companion but it badly needed an upgrade after a sit-down-and-get-serious accuracy test. After fitting the BarSto Precision barrel, my confidence in the piece skyrocketed. Here are the results.

5-Shot Groups at 25 Yards, Colt Commander Before/After Fitting BarSto Barrel		
Load	Group Before	Group After
Winchester 230-gr. USA Ball	5.0"	3.5"
Black Hills 230-gr. JHP	3.5"	2.5"
Hornady 200-gr. XTP	4.0"	2.25"
Nosler 185-gr. JHP Handload	3.6"	2.25"

Ammunition means a lot. Federal Match has legendary properties.

The 200-grain SWC at left is a handload using an Oregon Trail bullet. The Remington Golden Saber at right is much more expensive but often quite accurate.

As a bonus, the pistol fed all wide-mouth hollow points after fitting the perfectly polished BarSto barrel. Remember, we have not yet fitted high visibility sights. I fired these groups with the aid of Hansen Eagle Eyes shooting glasses.

Now for the final question: how much accuracy is enough? Will a five-inch group at 25 yards save your life? Of course it will because gunfights occur most often inside 10 yards. But then we wish to be all we can be. Where is the demarcation line between acceptable and unacceptable? I believe that a middle of the road pistol such as the Kimber Custom II or the Springfield Loaded Model should exhibit accuracy of 3 inches for a five-shot group at 25 yards. The Kimber Gold Combat or Springfield TRP should deliver to the tune of a 2.5-inch group, although many examples will do better. The next leap, to average groups of 1.5 inches as demonstrated by the Rock River pistols or the Les Baer, is expensive. Much depends upon your skill and the ability to deliver such accuracy. For most of us most of the time a 3-inch 25-yard group is acceptable. It takes considerable practice and ammunition to reach the point that an average 1911 is limiting your performance.

Notes on Ammunition

You really need to handload to produce true match-grade ammunition. Unless you have a Brinks truck full of money following you around, you will find even the least expensive factory ammunition prohibitively expensive. By carefully choosing your components and working up a load, you will find the sweet spot that offers the best accuracy in your particular 1911. The most accurate load is seldom the hottest load. I have found that combinations sensibly below the 230 grains at 850 fps are often the most accurate.

We do need a factory benchmark loading in testing handguns. I find that the Black Hills 230-grain RNL is often match-grade accurate, although it is offered in the Blue Box remanufactured line. Another good choice from Black Hills is the 200-grain SWC. CorBon has made considerable inroads in the match community with their 230-grain Performance Match. This is a fine choice for testing the accuracy of factory target pistols. The Hornady 200-grain XTP is the choice of many professionals.

Remember: garbage in, garbage out. Use good quality factory ammunition or good handloads in testing accuracy. For match grade loads I have used the economical Oregon Trail semiwadcutter bullets in both 180- and 200-grain weights. In jacketed bullets the Nosler 185-grain JHP has been a great performer. The Sierra 230-grain JHP has been a particularly good performer in the traditional weight.

1911 SIGHTING SYSTEMS

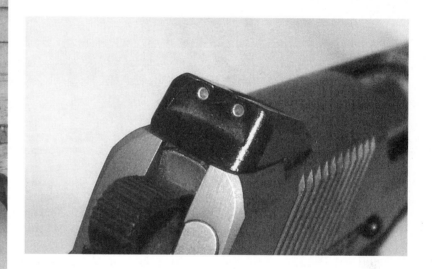

Chapter 17:

The original 1911 sights were embryonic military style sights. They were more than bumps on the slide, but not much more, and they were not ideal for accurate fire. The 1911A1 featured improved sights but until the days of the National Match pistol there was little to choose from. Custom pistolsmiths fabricated high-visibility sights of various types and while these were an improvement in some ways, few were practical. Many were so tall and awkward they would not allow the pistol to be holstered in a conventional scabbard.

Adjusting a Novak sight for windage isn't difficult, but use the correct tools.

This dusty set of sights is mounted on the author's carry gun. Novak sights are ideal for personal defense use.

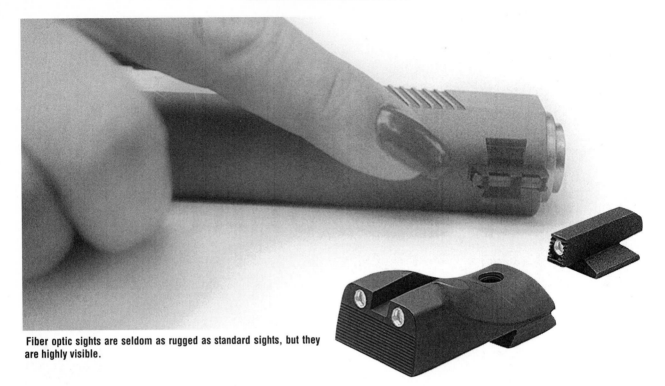

Fiber optic sights are seldom as rugged as standard sights, but they are highly visible.

Kimber night sights are available as an option and should be ordered on every personal defense pistol from Kimber.

Among the first practical improvements on the 1911 sights were the old King's Hardballer sights. There sight sets featured a taller rear sight and a post front sight. Even today, these sights are by no means outdated. They are good choices for combat shooting. These sights are very similar to the sights fitted to the Colt Series 80 and the Springfield Mil Spec. I have always thought that Colt missed the boat when they did not add an improved set of sights to the Series 70, but they did update them on the Series 80. These early combat sights are relatively inexpensive and offer a better sight picture than the GI sights. However, I have conducted comparison testing between these sights and GI sights and overall the advantage of the improved or mil spec sights is slight. Tests do not lie, and while I perceived the improvement as greater than the tests showed, a thorough all-around program comparing the Springfield GI pistol, a Colt 1918, and the Colt Series 80 and Springfield Mil Spec showed little practical improvement when the types were fired by novice shooters.

It is relatively easy to upgrade to some types of 1911 sights while others will require the services of a machinist/gunsmith. While we can upgrade, the superior course is to purchase a handgun with credible sights in the first place. The sights should be chosen for quality, practical accuracy, non-snag construction, and durability. This is a tall order but one that modern sights fill well. Among the first practical high-visibility sights were the Novak Lo Mount. These sights feature a pyramid-like rear sight that offers an excellent sight picture. The sight will not catch on clothing during the draw

and offers a virtually snag-free contour. The front sight is a bold post that may be from .200" to .249" high, depending on the application.

Reducing the vertical profile of a pistol sight is important because the sights rub on all manner of things including the holster and clothing. There are a number of considerations including short range fire, medium range fire, long range fire and snag-free presentation. Testing something as subjective as handgun sights is difficult. It is easy to note that the Novak sights are superior to Mil Spec sights, but to compare the Novak to Kimber sights is more difficult. This is where subjective opinion arises. The rear sight should have a bold profile that is easily picked up quickly. The pyramid style sights now available offer a good sight picture and do not trap shadows. When all is said and done, the Novak and Kimber style combat sights are at the top of the heap and offer excellent all-around utility. There are choices in the types as well. Plain black, white three dot and tritium night inserts are the most common types. Novak also offers a gold bead front sight. The gold bead front sight is among the very best choices. This bead gives an excellent all around sight picture, can be seen in the dark with a minimum of ambivalent light and is immune to oil and solvent.

Luminous iron sights are an excellent option, but they are not without drawbacks. For example, during

This pistol is well equipped with a Surefire X 300, 10 8 sights, Wilson Combat grips and low flash ammunition.

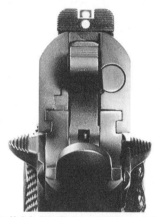

This is the famous Heinie 8 ball set up. It works well for most shooters.

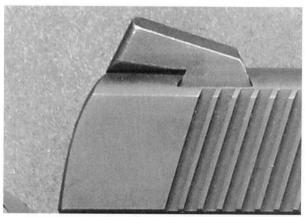

The low profile of the Novak sight now graces over 2,000,000 pistols.

daytime or bright light shooting, tritium sights often reflect sunlight. The same is true of nickel plated sights, but the tritium insert is not as reflective as nickel. Depending upon how deeply the shock mounted insert is buried in the sight, sunlight may play on the tritium sight. Tritium sights also will work loose. Usually the front sight is the one to take flight. I have only had this happen once, and it was at the 10,000 round mark, but it does happen. I replaced the sights of this particular pistol with Wilson Combat night sights and continued to bang out 10,000 additional rounds without any further problem. It is a relatively simple matter to replace the tritium insert; this is simply something to be aware of.

I once strongly preferred black sight over white three dot sights. With the coming of age and a loss in visual acuity, I now find the white dot sights work well for me. With unaided vision, blurred sights are a real problem.

Fiber optic sights or white dot sights help a great deal. I can recommend the Novak sights with the fiber optic option, but in the past I have suffered the loss of the fiber optic component with relatively light use of sights of other makes. The Novak is quite robust. Perhaps they did not introduce their version until it was perfected. An elegant option I find useful is the Novak Gold Bead front sight. All who used this sight appreciated the gold bead. It shows up in most dim conditions and offers an excellent visual aiming point.

There is more to the equation that how the sights look and how well you are able to quickly pick up the sights. Some are too sharp for efficient holster use. The sights need to be snag-free when carried in tight-fitting concealment holsters. The original Novak Lo Mount is the king of concealment but Wilson Combat sights also do a good job. The sights that absolutely must be avoided are the add on adjustable sights that hang over the

The Novak rear sight will not grab tender skin. That is efficiency by design.

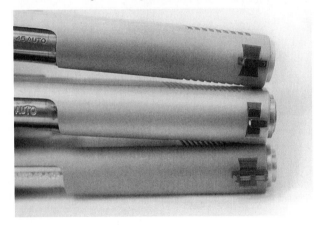

These are Novak sights but all Novak sights are not created equal. Note the difference in the dovetails.

rear of the slide. These are contraindicated for service use and are not my favorites for target use. A proper target sight should be low riding, properly set into a machined dovetail, and rugged enough for duty use. The inexpensive add-ons are not very robust and when they protrude from the rear of the slide you are asking for them to be knocked off on a door jamb. They are good examples of a false economy.

Adjustable sights were once questionable on personal defense handguns. The Colt Gold Cup, as an example, is fastened by a single hollow roll pin. This is no recipe for hard use. Even adding a more satisfactory solid pin is not always enough to properly secure the sight. On the other hand I have a custom mounted Bomar rear sight done by the Action Works of Chino Valley, Arizona. This is a secure mount with a vault-tough sight. The factory adjustable sight used by Les Baer is similar. Both are dirt tough adjustable sights well worth their price. Bomar unfortunately is out of business, but the Baer sight is at least the equal of the Bomar. Much the same applies to the modern Kimber adjustable sights. The unit mounted on my personal Eclipse has never given the slightest trouble.

An aftermarket sight I have used with good results comes from Caspian. This compact tactical sight offers good adjustment but is low profile and has survived hard use. I think that it is safe to say that modern adjustable sights are available that give every advantage in zeroing the pistol while they are mechanically rugged. Not all adjustable sights are, not by any means. A combination of a less rugged sight and mounting the sight in the conventional dovetail, resulting in the sight riding over the rear of the slide, is a combination doomed to failure.

Sight Regulation

It is easy enough to adjust the sight left to right, but I find a distressing number of modern pistols fire low at 16 to 25 yards. Filing the front sight or fitting a taller front sight is needed. Firing high is addressed by fitting a taller front sight. If your pistol fires to the point of aim as issued, treasure it.

THE MANY CALIBERS OF THE 1911

Chapter 18:

The .22 and the .45, the two most useful 1911 calibers in the author's opinion.

It isn't surprising that the 1911 has been chambered in many calibers. Some were an expedient, as with the Viet Cong-captured 1911 converted to 7.62x25mm. Others were a necessity. Some nations prohibit certain military calibers but do not legislate against handguns in other calibers. As a result, the 1911 could be chambered in .30 Luger or .38 Super in nations that prohibit the 9mm and .45 ACP. The 9mm is a light recoiling conversion for recreational shooting. The .38 Super has merit on the basis of penetration and was used during the 1930s in battle against our mechanized thugs. The 10mm is seen as many as an improvement over the .45 ACP. Colonel Cooper

The 9mm is available in lead, jacketed, hollowpoint and even Blunt Action Trauma (BAT) loadings. It is versatile.

The .38 Super was designed to have greater effect than any other caliber of the day on automobiles. It is still a formidable cartridge.

The 10mm and the .38 Super are usually more effective than the .45 against light cover, but efficient ammunition choices may change the picture.

The .40 Smith and Wesson is a highly developed cartridge that works well in the 1911—but it is not a .45.

reported that there are things you can do at 50 yards with the 10mm that cannot be done with the .45. The .400 CorBon has its own appeal and the .45 Super and .460 Rowland are improvements over the .45 ACP in terms of power. The .45 Super was envisioned as a law enforcement cartridge and the .460 as a hunting cartridge. There is some crossover in performance.

Let's look at the popular 1911 calibers and their reason for existence. While I regard the .45 ACP as the best choice for all-around use, some of these calibers have good points. The best choices are probably the .22 Long Rifle, .400 CorBon and .45 Super as they allow an easy conversion of an existing pistol, which can use .45 ACP again with a simple barrel change. There are those who will sing the praises of one caliber or the other. Again, I will repeat that my education and training combine with experience to make my choice. Experience is a road map of reality.

.22 Long Rifle

You need two calibers if you are a 1911 fan. These are the .22 Long Rifle and the .45 ACP. The .22 offers low recoil and low expense. It's the finest training cartridge available. It is also useful for target practice and small game hunting. Without the distraction of flash, blast and recoil you are able to concentrate on sight alignment, sight picture and trigger control. The .22 can be wonderfully accurate.

There are two ways to obtain a .22 caliber 1911 handgun. First, you can purchase a purpose-designed pistol in this caliber. Kimber offers a first class rimfire 1911. You can purchase the low end Chiappa 1911-22 at less than $300. While a discerning eye will be more pleased with the Kimber, there is also pleasure to be found in a modest investment that functions well. The Kimber is more accurate on average than the second choice, the .22 conversion units, and this includes a Kimber conversion on a Kimber frame. The purpose-built Kimber .22 is a fine rimfire and very accurate. There are those who do not see shelling out as much for a .22 as for a centerfire pistol and I understand their sentiments. Just the same, it is as difficult to produce a reliable and accurate match grade .22 as a .45. The Kimber .22 is a wonderful trainer and a great recreational shooter.

The 1911 has been blessed with the availability of rimfire conversion units since about 1935. The early Colt conversion units were lambasted as less than reliable but I have not found this to be true. As long as certain cautions were followed, the conversions worked. There is a type of floating chamber at work that was designed to give the slide a kick to simulate .45 recoil, as the story goes. My assessment is that it is more to the point that the floating chamber gave the slide greater impetus to work correctly with the .22 caliber's modest recoil energy. An old trick that works just fine with the original Colt conversion unit is to coat the float-

The .45 GAP is a success story for Glock but less suited to the 1911.

ing chamber with STP oil treatment. With this accomplished the Colt conversion is reliable with high velocity ammunition. .22 caliber ammunition is dirtier than center fire ammunition and the pistol needs to be cleaned more often, probably as often as every 300 rounds for good function.

The typical modern conversion unit consists of a slide, barrel, recoil spring, and magazine. The .22 conversion unit converts a 1911 to a blowback action. In order for the modest momentum of the .22 to enable the slide's movement, the slide is produced in aluminum. These conversion units are available from Jonathan Arthur Ciener, among others, but Ciener is the premier maker of 1911 conversion units. These conversion units are in use worldwide with an excellent reputation. They must be cleaned often for best reliability, and kept lubricated. In return they give you good accuracy and excellent economy.

Tactical Solutions uses another type of action. This is among the most accurate and well made conversions ever offered. While more expensive than the aluminum slide version, this conversion offers match-grade accuracy. The Tactical Solutions conversion mounts to the 1911 frame and the barrel is fixed as with the other types of conversion. But there is no slide to recoil; rather, the bolt recoils as is the case with a Ruger Standard Model or Browning Buckmark. This system is more expensive but it works very well. I have mated the Tactical Solutions conversion to my Rock River Arms 1911 with excellent results. It is not unusual for Winchester high velocity loads to group five shots into just over an inch at 25 yards. I have fired a number of groups with the Winchester Dyna Point that registered a group just under an inch, but this is not the average, just a lucky day! For the person who demands the most of their .22 conversion over and above inexpensive training and plinking, this is the unit. There is a picatinny rail option, but I ordered my conversion with iron sights.

The standard Wilson Combat unit always works well. Like all conversions, there are cautions. The Wilson Combat will deliver good accuracy and function but will begin to function sluggishly at about 300 rounds and need to be cleaned. This is true of all .22 conversions. In my experience a purpose-designed .22 caliber 1911 will go more rounds between cleaning than the conversion units. 300 rounds may seem like a lot of ammunition but with the .22 conversion and a few magazines and interested young people, a brick of 500 rounds will disappear in the blink of an eye! A good opportunity to learn cleaning skills.

The .22 conversion is an essential. I would recommend that the beginner purchase a good .22 caliber conversion unit and forego the purchase of a second 1911. I regard the device that highly. As for personal defense, the .22 is at a grave disadvantage. Its only advantages, and they are considerable, are accuracy and economy.

.30 Luger

In a number of nations the 9mm and .45 are outlawed for civilian ownership as military calibers, although handgun ownership is not prohibited. Handguns normally chambered for the 9mm Luger cartridge are offered in .30 Luger. The .30 Luger is better known than the .38 Super, making it the better marketing choice. A 93-grain bullet at 1200 fps is fast enough but in the real world will prove little more effective than the .32 ACP. I place the .30 Luger in the same category as the .32 H&R Magnum and the French 7.65 Long, although the .30 Luger is hotter than the .32 Magnum. I have seen Colt Commanders in .30 Luger, sometimes offered with a spare 9mm barrel. They were advertised as "re-imported." As for ammunition choice, the Fiocchi jacketed soft point load is reliable and accurate, and of high quality. If limited to a .30 Luger 1911 I would shoot straight, hope the bullet struck bone and pray for the best.

9mm Luger

It isn't surprising that the 9mm is outpacing the .38 Super in popularity in the 1911 platform. The 9mm offers inexpensive factory ammunition and it is dirt cheap to handload. I have fired quite a few and genuinely enjoy the 9mm 1911. For some of us the 9mm 1911 seems sacrilegious but this aversion disappears when you fire the piece. They are a great deal of fun to fire. For those who cannot tolerate .45 ACP recoil the 9mm is a reasonable counterpoint. My question is relaiblity. I have used several 9mm 1911 handguns converted from .38 Super. My results have not been as good as concerns reliability. It seems the 9mm 1911 is prone to malfunciton. The action and the magazines are designed to handle a longer cartridge, the .900" cartridge case of the .38 Super and .45 ACP. The 9mm is a shorter cartridge and more prone to short cycle. The 9mm has proven accurate enough for personal defense and self protection, especially with the BarSto barrel. And I have to add that all of these conversions have not been unreliable; some have proven very reliable.

I am not a 9mm fan but we cannot ignore the 9mm +P+ loads that police agencies report have given excellent results. The CorBon 115-grain JHP at 1350 fps from a Commander length barrel is a credible defense load. There is less reason than ever to choose a .38 Super over a 9mm other than the reliability issue. Recently, I have been using a Colt .38 Super with a spare BarSto barrel in 9mm Luger. My magazines have been Wilson Combat

ETM in 9mm. I am approaching 3,500 rounds of trouble-free firing, primarily with my own handloads. The majority of these loads have used the Oregon Trail 122-grain FP and a modest charge of Titegroup powder. I have also used a number CorBon +P loads, from the 90-grain JHP load at 1490 fps to the CorBon 115-grain DPX at 1200 fps. Function has been excellent.

A 9mm 1911 can be reliable. In the end, economy and low recoil are the main advantages of the 9mm cartridge. The wound ballistics are not in a league with the .45, but with the best 9mm loads performance moves into the acceptable category.

9mm Velocity, 5-inch Barrel	
Hornady 115-gr. JHP	1121 fps
Federal 115-gr. JHP/9BP	1160 fps
Federal 115-gr. JHP +P+	1355 fps
CorBon 115-gr. +P	1360 fps
Fiocchi 147-gr. XTP	969 fps
Winchester 127-gr. SXT +P+	1256 fps

.38 Special

The .38 Special has been chambered in a number of National Match pistols converted to accept only 148-gr. flush-loaded wadcutters. There were factory versions as well as custom versions. This is a very specialized type of handgun that was popular in its day and shows the ingenuity of gunsmiths and the versatility of the 1911 frame. It was in effect Colt's counterpart to the Smith & Wesson Model 52.

.38 AMU

The .38 Army Marksmanship Unit cartridge is simply a .38 Special with the rim turned down in self-loading fashion and an extractor groove cut in the case. The Army even convinced the major makers to offer commercial ammunition. Beware the .38 AMU! To the best of my knowledge every .38 AMU pistol was converted from a .38 Super Colt. The slides are marked .38 Super but the barrels are .38 AMU. The Super chambers were reamed and sleeved. I am aware of a near blowup when a shooter fired a .38 Super round in a .38 AMU. The barrel was ruined. These are no longer practical conversions but in their day they were quite interesting.

.38 ACP Super

The .38 ACP was chambered in the original Colt 1900 self-loader. The .900" long cartridge case was carried on to the modified 1905 autoloader and the .45 ACP cartridge. The .38 Super is a .38 ACP on steroids that was first offered in the 1911 in the late 1920s. If you

The .38 Super is loaded to full power by one company, CorBon.

own an original 1900 .38 ACP, <u>never</u> fire .38 Super in the piece. The .38 ACP was no hotter than the 9mm Luger, generating about 1050-1100 fps with a 130-gr. bullet. The .38 Super jolts the same bullet to 1300 fps in original loadings. Today the average generic ball load in .38 Super is closer to 1200 fps.

There is some confusion as modern .38 Super is often marked .38 ACP +P. When the SAAMI began designating ammunition as .38 Special +P or 9mm +P they felt that it would make sense to label the .38 Super a .38 ACP +P, although the .38 ACP is in production only on an irregular basis. The .38 Super is a hot cartridge that is considerably stronger than the 9mm Luger if you use handloads or CorBon ammunition. The general run of factory ammunition is no hotter than the 9mm Luger. Its major advantage is in reliability. The .38 Super is usually as reliable as a .45 ACP in a quality handgun. There is some evidence the Super is the most reliable of all 1911 calibers, but it would take more ammunition than I have to prove this. The Super is easier to handle than the .45 due to the low recoil but offers sufficient velocity to instigate expansion of hollowpoint bullets. The Super uses the same bullets as the 9mm but drives them an average of 100 fps faster. Penetration of light cover is superior. The rub is, the only ammunition that I am aware of that maximizes the Super comes from a single source, and that is CorBon.

The Super is a choice made by a small but experienced group of handgunners. It must be respected.

.38 Super Ballistics, CorBon Ammunition

CorBon 100-gr. PowRBall	1515 fps
115-gr. JHP	1460 fps
125-gr. JHP	1325 fps

I did an in depth feature on handloading the .38 Super for *Handloader Magazine*. It is worth a read if you are able to obtain a back issue from Wolfe Publishing.

Special Notes on Converting the .38 Super to 9mm

Usually all that is needed is a quality drop-in barrel and 9mm specific magazines. Metalform is a good choice of affordable quality magazines. I have used BarSto barrels with excellent results. Converting from 9mm to .38 Super is more difficult. The 9mm has a .384" breechface and the .38 Super measures .405". The 9mm breechface must be opened in order to allow the slightly wider .38 Super casehead to function properly. The reason we use the 9mm barrel is economic. 9mm ammunition is much less expensive and so is 9mm brass. Just the same, with a good supply of Starline brass laid in I load for the Super often. Still, this is a neat setup and an enjoyable conversion.

The Hot .38/9mm Rounds

A bit of history is necessary to appreciate the hottest of the mid-bore rounds available. I remember reading with interest a feature Jeff Cooper did in *Guns and Ammo* called the Super Cooper. Cooper took a 6-inch Bar-Sto barrel and cut down .223 brass and managed to load his Super Cooper with a 124-gr. bullet at a startling 1700 fps. He remarked that the cartridge would shoot flatter than anyone could hold. Cooper is best known for his personal defense work but he was also an enthusiastic hunter and experimenter. The Super Cooper jolted the 124-gr. bullet to 1700 fps and also a 90-gr. bullet to nearly 2000 fps. This is fantastic but he did so. In some ways the yearning for a fast small-bore is based on the reputation of the .357 Magnum revolver cartridge. The full-power Magnum is a respectable cartridge. A self-loader without the disadvantages of heavy recoil and muzzle blast but which came close to .357 Magnum ballistics would be a formidable and saleable handgun. The Super Cooper is mimicked by the 9x23mm Winchester. The 9x23mm is basically a .38 Super without the semi rim, but loaded about 10,000 psi hotter. The 9x23mm will jolt a 125-gr. JHP to 1450 fps. The equals or exceeds the performance of the .357 Magnum revolver cartridge. At a long 100 yards, the 9x23's 124-gr. bullet is still making tracks at 1100 fps. This is a true high-performance cartridge with many advantages. Unfortunately it is dead or has one foot in the grave.

In a 1963 *Guns and Ammo* report we saw the birth of the .38-45 Clerke. Bo Clerke was a respected pistol smith who developed a necked-down .45 ACP case to use .38 caliber projectiles. The intent was not to hotrod the 1911 but to produce a pleasant-to-fire and economical conversion without the expense of the .38 AMU and .38 Special conversions. This cartridge is now offered as the .38 Casull. In a 6-inch barrel the necked-down .45 delivered 1800 fps with a 124-gr. bullet. This is hot as a depot stove and very interesting. A 6-inch barrel 1911 with a 30-pound recoil spring may not be very practical, but it is an attention getter.

10mm

Colt introduced the Delta Elite in 10mm after the failure of the Bren Ten pistol. This saved the 10mm cartridge from extinction. Almost immediately some of us realized the 1911 is not the best home for the 10mm cartridge. Most of the loads then available were too hot and the foreign-produced loads used bullets that would not expand unless they hit a brick wall. I have tried the 10mm and find it an impressive cartridge but prefer the .45. Part of the problem with the Delta Elite was the Mickey Mouse recoil rod used by Colt. With a good full

length guide rod and a Wolff 24-pound gun spring, my Delta Elite was quite reliable and long-lived as well.

Many early 10mm pistols were criticized due to a lack of accuracy. This too was related to inconsistent springs. A too light recoil spring would allow the pistol to batter itself and lockup was not consistent. Also, many shooters did not understand spring technology. They would fit a light hammer spring and a heavy duty recoil spring. Much in the same fashion as mistakes made with the Gold Cup, this allowed battering as the hammer did not offer sufficient resistance to the slide in recoil. When the Delta Elite is fitted with proper full power springs and a heavy duty recoil spring it is reliable, long lived and accurate. There are things you can do at 50 yards with the 10mm you cannot do with the .45. The 10mm is no .41 Magnum, but it is a powerful cartridge with good performance. I would be perfectly satisfied with a properly set up, reliable 10mm 1911 pistol. There are many loads available including specialized hunting loads from CorBon. I would probably choose the CorBon 155-gr. DPX for general defense use. If you are a handgun hunter the 10mm offers advantages on thin-skinned game.

.40 Smith and Wesson

I have never liked the .40 Smith and Wesson. I find the recoil of the .40 harsh in the Glock pistols. If I worked in an agency that approved the .40 and nothing else but allowed the 1911, then I would have no choice. There are agencies that mandate the .40 but allow other quality handguns to be carried. An acquaintance of mine worked such an agency and I have fired his .40 caliber Commander. I strongly prefer the Colt to any polymer pistol. I do not like the .40's propensity for pressure spikes and I prefer not to try to feed such a short cartridge in the 1911 pistol. Feed reliability simply cannot be as good as the 10mm.

For God's sake never attempt to fire .40s in the 10mm! The shorter case may be pushed forward in the chamber and you will have a very dangerous situation if it ignites. I have to give this to the .40: it is a semi-big bore and it is an easy cartridge to control in the 1911, my earlier comments notwithstanding. In a converted 9mm the .40 isn't that great; in a .45 converted to .40, well, the equation is different. Accuracy seems more than acceptable. If you have fired the Glock M22 or the Beretta 96 you will be surprised by the easy-rolling recoil the .40 generates in the 1911 platform. The Winchester 180-gr. SXT is as controllable as a 9mm in the .40 caliber 1911. The hotter loads are not in 10mm territory but respectable. Handloading the 1911 .40 is a simple matter compared to the Glock. With the 1911 you have a supported chamber and far less swelling of cases: simply normal case head expansion. A Commander in .40 is a good pistol but I cling to my reservations concerning pressure spikes and feed reliability.

.40 S&W Ballistics

135-gr. CorBon	1290 fps
155-gr. Black Hills	1130 fps
180-gr. Winchester	980 fps

.400 CorBon

The .400 CorBon is a .45 ACP case necked down to .400" (10mm). The premise is to offer a high-velocity cartridge close to 10mm velocity with the good feed reliability of the .45 ACP cartridge. With high velocity bullet expansion is ensured. The bottleneck case shoves the bullet into the chamber offering ideal feed reliability. I have never heard of poor feed reliability with the .400 CorBon. I plugged an Ed Brown barrel into an old Ithaca pistol and accuracy was excellent. I have heard that some have needed to open up their magazine feed lips to ensure feed reliability, but using Wilson Combat magazines I have not. I have endured every handgun malfunction known except a malfunction in converting a handgun to .400 CorBon. Be certain to check all magazines to be used with this conversion! I check all duty magazines in any case but this is particularly true with the .400 CorBon.

I have found that .400 CorBon accuracy is excellent, for the most part. We are using good-quality custom barrels, true, but just the same the accuracy potential of the cartridge seems high. I have fired the 135-gr. hollow point load from CorBon extensively. A .40 caliber (10mm) 135-gr. bullet at 1450 fps must be respected. This load is brilliantly accurate, as are many CorBon loads. This is 100 fps hotter than the same bullet in the .40, but the larger case makes for lower pressure. What I like about the .400 CorBon is that you may use the standard .45 ACP pistol for most uses and simply drop in the .400 barrel if you decide you would rather deploy this cartridge. This is a specialist cartridge but a very good one.

.400 CorBon Ballistics

CorBon 135-gr. JHP	1450 fps

.45 GAP

Most .45s are improvements in power over the .45 ACP, but .45 GAP is a cut-back .45 ACP. The .45 Glock Auto Pistol was designed to allow Glock to produce a .45 caliber pistol with a grip frame that would accommodate average- to small-size hands. There are also compact 1911 pistols chambered for the .45 GAP. These pistols are thinner from front strap to back strap by 1/8 inch compared to the .45 ACP. In a special situation in which a shooter has small hands and unusually short fingers, this advantage may be critical. However, the .45 GAP is not one of my favorite cartridges. It is a better round than the .40 Smith and Wesson in the Glock, but I see no real need for it in the 1911. The shorter GAP round is running at pressures in the .45 ACP +P range, yet its performance is squarely in the .45 ACP standard velocity category (despite much hype in the popular press stating otherwise). The Speer Gold Dot round clocks 950 fps with the 185-gr. bullet. Winchester took the bold step of introducing a 230-gr. load – "they" said it could not be done – that runs at 830 fps or so.

The GAP uses a small pistol primer and a special recut extractor groove, which means it is not suitable for use as a sub-load in the .45 ACP. One writer recommended cutting down .45 ACP cases for use in hand-loading and claimed he had good results. I do not see how, since the extractor groove in the .45 ACP would not be compatible. The reason the .45 GAP uses small pistol primers is because the ejector in the converted .40 frame Glocks runs so close to the cartridge that a large pistol primer could be dangerous.

Overall, the .45 GAP is a boon to law officers who would be saddled with the .40, but I do not see it as a good choice in the 1911. When you have buckets of .45 ACP brass as I do, the GAP or any other cartridge simply isn't attractive, but when you look at the GAP's performance, its passionately-proclaimed superiority is soundly refuted.

.45 GAP Ballistics

Speer Gold Dot 185-gr.	950 fps
Speer Gold Dot 200-gr.	900 fps

The .45 ACP case, left, compared to the longer .460 Rowland.

Historical Footnote: the .45 NAACO

Among the first long-case .45s was the moribund .45 NAACO, introduced as a hopped-up service cartridge. A Canadian company offered an overbuilt Browning High Power chambered in this caliber. I do not know what they were thinking. The world's armies were drifting toward the 9mm and the Canadian Army was using the Inglis High Power 9mm. The .45 NAACO illustrates that while some were downsizing, a larger, more powerful .45 was on the minds of many.

.45 Super

The .45 Super is a product of the fertile mind of gun writer Dean Grinnell, cop and writer Tom Ferguson, and gunsmith Ace Hindman. The .45 Super is simply a hot-loaded .45 ACP case. Although Starline Brass now produces high-quality heavy-duty brass, the first loads were put up in .45 ACP brass or cut down .451 Detonics brass.

The .45 Super would quickly batter a standard .45 to pieces. Hindman developed a system that enabled the pistol to handle such heavy loads, including an extraordinary guide rod system and heavy duty springs. These springs not only ensured function but alleviated recoil. Make no mistake, the .45 Super is a kicker but it is also often very accurate. Today Buffalo Bore offers good ammunition for the .45 Super. Its ballistics are outstanding. This is a sensible modification developed for western lawmen and outdoorsmen in search of more range and power. The .45 Super is not for everyone but it certainly offers a practical upgrade in power.

.45 Super Ballistics (Buffalo Bore Cartridge)

185-gr.	1300 fps
200-gr.	1200 fps
230-gr.	1100 fps

.460 Rowland

This is a cartridge near and dear to my heart. I did a comprehensive loading program for the .460 that was published in *Handloader Magazine*. The .460 was designed to approximate the ballistics of a .44 Magnum revolver in a 1911 chassis. Conceived by outdoors talk show host Johnny Rowland, the .460's mechanics were worked out by Clark Custom Guns. If CCG is involved, the conversion had to work!

When working with this type of pressure, the cartridge could not possibly be designed to chamber in a standard 1911. Such an accident would have catastrophic consequences. On the other hand, the cartridge had to feed in standard 1911 magazines. The problem was solved by having Starline Brass (a lifesaver for experimenters with such projects) produce an over-length .45 ACP case. The bullet was deep seated, resulting in a cartridge case with the same OAL as a .45 ACP, 1.250". But the cartridge could not chamber in a standard .45 ACP.

You cannot have your .45 chambered for this cartridge. The conversion is accomplished by fitting a Clark Custom barrel to an existing frame. A compensator and a 24-pound Wolff spring are part and parcel of the arrangement. Without the effective Clark Custom Guns compensator, the pistol would tear itself apart. The compensator is very effective. When firing loads as heavy as 230 grains at 1300 fps recoil was subjectively in the .45 ACP +P class. Muzzle blast, however, is stupendous. My photographer was so startled at the first shot (even though she had her eye and hearing protection on) she gasped an invective and the photograph, when developed, showed only tree tops! The .460 will literally blow debris out of the roof of a shooting shack. Recoil is controllable but catches up with you after 50 rounds or so. Your wrists will be sore. I have fired several thousand rounds including the wonderfully accurate CorBon loading. This has been spaced over several handguns. I cannot detect any damage or eccentric wear but this type of momentum cannot be good for the pistol. The end result of the conversion is a pistol capable of taking deer, boar and small bear to 50 yards. The .460 is arguably the most powerful cartridge available in a standard 1911, and the pistol can be converted back to .45 ACP by a simple barrel change. The conversion is gilt-edged accurate. For specialized use the .460 is the ultimate 1911 hunter.

.460 Rowland CorBon Performance

185 grains	1550 fps
200 grains	1450 fps
230 grains	1340 fps

RELIABILITY AND SAFETY CHECKS

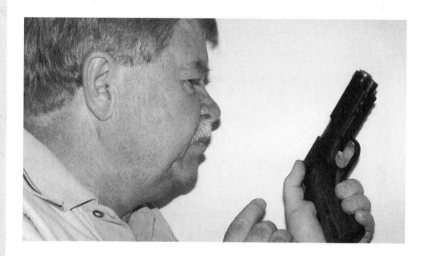

Chapter 19:

Testing the 1911 for reliability is straightforward and simpler than ever. Fewer pistols require a break-in period. A break-in period was practically standard operating procedure for a new 1911 pistol for most of my lifetime. Today, the break-in period is most often encountered with low-end and high-end pistols. Why? Because the low end Rock Island or Springfield GI may have burrs or a link to set. The high end Springfield TRP or Les Baer is so tight it will need a break-in. If you are not familiar with how to properly grip the pistol and to operate the controls and trigger, you cannot expect the pistol

These magazine followers are of a different design but each works well.

The author is performing the obligatory safety check on a new 1911.

to behave properly. If you are, then you should also lubricate the handgun and use quality ammunition. You also need to know how to properly field strip the pistol.

Field stripping the 1911 is easy enough. Frankly I usually break the pistol in with live fire first. It seems to make the field strip easier. We are getting ahead of ourselves but after firing, you will wish to clean and lubricate the pistol. I realize that a good 1911 will go thousands of rounds without cleaning but it will not do so without lubrication. Then there is the issue of unburned powder and lead deposits in the barrel. When the grooves disappear and there are only lands in the barrel, the lead deposits become difficult to remove. Accuracy is gone and pressure is much greater due to the noticeable obstruction of the barrel.

Proper field stripping of the 1911 is as follows:

Option One: Standard Pistols without the Full-Length Guide Rod

First, triple-check the handgun to be certain it is not loaded. Remove the magazine and lock the slide to the rear. Visually inspect the chamber and also insert the finger into the chamber. Next, carefully lower the slide. Place the slide lock safety on to keep the piece steady. While most 1911s can be field stripped by hand, I use the Wilson Combat bushing wrench to clasp over the bushing and rotate it to allow the recoil plug to be removed. The unit is under pressure! Do not let the recoil plug escape. Set the recoil plug aside. Next pull the recoil spring forward and out of the slide. Take the safety off and be certain the hammer remains at full cock. Turn the slide upside down and pull it to the rear until the half moon cut out in the slide is lined up with the matching notch in the frame. Press the slide lock out. The slide can now be pressed forward off the frame. Remove the recoil spring guide. Now, turn the barrel bushing counterclockwise until the lock in the bushing lines up with the slide to allow the barrel to be moved forward and out of the slide. The link must lie flat at this point. This is all of the field stripping that a beginner should attempt.

Simplicity itself: the 1911-A1 field -stripped. For normal maintenance, this is as far as one needs to go with the 1911.

Magazines are the heart of reliability.

Option Two: Standard Pistols with the Full-Length Guide Rod

If the pistol has a full length guide rod, the procedure is different. If the pistol has one of the two-piece guide rods with a indentation in the front for an Allen wrench, then simply un-screw the front section of the full length guide rod and remove this section and the recoil spring. Then proceed normally. With the one-piece type, you simply run the slide off in one piece, complete with the full length guide rod. Then you lift the full length guide rod and spring assembly out of the slide.

Some of the following recommendations require various skills at removing important parts such as the extractor. These reliability tricks will made the 1911 run smoother and in some case improve a budget-grade or well-worn 1911. But absolute finesse is needed. You can ruin the part if you attempt this upgrade in a ten-thumbed manner.

First, the initial testing: make certain the pistol is clean and lubricated. I like to drop oil on the bar-rel hood, on the front of the barrel, and on the cock-ing block and especially on the long bearing surfaces where the slide and frame are mated. I use a solid grip and fire from a benchrest. It is important to use good quality ammunition. I have had good luck with 230-gr. ball loads from Black Hills Ammunition, Fiocchi USA,

The CDP pistol is loaded with Black Hills ammunition and there are spare Wilson Combat magazines for the user to deploy. This is good kit with a proven record.

Winchester, Wolf and Zero ammunition. I occasionally use a handload I am confident in. Often the slide will fail to fully lock during the first magazine or so. A slight nudge with the finger should seat the slide. This short cycle should disappear within the first 50 rounds. If it

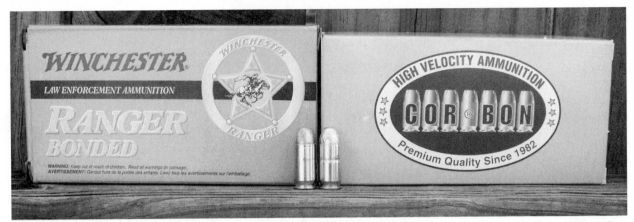

Know what you wish to do with your ammunition. The CorBon ball load is fine for accuracy and is always reliable. The Winchester FBI load offers a good balance of expansion and penetration. Either must be proofed in the pistol.

does not, there is a problem with the recoil spring or magazine or perhaps a deeper problem. A trip to the gunsmith or the manufacturer is indicated.

I am going to touch upon a few of the common upgrades that I use in addressing the 1911. These upgrades are part and parcel of the reliability package offered by reputable pistolsmiths. I recommend Don Williams of the Action Works. Don is a busy man but his work is first class. Let's look at the 1911 from top to bottom. These comments apply to the .45 ACP versions of the 1911.

Recoil Springs

The Government Model 1911 is supplied with a 16-pound recoil spring with few exceptions. My experience indicates that an 18.5-pound Wolff premium recoil spring is an aid in proper function. When using standard-pressure 230-grain loads I believe that function is more positive with the 18.5-pound spring. A Commander length pistol should use a 20-pound recoil spring. It is a tribute to Kimber that they know how to properly spring a pistol and this is a reason for the success of these pistols. Without exception I recommend the extra-power firing pin spring from Wolff. The Colt, Kimber and Para Ordnance pistols feature some type of firing pin block or drop safety. Springfield uses a lightweight firing pin with the heavy spring. In testing, this heavy firing pin spring has prevented the archetypical accidental discharge when the pistol is dropped on its muzzle. I modify my carry guns with this spring as a matter of course. The heavy spring results in greater safety and less chance of a stuck firing pin.

I never use a lightweight hammer spring, period. When you handle a Kimber, note that the hammer spring is full power. Some effort is required to cock the hammer. The Kimber also uses an appropriate recoil spring. A full-power hammer spring maintains the correct equilibrium between slide velocity and function.

The barrel on the right is not fitted properly. The lower lugs are taking a beating.

Low-power hammer springs have been used to allow the use of target loads in the Colt Gold Cup, but I do not believe they are strictly necessary even in this application.

I have often mentioned that the slide stop of the 1911 is a failsafe design. It is meant to be ridden over by the slide during recoil. Only a conscious effort should lock the slide back. I like to use a slide stop with a slight dimple where it contacts the plunger spring in order to keep the slide stop in place. I use the Wilson Combat slide stop. In standard types it is a simple matter to use a light punch to dimple the slide stop yourself. On occasion the slide stop nose meets a bullet nose and ties the pistol up. This most often occurs with 1911s advertised as top-end pistols when they are actually parts guns made up of a bucket of parts from different manufacturers. The cure is to carefully grind the nose of the slide stop. Do so carefully – a little goes a long way. I never under any circumstances use an extended slide stop. I have lost count of the malfunctions I have seen with these bastard devices. There are two drawbacks.

This is the 10-8 Performance Armorer tool. It is a handy tool for the 1911 fan.

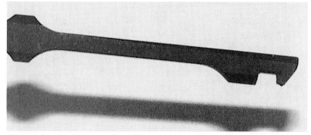

This extractor is properly cut for good function.

The thumb often meets this extended slide stop during firing, locking the slide. Second, the extra weight of the part sometimes causes the pistol to lock up under its own inertia. Avoid oversize slide locks if you are interested in a reliable 1911 handgun.

The firing pin stop was once a more troublesome item that what is found on most 1911s today, but then we used a lot of worn GI pistols when I first began firing the 1911. The firing pin stop would sometimes fall out of position when the pistol fired. The original cure was to peen the part. Today we have the Wilson Combat firing pin stop that must be fitted to the pistol. The original problem is no longer common but diligence will ensure that it does not come up again. Many of the inexpensive imports have firing pin stops with just enough fit and no more.

Extractors must receive their share of attention. The hook must be clean and sharp to perform well. The cartridge must snug into the extractor during feeding, which can be affected by a too light spring (refer to the section on recoil springs). Inexpensive handguns often have weak or even soft extractors. The best fix is to fit a Wilson Combat extractor and be done with it. Fitting the extractor is for a gunsmith, but you can check and be certain the extractor has sufficient hook to extract the cartridge.

The real issue is not extracting the cartridge but carrying it to the ejector. There are modern designs using an external extractor that claim superiority. Perhaps they may be but in the case of one well circulated 1911, the extractor hook is .125" tall and centered on the firing pin rather than clocked below it. The standard extractor is .175" tall. I am going to use the original. The new Para Power Extractor is lauded as an improvement. This extractor has 50% more gripping area than

the original. Which do I recommend? I cannot fault the Para but the majority of my pistols use the tool steel original from Wilson Combat.

Some of what we are doing will make the pistol more reliable and some is a cautionary upgrade for high round-count pistols. Looking at the feed ramp is perilous for an amateur gunsmith, but with respect and finesse polishing the feed ramp can be profitable. Examine the fit of the barrel first. The barrel hood must be perpendicular to the center line or bore axis. The barrel hood can be polished to an extent. I think that the primary area of concern on the barrel hood is the bevel at the rear on high grade pistols that was not found on early 1911s. This bevel helps lead a sharp shouldered bullet into the chamber. Yes, bullet noses rise that high and the barrel tilts to greet them. This bevel should be at a 45-degree angle. Don't overdo it and if you are not certain, don't do it at all. The inside of the chamber must be smooth. Most often it is but not always. A tool mark or a burr inside the chamber is best polished away with a jeweler's file.

Knowing what I know about the 1911's controlled feed action I am reluctant to polish the feed ramp. Just the same, at times this polishing is necessary. Once you reach the level of the Springfield Loaded Model, this is not normally necessary but with lesser pistols the feed ramp is seldom glass smooth. The frame and barrel ramps should be separated by a 1/32" gap. This is necessary for the proper stop, nudge into the extractor, and nose up into the chamber in the feed cycle. You must follow the curve of the feed ramp and very lightly polish this area. A little goes a long way. I have seen quite a few pistols with blown case heads due to a heavy-handed "throating." A local shop has a 10mm Double Eagle and a Rock Island Armory waiting for repair work at the moment. I believe the frame of the RIA gun may be wrecked. The 1911 has a supported chamber in comparison to the Glock but a certain portion of the case head is unsupported. A modicum of case expansion is normal.

The ejection port, breechface and ejector are all important and you should understand their function. There are a number of parts and accessories that I am going to strongly recommend you never use. One of these is the extended ejector. A too-tall ejector serves no real purpose and in my opinion is dangerous. If you are unload-

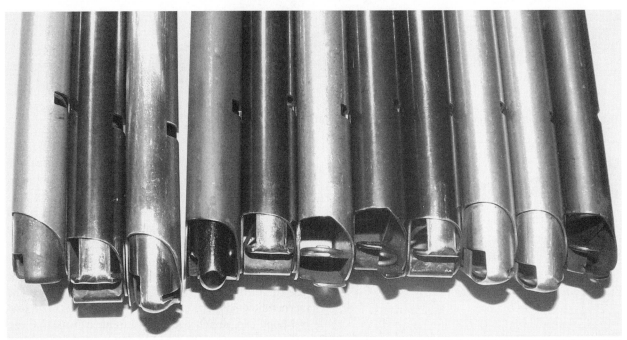

These magazines feature different follower designs but they all work!

This magazine follower is properly clocked for good function.

ing a live cartridge, there is a good chance you may rack the cartridge primer into the taller "competition" ejector. The standard ejector does a fine job of kicking the empties all over the north forty. The breechface should be smooth, but there are often tool marks on this machined surface. I would avoid purchasing a pistol with a rough breechface. The majority can be polished without any problem but if the marks are deep you may only dress them up a bit. If you remove too much metal, you may alter headspace, the distance from the breechface to the place in the chamber where the cartridge case mouth is stopped. You could have a burst case if you are not careful with breech face polishing.

The ejection port of modern pistols is universally scalloped or lowered unless you purchase a GI pistol. Even the inexpensive Rock Island line of GI pistols comes with an enlarged ejection port, the only visual deviation from the GI template. GI slide windows usually are just fine for ejecting spent cases. In administrative handling, when you are removing a loaded cartridge, or when you are attempting to eject a dud round, the GI port is less than ideal. The modern ejection port leaves .465" to .480" of steel between the port and the slide. A tip: be certain the inside of the ejection port is smooth.

Shock buffs are often recommended for high round-count, hard-use pistols. If you carry the pistol for personal defense, they are fine if you keep them in place during practice and remove them after every session. I doubt many of you if any will adopt this regimen. There are two problems with shock buffs. One is plastic shavings in the action. If you have never seen these in

a well-used 1911 fitted with shock buffs you and I are going to a different church. The second problem is that the shock buff limits rearward movement of the slide. If you were in a situation in which you had to swiftly eject a dud round, the shock buff would be an impediment. With the GI gun the drill might be impossible.

There are details that add up to an ultra reliable pistol that, as Colonel Cooper remarked, is as "reliable as a machine can be." Mediocrity is easy; good things take time. I mentioned the breechface. The firing pin hole is sometimes a bit rough. Using the Dremel, you can carefully polish the firing pin hole and bevel it slightly. Another overlooked option is to carefully polish the cocking block on the bottom of the slide. While this makes it less hard on the disconnect, this polishing also results in less eccentric wear overall.

This Springfield has been fitted a 10-8 Performance trigger. Black Hills ammunition and Metalform magazines are the sweet spot for this reliable handgun.

The final concern in reliability is in replaceable parts. The magazine is not intended to last the lifetime of the pistol. The detachable box magazine is a renewable resource. If the feed lips become bent or the magazine spring is worn, usually showing up as a failure to feed the last round in the magazine, it is time for a new magazine spring or a new magazine. The handgun grips must support the plunger tube. Poor grip design allows the plunger tube to flex. We will cover the choice of ammunition in the next chapter, but simply be certain that the ammunition is both feed- and cycle-reliable. If not, carry hardball. There is no other option.

Magazines are the heart of the pistol and there are competing designs. While this may be confusing, the cheapest magazine is never the best and is often false economy. Most magazines are made of the same sheet metal, about .024" to .025" thick. Magazine springs are about .045" to .048" thick. Magazine bodies, however, differ in length. The majority including the Wilson

Combat eight-round, the Novak and the McCormick are dead on at about 4.75 inches long. The Metalform top of the line grade measures 4.85"+ and the Wilson Combat ETM, the current technology leader, is 4.81". Here is the problem: most of the eight-round magazines are the same length as a seven-round magazine. With these dimensions they must accommodate a long spring but a shortened follower. When you use such a magazine it will usually feed just fine but when you insert the magazine into a pistol with the slide down, excess force is often needed to fully seat the magazine. That is why I regard my 1911 .45s as eight-shooters. I may load all eight rounds in the magazine but then I load the pistol by inserting the magazine and running the slide forward. It is asking a lot for the pistol to load from full compression to almost no compression. I strongly prefer the purpose-designed eight-round magazine, with the Wilson Combat ETM being the single most well-distributed.

Another consideration is the fact that the magazine springs are so tight in some magazines that they present a difficulty in lowering the slide if the pistol is empty. I have tested several and with the slide locked back, it is almost impossible to lower the slide against spring pressure. This sometimes results in excess wear in the groove the slide lock rides in. In other cases the slide lock will not lock on the proper shelf in the magazine follower but rather the slide lock will lock on the upper ledge of the follower, which is far from ideal. While we are on the subject of magazines, Dave Lauck of D and L Sports offers a magazine that is built like a Brinks armored car. The only hesitation I have in recommending these magazines is the fact that I have tested only two at present. Just the same, I have found them to be completely reliable and with no room for improvement.

Safety Checks

Most of what I learned concerning safety checks I learned from the late T. N. Hughston, but every gunsmith has a variation on the theme. These safety checks were in use as early as 1922 by armorers and possibly earlier. Safety checks are indispensable in examining a used handgun and sometimes a new pistol but they are particularly important to anyone who modifies their own pistol. They also serve to check behind the pistolsmith. These tests are proven and will spotlight the more serious problems encountered with 1911 safety. These tests are not independent but sequential and must be performed in the proper order.

First, cock the hammer, and then place the safety in the on position. Press the trigger then disengage the safety. The hammer should not fall. Next place the ham-

Maintenance means a great deal. The Commander, center, is on its third set of springs but has never malfunctioned. The Colt Detective Special has been running since 1960. The Bersa is relatively new and is shown for comparison. For just a little more weight you can have a .45.

mer close to your ear and carefully press the hammer to the rear. You should NOT hear a click. The click would be the sear reengaging the hammer hooks, an indication that the safety is allowing the sear to move out of place. Hammer hooks are relatively thin to begin with at only .022". After a trigger job you may find the hooks are too thin for positive engagement. For this reason I recommend that you purchase a quality aftermarket sear disconnect and hammer set when you wish for a light trigger job, not modify an existing action.

Next, we check the grip safety. The trigger is pressed without applying pressure to the grip safety. Press the trigger. The trigger must not fall and must not fall after the grip safety is engaged. Do not press the trigger but repeat the test with the hammer. These simple tests will indicate if there is an internal problem.

Finally we check the disconnect. Pay attention to detail, as this is a section in which the click test has a different character. First, press the slide about .25" to the rear. Press the trigger with the safety off and the grip safety depressed. The hammer must not fall. However, in this case you should hear a click when you do the click test, pressing the hammer to the rear, as the disconnect should reset.

Another test of the disconnect: bring the slide to the rear and lock it in place. Press the trigger. Release the slide to run forward while holding the trigger down. The hammer should not fall.

Half cock test: This test applies only with the original Series 70 and GI types, and the Kimber and Springfield pistols. Bring the hammer almost to the full cock notch and release. The half cock notch should catch the hammer. When the pistol is at half cock, press the trigger. The hammer should not fall.

Inertia firing pin tests for 1911 pistols without a Series 70 or Kimber type firing pin block: With the slide locked to the rear, use a pencil eraser to press the firing pin flush with the frame from the rear. The firing pin should not protrude from the firing pin channel.

Firing pin block test for Series 80 pistols: With the slide locked to the rear, use a small punch or pen or anything smaller than the firing pin and firing pin channel to press the firing pin forward. The firing pin should move very little and lock. It should not protrude from the firing pin channel.

Lubrication

A lack of lubrication is the most common problem with the 1911. It is a shame to be running a class on advanced tactics and some operator's Colt ties up because he has not lubricated the piece properly or at all. Ignorance of the fact is no excuse. The 1911 needs proper lubrication for reliable function. There is no room for discussion. The 1911 was designed in a day when mov-

ing parts needed lubrication. Even with my personal defense pistols that have some type of advanced finish such as Kimpro, I do not push the envelope. I know that NP3, as an example, is practically self-lubricating. But I have not done a torture test of the pistol. I continue to lubricate to my own specifications.

You cannot lubricate too much. The oil will run off, be blown out of the action, or find its way to your cheeks. On the other hand, the absence of lubricant will bring the action to a screeching halt. Remember, a light lube is usually OK for personal defense use. You will fire only a few rounds in personal defense. If the lube is gone in a few rounds, that's fine. But if the lubricant has run off or evaporated while you are carrying the piece you may be in trouble. If the pistol is not properly lubricated you will be in a jam – bad pun intended – if you have to use the piece in an emergency. I prefer that you lube the pistol before a class and check every 200 rounds. Understand the difference between wet lubricants and grease. On the range I often simply squirt Remoil into the ejection port. But a good quality grease that is laid into the slide rails works great for the long term. It will not run off in normal use but it will dry up and will need to be reapplied. It is not an onerous task to check the pistol for lubrication every week.

Some of the lubricants work well enough for preventing corrosion but are not the best for combating friction and for care of the long bearing surfaces. As for the self lubricating finishes, Bear Coat and NP3 have proven themselves in long-term use on several pistols. I have fired hundreds of rounds in NP3 coated pistols in particular, without lubricant, as an experiment. But I still lubricate the pistols for carry use. I cannot comment on the other types of finish. Pay particularly close attention to the internals of the 1911 if you live in a humid environment or if you perspire directly onto the handgun. I corroded a Star PD in this manner many years ago.

Manual of Arms for Lubricating the 1911

1. TRIPLE CHECK THE PISTOL. CLEAR THE CHAMBER AND MAGAZINE. LOCK THE SLIDE TO THE REAR.

2. Lubricate the slide rails; these are the long bearing surfaces.

3. Lubricate around the end of the barrel where it meets the barrel bushing.

4. Lubricate the cocking block on the bottom of the slide.

5. Lubricate the top of the disconnect.

6. Lower the slide.

7. Lubricate the barrel hood area well. This is a high-friction area. Rack the slide a few times.

Spring Replacement

Occasionally you run across an original Colt that is still running on the OEM recoil spring. It either has not been fired often or it is not running at capacity. The recoil spring should be replaced every 5,000 rounds for optimum performance, or every 3,000 rounds ideally. I recently went through my personal 1911 handguns and replaced every recoil spring with ISMI products, ranging from 16 pounds for GI pistols and 18 pounds for my tactical pistols to 20-pound springs for the 4-inch pistols. It is wise to change the firing pin spring every so often as well.

When a magazine begins to malfunction, there are causes other than the magazine spring that are suspect. The magazine lips may be bent or the follower may be well worn. Just the same, you can salvage an otherwise good magazine by changing the magazine spring. Springs are important. We would not let the springs and shocks run forever without replacement on the family van and we should not do so with 1911 springs. The longevity of the handgun and perhaps the shooter depends upon this simple replacement.

Tools

For machine work I send my pistols to a pistolsmith. Many of these men are backlogged and a wait of several months for major work is in order. There are procedures we can perform by ourselves, however. Often I use books on gunsmithing for reference. Sometimes I find the writer is preaching from the pulpit down instead from the congregation up. When he begins to describe the best lathe and drill press for the job, well, you had best be operating on a professional basis to amortize this type of outlay. The learning curve is steep as well. The best gunsmiths apprenticed under someone. Many of the cutaways handguns you see illustrated in gun-smith's books were mistakes, so they were made into cutaways. The road to becoming a pistolsmith is a long and challenging one, to be respected.

To perform good work we need tools. I have collected quite a few as they were needed. All are necessary. Remember, some of these tools are good to carry to the range in the tote bag. Don't be the fellow who finds himself at the range without a bushing wrench, screwdriver, lubricant and a means to adjust the sights. A quality screwdriver set is a minimal investment for a qualified handgunner. The Competition Edge Dynamics screwdriver with built-in tool kit, the CID 1911 tool kit, is very good kit. The Chapman screwdriver set has been around for some time and remains unbeatable for pistol work. This is a specially finished and hardened tool that allows you to work on firearms without buggering the screwheads and which gives plenty of leverage. The nut drivers and ratchet are a great resource. These tools seem to last forever, but I keep spare sockets as insurance against the occasional loss.

I have also used the Grace USA brass hammer and punch kit. This takes the worry out of dealing with external extractors and other parts. Universal Outfitters has introduced an exceptional set of grips with an internal bushing wrench I particularly enjoy. Then there is the Caspian Pocketsmith, a 1911 man's version of the Multi Tool. There is the usual screwdriver but also a purpose-designed bushing wrench incorporated into the pliers that are part of the Pocketsmith. This is a first rate tool designed to assist in working with the 1911 frame and slide. Another tool, a rather neat and simple addition to my tool kit, is the 10-8 Armorer's tool. This is a must have tool when dealing with extractors. When you use these tools, avoid the "By God, it is coming off!" attitude. Use a bit of finesse and everything will proceed smoothly.

AMMUNITION AND AMMUNITION TYPES

Chapter 20:

Ammunition is an important and interesting subject. There is some validity in the argument that in the final analysis the handgun is only a projectile launcher. If your ammunition is unreliable or underpowered, your life is at risk. I do not agonize over minutiae of performance but it is obvious that there are some loads that offer more performance than others.

There is intense competition among the ammunition companies. A real difference or a perceived difference is an important selling point. Performance is important to consumers although they do not

The Barnes X bullet may be the wave of the future.

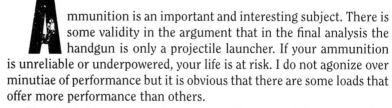

This is a recovered bullet from a Black Hills TAC load. Impressive performance!

These expanded bullets offer different philosophies on expansion and penetration but all performed as designed.

always understand what type of performance is desirable. The development of quality personal defense loads is reality-driven. Extensive testing and updating are important. I do not wish to debate the difference between specific competing loads because to do so would date the work. Loads come and go, the desirable performance is unchanging. To hash over competing loads that may be replaced in a few months would be counterproductive and unprofitable for the reader. On the other hand there are loads that have been in service a decade or more, and in the immediate future the reader will profit from an overview of the available ammunition.

We will look at the general performance of modern handgun ammunition and the most desirable traits. It is safe to say that Black Hills, CorBon, Federal, Fiocchi, Hornady, Remington, Speer and Winchester will be around for some time. These companies produce high-quality ammunition. The exact specifics of the loads differ but each company gives you a wide choice. Interestingly the smaller companies such as Black Hills and CorBon have used Barnes, Hornady, Montana Gold, Sierra, Speer and other bullets in their loads. Fiocchi uses the Hornady bullet in their XTP line produced in Ozark Missouri. This makes for flexibility. Smaller companies can move more quickly to improve their bullet choices.

Quality ammunition is at a milestone of sorts. The better loads now carry a tariff of a dollar a shot. For most of us this means careful selection. It is easy to invest a C-note in proofing a handgun for a chosen load. Companies producing less than first-quality ammunition have capitalized on this situation. I can only state that no matter the price of the ammunition, it must be proofed in your handgun. The most important ammunition choice made is in personal defense loads. But there are other loads that are important. You may fire 1000 or more practice loads for every personal defense load you fire on the bench.

Let's look at some of the better choices.

Practice Loads

Factory generic ball ammunition is the single most popular training load. Black Hills 230-grain FMJ or even less expensive 230-grain round nose lead loads are used by the thousands in training. Winchester offers a white box USA load. Fiocchi offers a similar load using a FMJ bullet. Wolf is the price leader at present with a steel cased loading. While we would never accuse ball ammunition of being match grade accurate, all of these loads are accurate enough for practice. Some are accurate enough to win matches, as is the case with the Black Hills 230-grain RNL loading. Most of these factory loads break 780-820 fps.

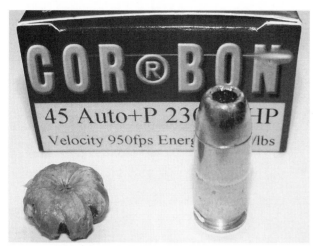

Cor Bon's 230-grain JHP is a front-runner in any personal defense selection process.

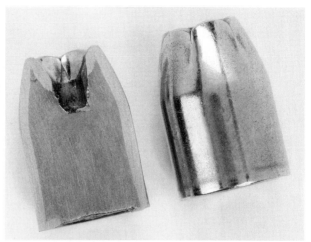

Winchester's Bonded Core technology is the choice of the FBI, circa 2010.

Another important resource is remanufactured ammunition. This is simply ammunition loaded using fired brass that has been recycled. I am very enthusiastic about remanufactured loads. I often use the Mastercast brand in practice. I enjoy handloading and find it economical, but I do not have time to load all of the ammunition I need. Remanufactured ammunition makes practice affordable. These loads are loaded on the same machinery used to load factory fresh ammunition. They simply incorporate used brass into the equation. The primary difference is that remanufactured loads do not have the same case mouth and primer seal as premium loads, which is immaterial for their intended use. The brass may not be as consistent, which limits accuracy potential but at typical training ranges the difference, particularly in fast paced combat shooting, is slight.

The Black Hills 230-grain RNL load I have mentioned often finds the sweet spot for accuracy in my 1911s. There are few combat competitions this load would not be adequate for. Most of these loads are rated sensibly lighter than the standard 230-grain military loading. This is good for control, comfort and long firearm life. For general practice and shooting, particularly with young shooters, I keep on hand a handload that propels the Oregon Trail 180-grain SWC at 850 fps. Most 1911s will function with this load and it is often brilliantly accurate. You do not have to beat yourself or the pistol to death in training. At a later tier in training it is important to master service loads, but I believe that marksmanship is best served by beginning with standard loads.

230-Grain Ball Loads

You have heard the credo, "they all fall to hardball." The original 230-grain jacketed round nose bullet enjoys a good reputation for effect on motivated targets. This load has excellent penetration, good accuracy, and is controllable in rapid fire. There is no better choice as a military handgun cartridge, although I would probably order some version of the Hornady 230-grain jacketed flat point bullet for service use. This bullet offers a flat meplat that is less likely to skid off bone and it is more likely to penetrate in a straight line. Most modern 230-grain ball loadings are intended for practice.

A GI .45 with hardball ammunition is a formidable instrument and the only reason you would be outgunned is from a lack of practice. Just the same, it behooves us all to use modern expanding ammunition for personal defense. After all we now have a load, Cor Bon PowRBall, that is as feed reliable as any ball load. I have tested most of the available loads and quite a few are impressive. I have seen the effect that expanding bullets have on game and the difference is noticeable. An animal struck with hardball tends to run a ways as it bleeds out. An animal struck with an expanding bullet that stays in the body tends to go down more quickly. This is especially true when the bullet chosen had sufficient penetration to rake a considerable distance in a quartering shot.

Match Grade Loads

The pursuit of accuracy is alive and well. I rely primarily upon my personal handloads for match grade loads. There are certain combinations that I find deliver wonderful accuracy. Most of these center upon the Nosler 185-grain JHP in jacketed bullets and the Oregon Trail 200-grain SWC in lead bullets. There are various factory loads that are usually accurate but many have proven difficult to impossible to obtain in recent years. When you need dependable accuracy for match shooting there are a relatively few factory loads that are dependable. The CorBon Performance Match loads have been a great boon to competition shooters. The .45 ACP 230-grain load has demonstrated extreme accuracy in

The final test: range work. No load, no matter how promising, is suitable for defense use if it is not 100% reliable.

my Les Baer Monolith and should do the same for you. A credible option is to have Custom Reloads of Dallas make up a match load for you. This service works two ways: you can specify they load a combination for you that you have worked up and found accurate. I did so with a combination involving Titegroup gun powder, Starline brass, and the Hornady 230-grain XTP. The second choice is to contract with CRD to work up a match grade load for your use. There is a difference in loads and while a number of factory loads have a good reputation for accuracy, when the big bucks and prizes are on the line you need the best.

Personal Defense Loads

Despite the best intentions of product designers, you cannot circumvent physics. There is only so much you can do with the basic energy stored in a cartridge. The bottom line is the depth of penetration and the size of the wound. The bullet needs not to just get to the vitals but penetrate them, hopefully leaving a wound larger than the original caliber of the bullet. Expanding bullet loads are designed to increase wound damage. Another consideration is public safety. A hollow point bullet is less likely to overpenetrate or to ricochet. When the open nose bullet catches a concrete drive or a streetlight pole it usually flattens. This is an important consideration in an urban environment.

Before we proceed to advanced criteria in choosing personal defense loads, let's look at the basics in reliable cartridge evaluation.

I have a program for proofing personal defense loads that I consider vital. If the load is not feed-reliable and does not feature good cartridge integrity, then it is not suitable for personal defense. No amount of ballistic advantage can make up for a malfunction. While I use a variety of loads for practice only, carefully proofed handgun loads are carried for personal defense. I demand good case mouth and primer seal. But how do we determine which loads are reliable?

I do not begin by firing them. That is a waste of time. I only fire for accuracy and reliability if they pass the initial test. I soak respective examples in water, oil and powder solvent. I let them set overnight. I then attempt to fire them. If they do not fire it is most often the powder that fails, not the primer. Ignition seems to be the easy part. If the ammunition doesn't pass the first test then it is for practice only. Next I hand-cycle a single round through the action 10 times at the minimum. This checks case mouth seal. The bullet must not be driven back into the case. When you consider how often you may load and unload a personal defense handgun, this is a reasonable test. The case mouth test also gives us an idea of feed reliability. (I prefer a cartridge case with a cannelure that grips the bullet and stops it from moving into the case, but I do deploy loads that are perfectly acceptable without the cannelure.)

Next I proceed to the firing test. The load must feed, chamber fire and eject without a problem. Muzzle signature should be minimal. 230-grain hardball has little flash, usually only a few sparks. A good 230-grain JHP such as the Black Hills version also has little muzzle flash. Most 185-grain JHP loads such as the 1050 fps rendition from Black Hills have little flash but have an orange glow. This shows that little unburned powder is evident. Accuracy should be consummate with the proven ability of the handgun. As an example, my personal Kimber Eclipse has demonstrated accuracy on the order of two inches at 25 yards with the Black Hills 230-grain RNL and about three inches with most 230-grain generic loads. The Black Hills 230-grain JHP load

This is a specialty load with much promise, the CorBon short barrel loading.

will group into about two and one half inches. Before testing personal defense loads, I had a baseline. If the pistol groups less accurately with a good quality JHP than with a target load such as the Black Hills 200-grain semi-wadcutter, that is to be expected. But the group should not be significantly larger. There is some currency to the notion that a personal defense handgun need not be very accurate. That's a bunch of hooey. I want all the accuracy I can get.

Modern expanding bullet loads are highly developed, accurate, reliable and effective. The hollow point bullet features a long bearing surface and gives good balance. Sometimes a personal defense load is more accurate than a match-grade RNJ load. As an example, my Les Baer Monolith has an affinity for the Hornady 230-grain XTP +P. Don't swoon, the finely wrought Baer pistol handles +P loads just fine and is very accurate and flat-shooting as far as I can hold with this load. The 200-grain XTP I often handload to around 1,000 fps is as accurate when I follow good load practice.

An expanding bullet does not solve all of your problems. You have to deliver the bullet to the area that will do the most good. A properly-delivered flat point is more effective than an expanding bullet that misses by several inches. But even a partially expanded bullet is more effective given equal shot placement. I do not think that perfect expansion in the cards. But most expanding bullets expand to some degree upon meeting flesh and blood. Rather than pushing a .451" bullet

an expanded bullet creates a wound channel of .500" or more. Once the mushroom is present, the bullet cuts flesh rather than pushing it aside. While we can check bullet expansion by various artificial means, none exactly duplicates the effect seen in flesh and blood. As an example, if the bullet expands to .68" in 14 inches of gelatin – just about ideal – where exactly did it expand to .68"? I do not lose any sleep over the matter. I test my ammunition thoroughly on the range and know that it will feed, go bang every time, function, and hit the target. Expansion is a bonus.

There are three basic depths of penetration in personal defense loads. These are shallow, medium and deep penetration. You cannot always gauge the penetration by bullet weight or velocity. High-velocity bullets do not always fragment. Much depends on the design. Some of the low-velocity loads plump up well after moderate penetration. The consensus is that the bullet must penetrate to a depth of 12 to 14 inches in gelatin. Hardball will penetrate to about 30 inches, so 230-grain hardball is unnecessarily penetrative. The bullet should expand to 1.5 times its diameter, or to about .68 caliber. There are several loads in this ideal range. The Black Hills 230-grain JHP penetrates to this standard but expands a bit more. The Winchester Bonded Core load is spot-on. A 230-grain JHP that penetrates and expands adequately is probably the best bet in personal defense.

There are some who prefer the faster Hornady 200-grain XTP. This load penetrates to 16 inches with consistency in gelatin while expanding to .68 caliber. For those living in a true-four season climate this may be the load of choice. The original Super Vel load used a 190-grain JHP. With the lighter bullet it was deemed necessary to reach a velocity of over 1,000 fps, then thought vital to instigate expansion. We have come a long way in bullet technology. The 230-grain bullets reliably expand even at less than optimum velocity as when fired in short barrel handguns. But there are good points to the 185-grain loads. As an example, the 185-grain CorBon JHP breaks over 1100 fps from a Government Model .45. This load does not penetrate to the 12-inch standard and often fragments. Some feel that this is ideal performance against soft targets.

One of my young female family members finds the CorBon load cycles her Commander faster. She notes it is ZIP ZIP and her recovery from recoil is enhanced. She also feels that the 185-grain load offers less recoil than the 230-grain loads even though the CorBon is a +P load. For Jessie, the 185-grain loads are ideal. Confidence means a lot. A rule beater is the Cor on DPX, using the all-copper Barnes X bullet. Loaded sensibly lighter than the +P 185-grain bullet, the DPX loading penetrates to practically the same degree as heavier bullets with good expansion. There are some who feel that the DPX and other all copper bullets are the wave of the

The Federal Hydra Shock +P is seldom seen but offers interesting performance.

future. They may be, and while the performance cannot be faulted they are more expensive than standard bullets. I have confirmed their accuracy and expansion potential. They also seem to offer the same safety factor as conventional expanding bullets.

When it comes to penetration, it is true that many of us would like to limit penetration in the home or the apartment building or even the mall. This is a laudable public safety measure, but what if the bad guy takes cover behind your sofa? What if you are in the open and must respond to a drive-by and penetrate a vehicle door? What if the adversary weighs 300 pounds and is clothed in heavy winter garments?

I think that the 230-grain loads have earned a reputation as the hammer of the .45 ACP loads. The balance of expansion and penetration with these loads is often ideal. Another important consideration is function. The 1911 was designed to be feed and cycle reliably with 230-grain loads. The 1911 is remarkably reliable with modern loads, but the 230-grain load or a load with the same power factor is most reliable. There are outstanding light-bullet loads that have proven reliable in my 1911s, however. For example, the recently introduced Black Hills 185-grain TAC XP +P load has proven completely reliable in my personal Kimber CDP. I have adopted the CDP partly because it is fully ambidextrous. I am able to draw the pistol with my non-dominant hand and use it well. When firing with the weak hand, malfunctions show up. Black Hill's light bullet load is completely reliable from any firing position. As a bonus it proved capable of severe accuracy, placing five rounds into 1-5/16" at 25 yards from a solid bench rest with the Kimber Eclipse. I think this load is good enough to ride with.

In short, choose a reliable loading with a good balance of expansion and penetration and shoot straight. You will be ahead of the game.

Best Buy Loads?

We are beginning with the world's most efficient personal defense cartridge, so is there a means of compromising and economizing and still maintaining good performance? The loads mentioned that break the price barrier of a dollar a bullet are triumphs of modern defense technology. But there are a handful of loads that offer good value. Some loads are simply cheap copies of premier American defense loads, but without the extensive test and evaluation that goes into the American loads.

There are two loads offered in 50-round boxes that are a good example of quality defense loads. The first is the Winchester 230-grain JHP offered in the personal defense line. This load usually breaks about 820 fps. The load expands and penetrates well and offers modest recoil along with Winchester quality control. The second is the Fiocchi 230-grain JHP. This load is pretty brisk at over 850 fps, and offers good expansion. This Missouri-produced load usually feeds in GI pistols in my experience. You could do worse than choosing either of these loads and hitting the target every time.

45 ACP +P in Depth

+P loads bump the pressure of the .45 ACP up from 18,00 psi to 21,00 psi. While still relatively sedate compared to the 30,000 psi 9mm Luger, this is a significant boost in pressure for the .45 ACP. The .45 ACP's advantages as a low-pressure pistol cartridge include long weapons life and little chance of battering. By increasing the momentum of the slide, battering is likely to increase. Firing a 1911 extensively with +P loads has been likened to running the family sedan at 100 mph for 100,000 miles over a bumpy road.

There are ways of setting the pistol up properly for +P loads, foremost of which is using a W C Wolff +P rated recoil spring and heavy duty firing pin spring. The firing pin spring is for increased safety when the slide recoils to prevent the firing pin from running forward during recoil. I do not like any setup that interferes with the use of standard loads. As a rule, the heavy duty springs are compatible with standard ammunition. I have used Wolff gun springs for two decades in handguns intended for all types of loadings. They are good kit.

When moving to +P loads you must consider the advantage. If there is no advantage in performance, then there is little point in using a +P load. By testing penetration and expansion in media, we determine if there is any advantage in adopting a +P rated load. Some may desire rapid expansion or even fragmentation. The CorBon 185-grain JHP delivers. The CorBon 230-grain

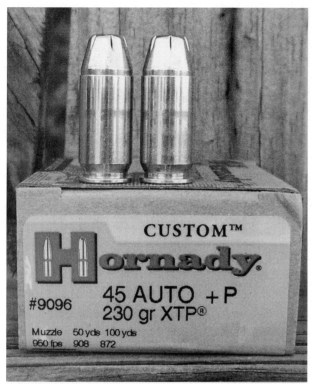

The Hornady XTP +P is faster at 100 yards than many competing loads at the muzzle!

JHP is less well known but delivers an excellent balance of penetration and expansion for those desiring more penetration.

If you are searching for the ideal personal defense load then you must first qualify the performance of a standard pressure load before deciding that the standard loads are not enough. I have performed extensive testing of most of the available handgun loads. As a baseline I used the Black Hills 230-grain jacketed hollow point. This is a good loading with a balance of expansion and penetration I find ideal for personal defense. Accuracy is match grade and for other reasons the load just feels right. I am certain there are those who feel the same about their personal defense loads and who have equal proof of the pudding. But using the Black Hills load as a baseline, I compared the performance of over a dozen +P rated loads. Many expanded more rapidly but at the cost of penetration. Others fragmented. A few offered more penetration at the cost of bullet expansion. In the end, only two +P loads existed that I felt offered a genuine improvement in performance over the standard loads I usually deploy. These were the CorBon 230-grain JHP +P and the Black Hills 230-grain JHP +P.

It isn't surprising that you have to go to +P rating to achieve an improvement. The CorBon load offered a measurable advantage in expansion due to increased velocity. Accuracy was also good. The Black Hills +P of-

fered considerably more penetration. Each produced about 10% more recoil and increased muzzle flip compared to standard pressure loads. Only the end user can answer the question of worth. Remember, these loads demand attention to your training. It is unethical not to practice if your loved ones depend upon your skill at arms. You need trigger time. You may find yourself in a situation in which you wish you had practiced more often.

As for bullet performance, I do not necessarily believe that gelatin is an accurate predictor of bullet performance in a living creature but I do believe that gelatin is a good comparison medium. I compare loads using many products, but frankly good old wet newsprint, properly done, gives me results within 10% of the results I have obtained with FBI grade gelatin. Wet newsprint is a good choice but be careful. Bullets sometimes take a turn and burst from the side of the bucket and many penetrate completely into the ground.

Specialty Loads

Glaser Safety Slug

The Glaser 145-grain +P load averages 1299 fps from my 5-inch Gold Combat. This loading uses a compressed charge of birdshot sealed in the jacket by a synthetic plug. The goal is for the Glaser to feed and function perfectly, then to penetrate in a shallow wound so that the birdshot fans out, shredding tissue. The safety aspect comes from the Glaser's well-known and proven proclivity to fly apart and disintegrate on hard surfaces such as light poles and city roads. The Glaser is a true safety slug in that regard. Per my experience, since Dakota Ammunition (CorBon) purchased Glaser and has undertaken production, the ammunition has been both reliable and accurate. The Glaser is not as consistent as a conventional copper jacket and lead core bullet, but it does offer combat accuracy. In most Government Model 5-inch barrel handguns, the Glaser will cut one ragged hole at seven yards. Two to three inches at 10 yards is common and four to five inches at 25 yards is average, although some handgun and load combinations do better. The Glaser usually penetrates about 6.5 inches of gelatin.

I will repeat what I have often said concerning the Glaser. If it performs as designed, it produces a complex wound that is difficult to repair. If the safety aspect is more important than penetration, then this is the round for you. The Glaser Silver is faster and offers a claimed one inch greater penetration.

Air Freedom

The Air Freedom round offered by Extreme Shock is a modern round with much to recommend. It is slightly slower than the Glaser in my test program, and its ac-

Black Hills offers an all-copper TAC load as well as the traditional 185-grain JHP. Both offer good performance.

curacy is comparable to the Glaser's. Penetration is a shade less on average, on the order of perhaps .5 inch in average penetration. The Air Freedom round is a credible alternative to the Glaser, a specialty load that offers good function and accuracy per my testing.

As you can see there are many options in ammunition. The primary requirement of any load is that it is reliable. You cannot accept anything else. Practice ammunition need not be as resistant to the elements as duty ammunition but it must be reliable.

HOLSTERS AND CONCEALED CARRY

Chapter 21:

When it comes to concealing the 1911 we have several advantages. The pistol is flat enough; no other big bore handgun is as flat as the 1911. This allows designers a great deal of freedom in holster design. For example, the DesBiens covert IWB is ideal for the 1911, with its high-quality leather and thin design. Retention is good because of the long slide of the 1911. A short-sided heavy-handled pistol such as the SIG P220, in comparison, is more difficult to holster properly. Blocky-slide pistols are a horror, although Milt Sparks in particular has designed successful holsters that

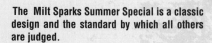

The Milt Sparks Summer Special is a classic design and the standard by which all others are judged.

The craftsman at DeSantis Leathergoods is molding a 1911 holster.

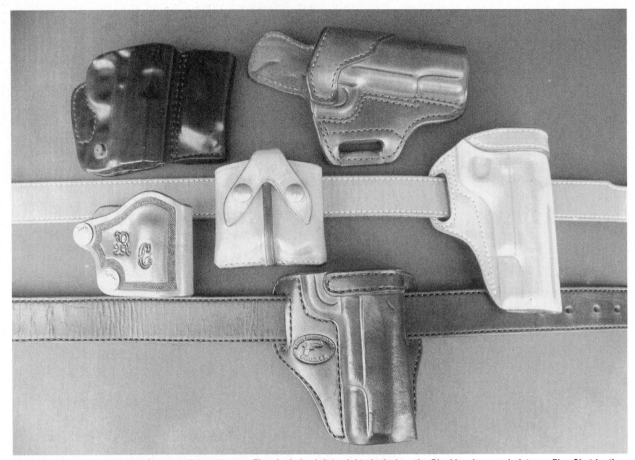

These holsters are a good set for most circumstances. They include, left to right clockwise, the Blackhawk range holster, a Five Shot leather scabbard, the Rafter L belt and holster, a Haugen Handgun Leather crossdraw and the Saguaro belt slide.

conceal the Glock and SIG well enough. In compact versions, the 1911 is short enough for deep cover and in some versions the pistol is as light as any capable combat handgun. I have carried a Government Model for many years but I admit that I carry my Kimber CDP in a K and D concealment holster more often than not these days. I very seldom carry a tactical type or a 1911 rail gun concealed, although I own a Secret Squirrel rail gun holster. I pay attention to draw angle – there is something about a properly designed holster such as the Milt Sparks Axiom that holds the pistol's butt at the right angle for a rapid presentation.

The 1911 lends itself well to concealed carry but, just the same, concealed carry is a learned process. You must be comfortable and at the same time always be aware of the position of the handgun. There is a big difference between a smooth transition to carrying a handgun and appearing as if you are a handgun with a man attached. It may be argued that an objective truth does not exist in holster selection, that it is all relative to your position. To some extent this is true but an error in the application of concealed carry discipline may have severe consequences. You must choose a quality holster.

The holster has several functions. Among these are:

Retention. The handgun must be secure, no matter what type of physical activity you engage in. I have been turned upside down during a scuffle while wearing a concealed handgun in a Milt Sparks Summer Special holster. Retention kept it in place. A holster without proper molding and retention will wear more quickly and become a chafing nuisance. Leather holsters retain the handgun by the long bearing surfaces and slide; Kydex holsters embrace the trigger guard and muzzle. Soft, floppy holsters embrace nothing.

Draw Speed. The holster must offer a rapid presentation. The holster and the handgun are a synergistic blend when properly designed. Take a look at the Nick Matthews belt scabbard, and you will note that while the holster holds the 1911 securely, the gun butt is angled into the draw. When I was a young man I made a fast presentation under stress and the holster came out with the handgun. (I survived and a single shot solved the problem.) The debacle was a result of my own ignorance. A well-molded holster will offer retention and also draw speed. As Dale Fricke is able to illustrate with his Gideon Elite holster, Kydex holsters have come a long way and now offer good speed and retention. This was not always true.

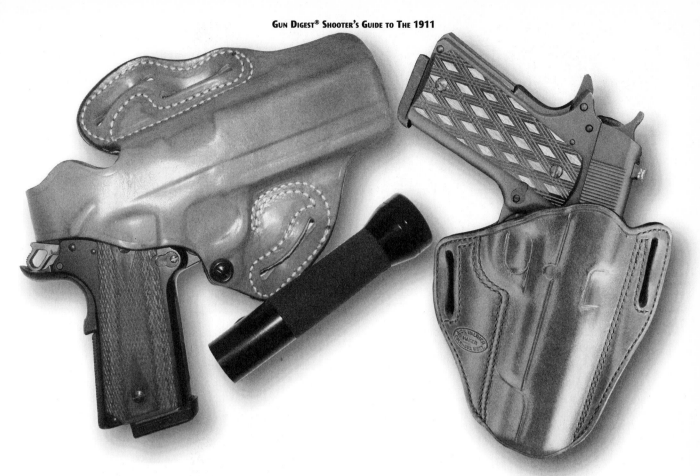

This classic thumbreak from DeSantis is molded for a rail gun.

Rick Waltner's belt scabbard is versatile and very well turned out.

Events unfold in seconds. The presentation is a salient point in personal defense training and a perishable skill that must be practiced. A poor holster does not allow good speed. At this point I must state that nothing is more amateurish than to adopt a good holster and a poor, thin belt. A thick, rugged holster belt is essential to rigidity. The holster must be in the same place draw after draw. Rafter L offers good custom grade belts, while Don Hume is the leader in mass produced gun belts at a fair price.

Comfort. The fundamental appeal of leather may be appearance but a good leather holster is also more comfortable than a Kydex holster. The holster will not be completely comfortable and never unnoticed. A holster and gun are comforting, not comfortable. A proper design of adequate thickness will protect the body from the sharp edges of the handgun, and also protect the handgun from the body's harsh corrosive salts. Note the sweat guard found on the majority of Tauris holsters as an example. This lip, an option with most makers, is a good example of protecting both the handgun and the user. If the holster is properly worn on a well-designed gun belt, then it will be comfortable. A loose holster flopping on a thin belt is a lost gun or a fumbled draw waiting to happen.

Choices

When it comes to handgun leather the choice is highly personal. A wrong choice may resound fatally at a later date. A poor choice may result in a lost handgun and the revocation of your carry license. Several decades of concealed carry have given the author some perspective. The holster must fit the circumstance. I most often carry my Colt Defender in a Milt Sparks Summer Special holster in the summer. During the winter months, I would have to dig through several layers of clothing to draw the piece. This is when I switched to a larger pistol and the Milt Sparks Axiom belt holster. The Axiom is the latest development in a holster, offering rapid on and off belt snaps. While they are quickly actuated, the loops are perfectly rigid and offer real security. I am not a fan of paddle holsters and the Axiom offers excellence of design with a degree of convenience that is popular with the modern high-speed low-drag class.

If the holster you choose is unsuitable for daily chores then it will not be worn. The holster must fit the circumstances. Your lifestyle and environment must be considered. The mission of the holster must be understood. As an example, the Covert OWB #1 from DesBiens Gunleather (DGL) is an excellent strong-side scabbard with a highly desirable forward

The Secret Squirrel Practical is an ideal holster for most uses. Note the Sharkskin trim.

In this illustration Jessie is wearing an inside the waistband holster outside of her daisy dukes to illustrate that the longer the holster the more chance of being pinched when you set. This Milt Sparks Summer Special is just right.

The Maverick holster from Gunfighters LTD is inexpensive but a good option for deep concealment of the Commander .45.

rake and real speed. It is well suited to carry under a suit coat. I would not try to conceal a handgun under a sport shirt with this holster. I will move to the DGL IWB holster in that case. Comfort, balance and speed must be balanced with retention. When you choose a concealment holster, however, another consideration is often overlooked. This is ease of insertion or reholstering. If you draw the piece, you must be able to holster it with relative ease   and safety. Look at the reinforced holster welt   at   the mouth of the holster of a quality scabbard such as the Nick Matthews OWB. If you draw from this holster, you will be able to reholster with a minimum of practice. The Matthews IWB holsters share the same quality.

It takes time to acclimatize to carrying a handgun. Don't expect the kit to be comfortable but you will get used to it to it with time. Avoid combinations that allow the handgun's sharp edges to gouge the shooter. For the purpose of this discussion we are primarily concerned with concealed carry holsters. Even when carrying in the field I keep the handgun under a coat or jacket.

When you are choosing a holster you need to consider draw angle. As an example, my DesBiens Covert OWB is a pancake style that offers a rear rake. Rear rake means the muzzle is angled to the rear. This allows a more natural draw. For the purposes of exploration, I ordered a Rick Waltner holster with a more neutral rake. This type

of holster is suitable for taller individuals and I find it comfortable when in the field as well. A forward rake is rare and works only with very tall individuals. For most of us the rear rake and the generic FBI rake is ideal. What material you use is personal, but leather – cowhide – is still among the most versatile and useful of materials. My ratio of cowhide to anything else is more than 10 to one. But a genuine top choice that is worthy of consideration is horsehide. Horsehide is stronger and lighter ounce for ounce that leather and also more resistant to moisture. I have used Null Shell Horsehide holsters for years. The Null Speed Scabbard is a well designed holster with impeccable craftsmanship. Null's holsters are a study in efficient design. He offers a pancake style holster that hugs the body with good concealment and also the

Speed Scabbard, which has more offset from the body. Either is well made but be certain you choose the one that is suited for your dress.

Exotic materials are often used in holsters, with striking results. I sometimes deploy a Rocking W ostrich hide holster. While well designed and quite use-ful the holster is very striking when worn with a high-end 1911. You should spoil yourself at times and the Rocking W holster is one example of a handgunner's rock candy. Secret Squirrel Leather also offers exotics, including a few that are rather understated. One of these is the Practical, a strong-side holster that I have

In this illustration we see several strong-side holsters with different tilts. Left to right, Rocking W, DesBiens, Desbiens (DGL) and Rick Waltner. The sharkskin belt is from Kramer.

These are all strong-side belt holsters. Left to right clockwise, Rocking W exotic ostrich skin holster, a Tauris holster in service for over a decade, a DesBiens, and a holster by the late great Lou Alessi.

A look at some of the best leather on the planet: a strong-side scabbard from Nick Matthews, a strong-side holster from Barber gun leather, a Nick Matthews IWB, and finally the priceless Alessi holster.

ordered in leather with a alligator holstering lip (welt) band. This is a first class holster with much to recommend it. Secret Squirrel also offers an IWB design with adjustable belt loop that offers an unprecedented choice in comfort and cant and tilt adjustment.

The strong-side holster is by far the fastest and most comfortable. When you leave the strong-side holster behind then you have to have a good reason. But there are situations in which other types are demanded. Do not adopt a cross draw just because it is trendy. There are two reasons to choose the crossdraw: concealment and access. Before you leave behind the strong-side holster in a first class example such as the Secret Squirrel Practical, consider your needs. When you need more concealment the inside the waistband holster is ideal. As an example I have tested an IWB from US Gunleather for several weeks. This holster has well defined wings that support the weight of the holster, making the pistol more comfortable to carry. This is important with a full-size .45. The holster is worn inside of the pants between the trousers and the undergarments. The visibility of the holster is greatly affected. You no longer need a full-length covering garment to conceal the handgun. A pulled-out sport shirt or in some cases a heavy cloth T shirt may be used. The IWB does not protrude below the belt line. The wings position the belt loops away from

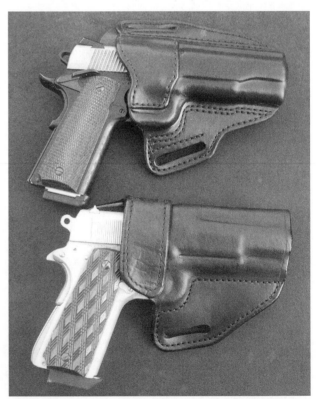

The Barber holster, top, and the Secret Squirrel, bottom, feature first class stitching and the contrasting welt many find so attractive.

We have great designs in abundance. The holster on the left from Barber offers a good sharp draw. The Milt Sparks Axiom, right, offers ease of attachment with easy on and off belt snaps.

The Milt Sparks Summer Special, left, and the C5 leather IWB, right, offer good designs for concealed carry. Both have been worn extensively.

the slide and offer good balance and a degree of concealment that allows a Government Model to be worn under the heavy T shirt – provided you have a good gun belt!

IWB holsters come in a wide variety. Some are practically shapeless but soft. The rub is you may get by with some of these holsters because the 1911 is flat and round. They would be excruciating with the Glock, as an example. DeSantis, a noted old-line maker and strong supplier of police holsters, has earned law enforcement contracts and holds an excellent reputation. They make some of the best production grade holsters on the planet. An inexpensive IWB from this maker is as inexpensive as you need to go. The two-in-one type features a thumbreak and does double duty as an IWB and OWB. If you are not able to tolerate a stiffer holster, this DeSantis may do the business. A better choice in my opinion is the DeSantis Inner Piece at a higher tariff. DeSantis also offers production holsters for the tactical rail guns.

There are few Kydex holsters I have learned to like but the Archangel IWB from Dale Fricke is an exception. This holster lies close and flat to the body, and rides above the belt line for a sharp draw. It is rigid and even though there is no true reinforced holster welt it will not collapse after the pistol is drawn and speed is good. I like the holster. Fricke's Kydex makes the grade and has become a popular choice.

Belt slide holsters are often simply constructed and intended for range use. They are neat and handy and I often use one of Walt Stipple's belt slides in such duty. It is affordable but well made. This is a minimalist holster that is a great holster for those who would otherwise thrust the piece in the waistband. For the compact pis-

tols I have adopted a belt slide from Dan Sanders, GDS, for use with my short barrel 1911s. This holster is more tightly molded than the usual belt slide and offers excellent retention. I do not like the idea of a long slide protruding from the holster, but his holster accommodates almost anything: a 3-inch pistol to a long slide 6-inch barrel. It is a neat trick.

Cross draw holsters are still popular with a hard core of shooters. The cross draw is a mixed bag of tradeoffs. The cross draw design is suitable for use by those who often are seated when at work, or those who are often in a vehicle. When seated you may adopt a ready position with the hands practically on the handgun grip. When driving, it would be difficult to reach a holstered handgun on the strong-side. Considerable effort is demanded to master the cross draw but once done, the cross draw is a credible holster. I have seen poorly designed cross draw holsters that tilted the handgun at an impossible angle. The leader at this time is the Haugen Handgun Leather Wedge, designed by Roy Huntington. This holster offers a draw angle that is ideal for concealed carry as a result of a wedge that tilts the holster at the correct angle.

Professional Grade Holsters

For those engaged in law enforcement and given a choice in holsters for the 1911, there are several standouts. The first was developed for the FBI. This is the DeSantis Hostage Rescue Team or HRT holster. This is a brilliantly designed strong-side scabbard that features a thumbreak for security. There are those who prefer to keep a safety strap between the hammer and firing pin of the 1911. Other agencies specify a thumb break

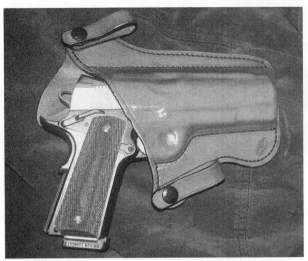

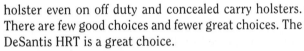

The Rhome DesBiens (DGL) IWB is supple enough for comfort and is a great aid in concealing a full size Government Model .45.

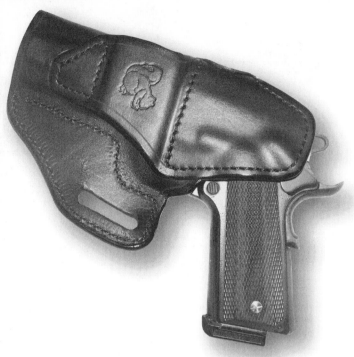

We do not often consider the reverse of the holster but it is very important. This is a Practical from Secret Squirrel. Note the care in stitching and in putting a complex holster together.

holster even on off duty and concealed carry holsters. There are few good choices and fewer great choices. The DeSantis HRT is a great choice.

A high ride scabbard of the first order that allows quickly taking the holster off and replacing it is the Milt Sparks Axiom. Those who work in an office or visit jails with restrictions on firearms may remove the holster and handgun and lock it away several times a day. (Psychologically, when an officer questions a subject, an empty holster degrades his authority.) I am no fan of paddle holsters due to security issues. I have seen too many holsters break at the joint and in force on force demonstrations I have seen paddle holsters ripped from the waistband.

Shoulder holsters get the weight of the handgun off of the hips. Some offer excellent balance. One is the West Woods Landing holster. This is a holster comprised primarily of fabric. It is comfortable, offers a sharp draw, and offsets the weight of the handgun with a dual magazine carrier on the weak hand side. The primary cause of a failure to fire in a 1911 is for the pistol to run out of ammunition. I have an affection for spare ammunition. This is good kit.

An exceptional holster that is pricey but well worth the tariff is the Lawman Leathergoods Dirty Harry. Originally intended to comfortably carry a 6-inch barrel Smith and Wesson Model 29 .44 Magnum the Dirty Harry is a good choice for the 1911. Rugged, with good adjustment, this holster is designed to last a lifetime and it will.

Dual Purpose Holsters

The old adage "jack of all trades, master of none" comes to mind. But there are a handful of holsters that are suitable as dual purpose holsters. Simply Rugged

fulfills the promise of their moniker. The Tribute is a tribute to Roy Baker, the man largely responsible for popularizing the concealable pancake holster. The tribute is offered with three belt loops for a wide range of adjustment. There is a special option of adding IWB clips. I could get along just fine with the Tribute.

K and D's Thunderbird offers both belt loops for outside the waistband carry and belt clips for inside the belt carry. These are first class holsters that have proven themselves in months of testing. I have enjoyed these very much. Michael Taurisano, Tauris holsters, offers a custom grade holster that I often use with my Colt Defender. The Double Shift holster features removable belt loops and offers the ideal draw angle for a light 1911.

Special Purpose Holsters

I don't believe in over-specialized holsters. The dual purpose holsters are good for all-around use, and there are strong-side belt scabbards that are surprisingly versatile. A good IWB holster fills the bill most of the time in my world view. One of the best designed and well made practical back up holsters I have ever used with the Badger Reload from DesBiens. This holster is designed to carry not only the backup 1911 – or another handgun of your choice – but also a spare magazine. This is a very neat rig that is the answer to requests from satisfied customers of other designs. This was not an easy holster to design or fabricate but one that solves a lot of problems.

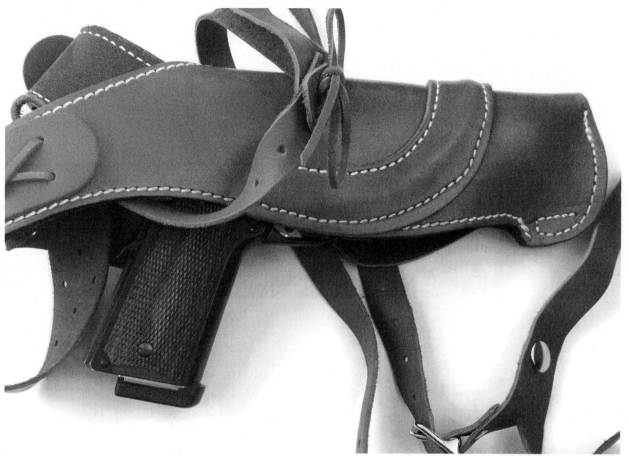

The Lawman Leathergoods shoulder holster is a legend in its own time that is once more available.

When to Replace Leather

You have to know when to bury the cow. If the thumbbreak on your holster is cracking, then it may malfunction under stress. If the belt loops are loose and wallowed out, it is probably past the time when an adjustment on the tension screw will help. Quality leather will last many years but a good quality holster will not outlast a good pair of boots or shoes by very long if used on a daily basis. Discoloration from the elements or gun oil isn't a problem but wear and tear is. Take a good look at your holsters often, treat them with Neet Foot's oil and other preservatives, and treat them like the lifesavers they are.

Holster Safety!

When holstering a handgun, keep the finger away from the triggerguard. Keep the safety of the 1911 on and keep your palm off of the grip strap. The slide lock safety and the beavertail safety are great safety designs but true safety is between the ears. Do not trust a mechanical device. If the holster has a safety strap, angle the 1911 in from behind and slip the muzzle under the strap. Pushing the handgun over the strap has resulted in accidental discharges when the strap engaged the trigger. It is true most of these discharges have occurred with revolvers or automatic pistols without a safety, but just the same trust no mechanical device. At all times, keep the trigger finger away from the triggerguard when holstering. Gun safety and holster safety lie primarily between the ears.

AFTERMARKET PARTS

Chapter 22:

Recently I performed a modest upgrade of a GI .45. I have performed similar upgrades over a dozen times. Naturally some of the early experiences were frustrating. I made bad choices and had not yet built skill. I gained experience in fitting parts but I also learned to avoid cheap parts. I have not used heavy machinery much but rather have relied upon drop-in-parts primarily. Drop-in parts are high quality aftermarket parts designed to fit most Series 70 or Mil Spec pistols with minimal fitting or no fitting at all. Some makers call them easy-fit parts. Some have been easy-fit and others, anything but. The best include those from Ed Brown, Wilson Combat and the Italian Sb.nc company. I have attempted to use parts that were bargain priced and purchased building and rebuild kits that turned out to be full of either GI parts or cheap cast parts. Buy cheap and you buy twice.

The Universal Outfitters grips also offer an integral bushing wrench. They are called the Grench.

When using a full length guide rod, the Springfield two-piece type is the most easily removed.

The 10-8 Performance trigger is among the few aftermarket designs suitable for hard service.

Both my skill and my religion have been tested by such misadventures. You need to know what to expect from aftermarket parts. The first obvious piece of advice is to purchase parts of at least equal quality to the handgun you are working with. Upgrading means improving. Don't put GI parts in a new Colt. If you are trying to repair a Llama you might beat something out on a rock. Don't use cheap parts on a good gun. Ed Brown as one example offers good quality parts of good metal and precise tolerance.

A common aftermarket part fitted to the 1911 is a barrel. While you can order a gunsmith-fit barrel and achieve stellar results I have also used drop-in barrels with excellent results. I have used a dozen or so BarSto barrels and a smaller number from Nowlin. I have also used the economy replacement ROTO barrel from Sarco. The Sarco barrel was a true drop-in in a GI pistol. The custom quality barrels were drop-in barrels in about one half of the cases. The others required minimal fitting. I have also fitted a Kart barrel with good results. I recently ordered a BarSto drop-in for my long-serving and much-revered Colt Combat Commander. As issued the Commander averaged four inches at 25 yards with Winchester ball ammunition and larger groups with some loads. The barrel bush-

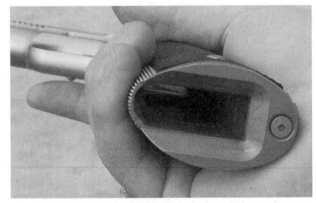

The Smith and Alexander mag guide is the best design we have run across, with excellent fit and finish.

ing could be pushed from side to side and there was lateral play in the muzzle. The Colt had been reliable and spoke in my favor but it deserved an upgrade. The drop-in BarSto almost dropped in. With minimal file work, it was a shoe-in. I had to address the upper barrel lugs. I fitted the barrel, lubricated the slide and barrel, and racked the slide a few dozen times. I fired a few rounds into the berm, and found function ideal. I also found that the BarSto polishing of the feed ramp allowed any hollowpoint to feed in the Colt, something not possible before. Accuracy was greatly improved.

This relatively modest magazine guide from Kimber is well suited for use with Wilson Combat magazines.

The pistol needs better sights but with the Winchester 230-grain SXT the Colt will group five rounds into two and one half inches at 25 yards. I am going to add better sights at a later date, but the improvement I've already noted is encouraging. I did not have to fit all of the lugs or the barrel bushing but I experienced considerable improvement.

In a pistol manufactured from 1911 to the present it stands to reason that there are going to be variances from one example to another. There will be some fitting and the part should be delivered oversize. I have never encountered a too small aftermarket part. Barrel makers err on the side of caution and give you a good product to work with. In my experience it is the hood and the lugs that need to be fitted by filing. A rule of thumb is to check fit with a bare frame first. Place the slide stop in the frame though the barrel link, holding the new barrel in place. The barrel should not move upward easily.

Sometimes when using a particular frame or slide we are married to a certain idea from the beginning. Few of us order a slide without the sight cut, but I have done so because I was ready to begin a project but unsure which sight I would use. I did know I wanted a Rock River Arms frame and slide but did not realize I would be using the Bomar sight at the time. Once you order a slide with Novak cuts you are married to Novaks, although you have quite a few options. The frame is another matter. The RRA frame came with the proper cut for a Smith and Alexander beavertail safety. So I used the Smith and Alexander beavertail with good results. I have experienced good results with other types, but the Smith and Alexander fits this high-grade pistol's profile. Some shooters may not realize the connection between the beavertail and the trigger as when the trigger is replaced with a long type.

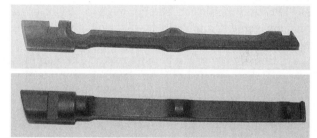

These are Wilson Combat extractors, for both the Series 70 and Series 80 – be certain to get the right one!

A surprisingly troublesome part can be the slide lock safety. Shooters will perform a trigger job and ruin it with a roughly fitted safety that grinds on the hammer and ruins it. I have come to prefer the Ed Brown slide lock safety for my use. Slide stop levers are important for proper function. I prefer the Wilson Combat version. This slide stop features a dimple that allows the plunger to lock in firmly. I tend to remain with a proven product.

Extractors are a critical part. The controlled feed function of the 1911 that is so vital to its reliability depends on a properly fitted tool steel extractor. The Wilson Combat Bulletproof extractor has proven durable and well designed. The extractor is practically a drop-in unit, with some minor fitting on the hump behind the extractor claw often being required. The use of the Wilson Combat part in high-end SWAT pistols makes it the most proven extractor.

Many shooters attempt to lighten trigger compression weight. Carefully stoning a heavy GI trigger can bring the compression to a smooth five pounds. Reducing the trigger from seven to five pounds is one thing. Any lighter and you need to use custom grade parts. I would not drop below five pounds on a carry pistol but

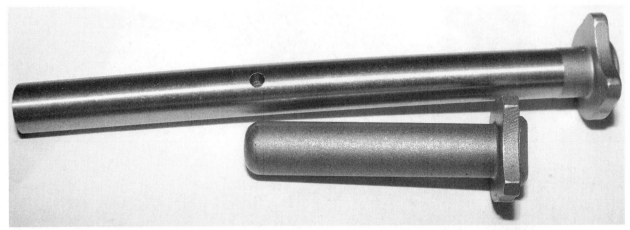

This FLGR is contrasted to a standard spring guide, both from B.T. Snc.

today a number are delivered with such light pulls. I am leery of attempting to perform a trigger job on the steel of some foreign pistols such as the Argentine Modelo 1927 and the suspect steel of modern 1911 clones. The engagement you have left when you are do may be unsafe. I prefer to purchase quality aftermarket trigger action sets from a reputable maker. The hammer, sear, and disconnect should be mated. A drop-in set is always drop-in in my experience except for the trigger. You need to change ignition parts in sets. A new hammer may not mate with the sear and so forth. You will save time and money by purchasing a complete ignition set from Ed Brown, Cylinder and Slide Shop or Wilson Combat.

The trigger usually needs fitting regardless of the pedigree. At one time only the Gold Cup was delivered with an adjustable trigger but today even Combat models are delivered with one – at least adjustable in appearance, as they are usually set and sealed at the factory. The set screw adjustment is either staked or loctited at the factory. The set screw allows adjustment of sear engagement and over travel. (All trigger work should be performed by a qualified gunsmith, without exception.) The 1911 trigger rides in grooves in the frame. The trigger face is pressed and the trigger travels to the rear, tripping the sear and dropping the hammer. There isn't much leeway for adjustment and overtravel ensures that the sear will be tripped. The adjustable trigger is used to set overtravel by butting the adjustment screw against the magazine release. The proper adjustment results in a crisp release with no overtravel. In factory versions the trigger is properly adjusted and then permanently locked in place. While you pay a bit extra for the trigger and the fitting required, the result is a better feel and smoother trigger compression. If an adjustable trigger is not properly adjusted it will not travel far enough to reach the sear, so caution is the guide when performing this work outside of the factory.

These beautiful custom handmade grips from our friends at handmade-grips.com will grace any handgun.

I would never fit a target trigger to a Colt Series 80 or any other handgun that uses the Colt positive firing pin block. Colt has done so successfully with the Gold Cup Trophy but odds are few people outside Colt are as familiar with the Series 80 as the guys at Hartford. For example, the timing of the trigger may be such that the firing pin block is not properly released. The firing pin will fly forward but strike the firing pin block, and in other cases the sear may not be completely pressed. The half cock notch might even beat the sear. The Colt Series 80 is a reliable system but keep the trigger system as issued!

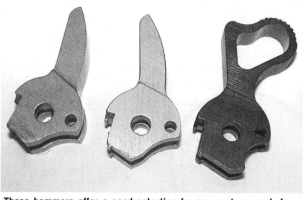

These hammers offer a good selection for any custom need, from BT Snc.

High quality aftermarket parts from BT Snc and Wilson Combat have been an aid to the author as he repairs various 1911 handguns.

Full length guide rods (FLGR) are not strictly aftermarket parts as they are delivered in many factory pistols, but they are a controversial item. While I use pistols both with and without a FLGR I am not going out of my way to add the device to my pistol. Many professionals feel that the FLGR is an unnecessary complication to the 1911. Alternately there are those who feel that the ability to quickly strip the pistol with the barrel and recoil spring assembly intact is an advantage. The FLGR also keeps the recoil spring in line and prevents it from kinking in recoil. This may be a minor issue. The 16-pound recoil spring is 6 inches long when relaxed, but about 2.25 inches of the spring is compressed when the pistol is assembled. The recoil spring guide supports about 1.5 inches of the spring and the recoil spring and the recoil spring plug another 1.4 inch. Not really a lot of slack there!

A final point is that the FLGR may prevent the pistol from going out of battery if struck against a barricade or other cover. In the case of a particularly tight pistol the slide may be bumped out of alignment and the pistol will not return to alignment. The FLGR may prevent the pistol from leaving battery in the first place. On the flip side one hand malfunction clearance drills are made more difficult by the full length guide rod. In many cases they are impossible. As for aiding accuracy by keeping the slide perfectly in line, it is difficult to prove an accuracy advantage in a pistol fitted with the FLGR. If I were heading for the sandbox I am certain that I would keep the pistol simple and use the conventional GI type guide rod and spring for ease of disassembly and cleaning. The bottom line is this: there are worthwhile improvements we can apply to the 1911. Good sights are not a drawback but the FLGR may be a drawback in extreme situations.

A certain fraternity is disdainful of magazine guides, sometimes called magazine chutes. They find the magazine guide a problem in concealed carry. I am not one of these. I appreciate my magazine guide-equipped pis-

tols. It is not strictly needed, true, as reloads are seldom needed in combat shooting. Browning developed the 1911 to use a flush fit magazine. I appreciate this. If you use a magazine guide as a practical matter you must also use magazines with a bumper pad. For SWAT teams and competitors the magazine chute results in faster loading time and administrative handling is much smoother. For those willing to practice, the Smith and Alexander mag guide gives the shooter every advantage. I have also used the easily added-on Wilson Combat magazine guide and the factory version from Kimber. All add slightly to the height of the handgun. They are best suited for use on service pistols rather than concealed carry handguns in the opinion of many, but I have no problems with the magazine guide. A caution with the magazine guide is that are not compatible with all bumper pad type magazines. Some magazines will not fully seat in all magazine guides. Be certain of the compatibility with your magazines before you upgrade.

The most common addition to 1911 handguns is aftermarket grips. We sometimes choose grips for vanity and other times to increase grip adhesion and control. While I sometimes use smooth presentation grips on certain types of handguns, I prefer at least a checkered grip for defensive use. Treated wood, aluminum and micarta are recommended for service-grade pistols. A very interesting new alternative are the striking titanium grips from Halpern. I have tested these grips extensively with excellent results. Halpern also makes G10 grips that are more conventional. G10 was radical a few years ago! The evolution in development and been generational and duly recognized. Shooters of my

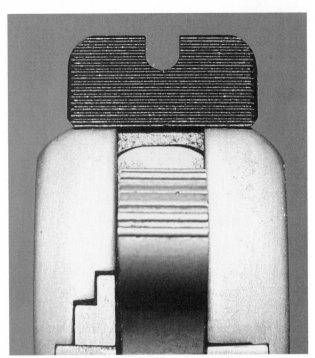

This rear sight from 10-8 Performance is an aid to shooters with diminished visual acuity.

generation growing up with checkered walnut grips will find the presentation grips from Herrett well suited to their tastes. My personal Kimber Gold Combat is among the last to be fitted with checkered rosewood; Kimber has gone exclusively to micarta with combat-type handguns. My Colt Gold Cup was delivered with cheap imitations of the Pachmayr – shame on Colt – but is now fitted with a set from Deathgrips.com. I

have examined grips that do not properly support the plunger tube and cheap plastic grips that broke under the stress of firing. The hollow plastic types are not suitable for service use. The Ergogrips.com plastic grip is of a stronger design and nearly as raspy as skateboard type, a good set for those on a budget. Many of the cheaper types featured a Colt roundel that fell out in short order.

I have used the half-checkered Ahrends Tactical grip with excellent results. Ahrends offers several styles that are popular with custom makers. My personal 1911 that is carried more than any other, the Colt Defender, wears a set of Ahrends stocks. Herrett Stocks defines the old-line style and feel of double diamond grips but also offers a classic alternative called the D45 that is among the all time best buys in 1911 grips. These grips feature small diamonds and black lacquer in a combination that simply cannot be matched for grip adhesion and comfort for the price. I own a set of Smith and Alexander stocks that have been in constant use on a training pistol for over a decade. Folks still comment "nice grips," even though they have turned a darker shade than when new as a result of contact with perspiration and oil. Universal Outfitters supplies a special grip with the Grench or grip wrench, a built in bushing wrench. That's utility! There are a good number of excellent grips available today, but there are also grips that should never be used. Do not spend good money removing usable grips for junk. Finally, enthusiastic handloaders will wish to mount Alumagrips. These aluminum grips are strong enough to withstand the explosive pressure of a burst cartridge. How do I know? Trust me on this one.

1911 TRIGGER ACTION IN DETAIL

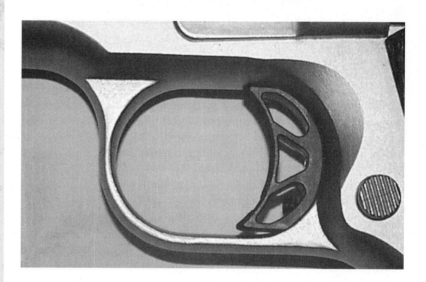

Chapter 23:

Among the single greatest advantages of the 1911 is its trigger action. The trigger is a single action type, meaning it drops the hammer and has no other function. The trigger does not cock the hammer. As a result the single action trigger is often smooth and crisp and controllable. Trigger compression is measured by the weight in pounds of pressure that are needed to move the hammer enough to break the sear and drop the hammer. I have tested many 1911 handguns over the years and have never recorded a factory trigger action lighter than 3.5 pounds and this light a pull is a rarity. GI types and the less desirable factory types run much heavier, from

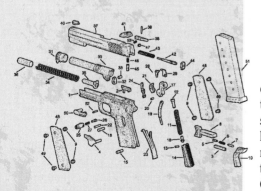

Be certain that you are completely familiar with the 1911 and its parts before venturing into modification.

The standard Para trigger offers good control.

159

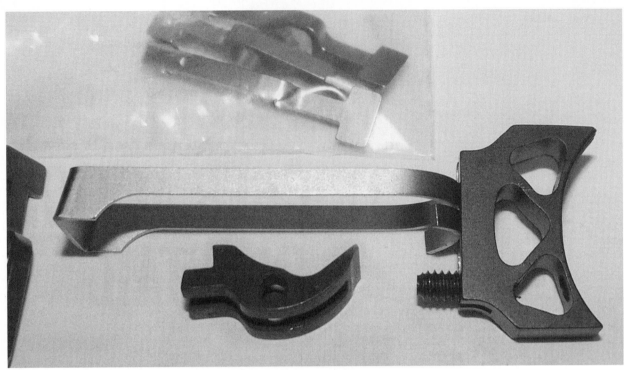

If you are going to perform a trigger job, use first-class parts. These are from BT Snc.

6 to 7 pounds. I have never recorded a factory trigger compression heavier than 8 pounds. Today, the general run of GI guns sports a trigger compression of 5 to 7 pounds. Many of the top-end pistols demonstrate a smooth 4-pound compression. Among the best factory trigger actions is the one found on my personal Kimber CDP at five pounds and very smooth.

Trigger pull weight is not the only story, however. Take up, or the initial movement required before we begin the "solid" part of trigger compression, is disconcerting, as is movement after the trigger breaks or backlash. A good trigger is clearly obtainable but much depends upon our person needs and experience. I do not think that a personal defense pistol should exhibit a trigger compression of less than four pounds. There are simply too many variables and the possibility of overexcitement or even a stumble when handling the handgun. During a struggle, for example, the average person may exhibit a hundred pounds of pressure on the pistol's grip, more than enough to unintentionally squeeze off a shot.

The short trigger stroke of the 1911 is obviously an advantage. Since trigger span is less, reach is less and there is less discomfort in reaching the trigger. You are less likely to suffer sympathetic action of the other digits as you perform the trigger stroke. It is critical that the 1911 trigger action is free of creep and backlash as much as possible. When working through a proper surprise break, rough spots and inconsistency in the trigger action will invite the best shooter to jerk the trigger in the belief he or she needs more force to break the sear. A good trigger action makes for a compressed learning period when mastering the trigger.

Many who attempt to master the 1911 feel that their shooting would be improved by an action job. If you are genuinely limited by the pistol's action, then a professional grade trigger action by a reputable gunsmith is an option. But I am going to restate the obvious. Performing a trigger job, trigger smoothing or action tune should be performed only by individuals who are competent and confident. While there are disagreements among those professionals as to exact procedure, no one feels that the 1911 trigger action should be undertaken by inexperienced individuals. I do not believe that older pistols such as a World War II-era Colt 1911 are prime candidates for a trigger action. The same goes for entry-level handguns. When GI pistols were put together, rapid manufacture was as important as anything and while most have proven reliable, they are not always easy to use well. The metal is not always heat treated sufficiently, especially in the internal parts. The occasional good action is found among entry-level pistols but getting them to five pounds clean would be the limit. Attempting to produce a clean, sharp trigger action of less than five pounds requires aftermarket trigger action parts in my opinion. Ed Brown, B.T. Snc and Wilson Combat are among a few offering first-class action parts. When an action job is performed on original parts, the engagement that is left in the hammer hooks after polish may not be sufficient, in my opinion.

Sometimes a trigger action feels lighter or heavier than it really is. The RCBS trigger pull gauge gives us the low-down on trigger compression.

In addition to GI pistols, the steel in many foreign pistols is so poor they need to be left as they are. A number of domestic 1911 handguns have suffered the same malady. Any good quality 1911 can be improved with the use of custom parts. There are simple steps short of a full action job that will make for a cleaner action but a true action job will usually require aftermarket parts. For brevity we refer to these as trigger jobs but action job or trigger action job is more correct.

To smooth the trigger action to an extent, we can take other steps. For example, the interface of the sear and the hammer may be carefully polished and lubricated with a quality lubricant such as Tetra Lube. This is a simple enough step but one that can be abused. When polishing the hammer contact surfaces we must never take so much off the hammer that it will slip on the sear. I have had this happen after performing a trigger action job on an Argentine Modelo 1927, a Colt clone of good repute. This pistol seems well made of good material but if you check the postal scale, the Argentine pistol often weighs an ounce or more than the Colt. The steel is denser. I had a terrible time getting a good trigger action and it seemed the metal was harder than that of a Colt. I attempted to keep the original angles and polish them but in the end the hammer followed the slide occasionally – not on firing, but when I lowered the slide on a loaded chamber. I did not abuse the pistol by dropping the slide on an empty chamber. The pistol was basically a learning experience and a gunsmith project. It was a profitable experience in every way. I eventually replaced the internals with all Ed Brown action parts. I would have disassembled and trashed the offending parts before I would have let anyone buy the handgun in the condition it was in.

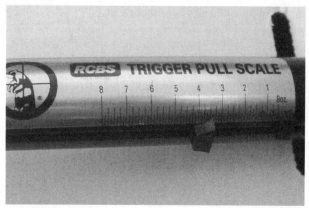

The RCBS registering trigger pull gauge is a great aid in comparing trigger actions.

Be aware of common action problems. Firing on dropping the slide or double firing is possible if the hammer does not have sufficient meat in the hammer hooks. Admittedly, this is rare; usually the hammer is caught by the half cock notch. (Remember your 1911 safety checks?) We must have enough sense not to keep using the handgun after it has exhibited such a fault. I am not saying a finely tuned trigger action will not occasionally drop the hammer to half cock if the slide is dropped on an empty chamber – which is abuse – but the hammer should never follow the slide when lowering the slide to load the chamber. Take care if you polish the sear and hammer. This is where the problem begins.

When you have disassembled the pistol, carefully study the hammer hook and sear and how they fit together. When polishing, it is fine to produce a smoother surface but the original contact angles must be maintained. And it is not all in the hammer and sear! The sear spring is another part that bears close attention. The sear spring places resistance on the trigger bar and on the bottom or foot of the sear. I have checked factory sear springs and we must be familiar with what a proper sear spring feels like. The spring is sometimes adjusted by bending to reduce pressure on the trigger. This expedient may reduce trigger resistance. But the resistance of the spring against the sear is also reduced in turn. Usually in pistolsmithing there is an opposite and equal reaction to everything we do, good or bad. I do not wish to reduce sear spring tension and find that the sear does not engage the hammer hook when the piece cycles. Cooking off two rounds at a single press of the trigger may be the result. If bending the sear spring is undertaken, then the bend should be very slight to almost imperceptible.

The 1911 mainspring has a bearing on the trigger action. The mainspring is simple enough in construction but must be understood. The function of the mainspring is to transfer energy to the hammer. While some old hands are adept at modifying the spring I prefer to switch and change springs in order to produce a smoother let-off. I have used the Clark spring in a custom pistol on several occasions with good results. The force needed to crack the primer or pop the cap is the deciding factor. Some primers are harder than others. Foreign primers are less reliable and a dirty pistol with a dirty chamber may combine to impede forward motion of the firing pin, resulting in a failure to crack the primer. Pressing the cartridge forward robs the firing pin of some of its energy. This may result in a light primer strike or a failure to fire if the mainspring is a light version. There is a reason the mainspring is rated at 22 pounds in service pistols. The mainspring also helps the pistol remain locked after firing. If the hammer spring is light then the slide has but little resistance in the hammer to overcome after firing. If the pistol cycles too quickly, it may create an unreliable and inaccurate handgun. Accuracy will be affected by erratic unlocking. Be particularly careful when working with a lighter mainspring in the 10mm or in a 1911 intended for use with +P ammunition.

Let's look at the trigger itself with emphasis on the bow. When changing to a light trigger action, an aluminum trigger is desirable. The trigger is lighter and less likely to rebound against the sear in recoil. The super light action and mainspring are fine for competition but we need to ask if the pistol will be used for personal defense. The trigger bow must move freely in the trigger channel.

I check all magazines that will be used in the pistol to be certain that they are compatible with the particular trigger. There are some magazines that are thicker than others. The Metalform magazine is not only high quality, it will lock and perform in pistols that seem to have problems with other types. Some of the GI magazines are thicker than modern aluminum body magazines. There is always the possibility of a burr on the trigger bow. The best cure for burrs is to stone them away. I perform this function as a matter of course when I do a trigger job. This type of work does not lighten the trigger action but results in a smoother and more consistent trigger compression. Bumps and hard spots in the trigger channel make for an inconsistent action.

Details

Probably the main complaint with otherwise decent factory actions is creep, i.e., movement after takeup and before the hammer falls. Creep is disconcerting to an accomplished shooter.

I have a number of procedures in my bag of tricks that are SOP in obtaining a first class trigger action. First I look at the sear and carefully stone it, trying to maintain the original angles. But the hammer also deserves attention. I check the hammer hooks and make certain they are no taller than a .020" feeler gauge. If they are, I stone them to a good polish while maintaining a perfectly square angle. I do so with the stone in the vise and by moving the hammer against the stone. It works for me and I never go below .019" hammer hook engagement.

I stone the disconnect to be certain that it rides the trigger bow correctly and smoothly. Now, the sear spring can be interesting and I am very careful with any modifications to it. The spring arms that run to the rear control the grip safety, while the middle spring bears on the disconnect and the far spring keeps the sear against the hammer. If the grip safety is springing back slowly, you can bend the spring arm toward the grip safety but this expedient is seldom needed. Bending the sear spring just slightly away from the sear may make for a lighter action but you must bend, reassemble and check. Always check the disconnect and make certain it pops up as designed.

Practically every good 1911 now comes with an adjustable trigger from the factory although the term "adjustable" may be a misnomer inasmuch as the trigger is pre-set at the factory. When installing a true adjustable trigger you will set it to break with as little movement as possible. The trigger screw bears against the magazine release and the set screw is adjusted one-quarter turn at a time. Get it right, make it tight, and check the action. Then loctite it in place.

CUSTOM PISTOLS:
THE BOUTIQUE WAY

Chapter 24:

I am an individual.

When I was growing up in the 1970s and learning to shoot handguns I never saw a custom handgun. I saw handguns that were nickel plated and a few with special grips, but none that had been modified in a mechanical sense. Colt and Smith and Wesson revolvers were found stock for the most part, especially in police holsters. My circle of elders never took a gun to the shop unless it needed work. I relied upon bone-stock handguns that smoothed with use. Then I began to read Jeff Cooper and Skeeter Skelton. Each went beyond simply changing handgun grips. They wrote of action work, modifying sights

With a stippled front strap, Ahrends grips, a Heinie rear sight and a Novak front post, the Action Works .45 is a great personal handgun.

The hard chrome and custom action work on this Commander are from Accurate Plating and Weaponry.

163

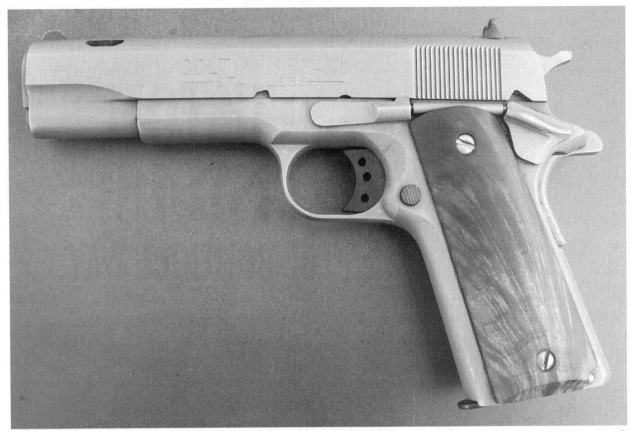

There isn't a lot of work done on this pistol but the work is to the point and useful. Herrett's Oval grips and Magna Porting make for a "light custom."

and even complete rebuilds. My first attempt at a custom handgun was a Smith and Wesson .38 first with the hammer bobbed. After I did an action job I was hooked. Jeff Cooper may have waxed poetic concerning the 1911 .45 but remember that he promoted the custom 1911 concept in personal defense as well.

I like to have a handgun that is a custom fit from A to Z, beginning with the grips and proceeding to the sights. But one thing I do not do is fix what isn't broken. If the pistol is for concealed carry I do not always add a magazine well, and I do not add anything extraneous. The first thing I assure myself of is function and reliability. If the pistol is not 100% on all counts, there is little point in spending good money on modification. Next I add the grips of my choice. I have enjoyed good results with Ahrends grips for too many years to remember. I also use Wilson Combat grips and lately I have enjoyed good results form Universal Outfitters. There are many choices, but the better the adhesion, the better the pistol will perform on a combat course.

Personalizing a pistol with custom grips, however, is not true customization. Custom work entails something the factory doesn't offer. Finding something you cannot get from the factory is more difficult these days, but there are custom touches that are unique to certain pistolsmiths. Custom quality is different as well.

This .45, from Action Works, is an ideal all-around service pistol with much to recommend.

A couple of decades ago I was dissatisfied with factory performance for the most part but got along with my Colt 1911s until I encountered Action Works of Chino Valley, Arizona. At the time there was not a single 1911 available with Novak or Heinie sights. Action Works put together several excellent handguns for me. I came to understand that a well-fitted handgun was tighter and more accurate and more durable. The less slop or the tighter the handgun returned to battery after each shot, the less eccentric wear. With expendable dollars care-

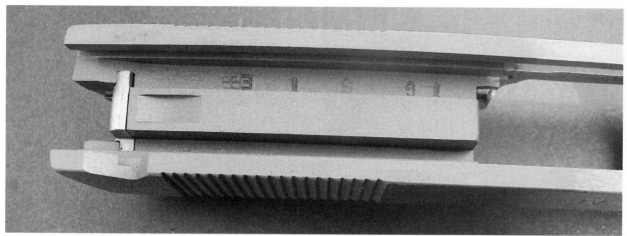

The Springfield GI has been gone over by Novak and the loading block polished and the extractor tuned.

fully hoarded, I began to put together several very nice custom handguns. Action Works was a dream realized. Even today, when we have both Novak and Heinie sights on special custom editions from the factory, I would be hard pressed to find a factory combination of a Bomar rear sight and Novak front as ordered from the Action Works. I also ordered a pistol with a Heinie rear sight and Novak front post. Such combinations are eye catching to those in the know and serve a real purpose. As an aside, with the price of the best custom shop pistols approaching $2000, why not go ahead and commission a truly special custom pistol that is to your liking?

I have enjoyed these custom 1911 handguns very much. While I have occasionally worked up a good Browning High Power and even completed projects with the Beretta and Glock, only the 1911 has truly kept my interest. Accurate Plating and Weaponry worked up a hard chrome Commander that was particularly appreciated in under the shirt carry. I experimented with extended safety levers, custom sights, and sometimes I added too much. I had frames modified in some instances and I came to appreciate a good trigger job.

Even today, with so many pistols available that are advertised by the factory as custom quality, a factory handgun has less finesse than a true custom pistol. The fitting and machine work on low-end pistols is embarrassing at times. I believe that you are best served with a GI pistol on the cheap. The craftsmanship involved in fitting a LW trigger and a good custom beavertail are not found on low-end pistols. Adding features to an entry-grade pistol is sometimes false economy. Again, it is what do we really need, what are our expectations, and what are we willing got pay for. Sating our desire is reason enough if the greenbacks are there.

There are a number of finishes available only on custom order from custom makers and nowhere else. One of these is Bear Coat. Bear Coat is a Teflon based finish that is very high on corrosion and wear resistance. With

This RIA pistol features Bear Coat finish, Gator Grips, a Smith and Alexander magazine guide, Ed Brown internals and Unertl luminous iron sights. This is a great pistol at a reasonable price for the work and accessories from Rocky Mountain Arms.

This pistol has been to Wilson Combat for sights and a magazine guide and to Robar Industries for NP3 finish. It looks pretty good for a pistol with over 20,000 rounds on the frame.

Bear Coat, the finish is self lubricating. This is a great advantage and while I always lubricate my pistols, the advantage of any Teflon based finish is great. I have used Bear Coat on several 1911 handguns and one hideout .38 revolver with excellent results. I particularly enjoy the two-tone versions.

Note the frame and trigger guard checkering on this pistol from the Kimber custom shop.

Novak's stamp means something. This is a GI .45 in stainless with Novak gold bead front sight.

True custom pistols are a different story from factory high-grade production. This front strap work is by Hilton Yam.

This is a high-grade factory custom, the SIS from Kimber.

The other finish that I recommend for hard use handguns is NP3. NP3 has given excellent service on my longest serving 1911. I wore the original finish to the point it was serviceable but quite unattractive. I had an alternate set of sights installed, tried another finish, and was not pleased. NP3 has served for some time. This is a mix of Teflon and Electroless nickel and in my opinion it is the better choice than either competing finish alone. NP3 is attractive, durable, corrosion resistant and self lubricating. Like all custom finishes NP3 has not been incorporated into any production pistol I am aware of, perhaps because of the added expense, but it is well worth the application on a private purchased handgun. NP3 is still a space age finish and among the best options for a hard use handgun.

FIRING TESTS

Chapter 25:

This chapter was the one that appeared to be the most fun as I worked up the final draft on this book. Conversely, it is the most work and absolutely the most difficult. I am thankful for my NRA instructor's course and the stress my NRA counselor placed on benchrest shooting. Firing handguns consistently, accurately, over a long period of time is an essential skill for a reporter and experimenter. The benchrest tests were fired on different occasions; seldom more than four pistols were tested in one day. We kept ammunition as consistent as possible, but with the prevalent ammunition shortages, it was not possible to use the same ammunition for each test. In fact, this would have been a disservice. I would rather have a broad test that shows what a num-

The author wrings out the Para Ordnance Sterling Edition in rapid fire and finds it good.

Our military intelligence officer found barricade fire as accurate as the bencrest. His skill is above average.

ber of handguns will do with a loading that is widely available and easily obtained. This includes examples of the best performance defense ammunition, target ammunition, and inexpensive practice ammunition. We attempted to use the more precise premium ammunition for accuracy testing.

The ammunition used in the test program included premium defense ammunition, precision target ammunition, custom loaded target ammunition, inexpensive generic ball, and my personal handloads. I did not use anything unproven. Every brand included is proven in years of use. In the case of Winchester ammunition, for example, I first fired a round of Winchester over 40 years ago and I still rely upon the brand. When Black Hills ammunition was founded I obtained and used the brand and still do. Today, their military contracts speak highly of the quality of this South Dakota based company. I have lost count of how many thousands of rounds of Zero Ammunition I have seen used in police training. I first tested the exotic CorBon ammunition when their high velocity rounds were introduced as the logical successor to Super Vel. Today few companies can boast of the coverage offered by CorBon. Hornady Custom has give us the XTP and Colonel Cooper's flat point bullet, the 230-gr. projectile that has proven so accurate. Fiocchi was once a mysterious high-quality European brand, but today they make much of the ammunition we use in an American plant in Ozark, Missouri. Wolf ammunition offers good practice ammunition at a fair price.

The 25-yard groups are obligatory because testing the practical accuracy of a handgun is important. I realize some favor a machine rest. The fact is, firing off the bench rest tells us more about the accuracy potential. The sights, a good trigger and general handling all are important in benchrest testing. A few words on accuracy: there were no dogs. Even the GI guns would save your life. As for accuracy, the spread between the best and the worst load, with each example being relative, is not as great as we may think. If you are a competitor aiming for a 50-yard bull then you must wring the last bit of accuracy from the load. I am not certain Federal Match or CorBon Performance Match will do what you need to do, but they are a good starting place. There are very few 1911s capable of an honest three-inch group at 50 yards. They have names like Les Baer and Ed Brown on the side of the slide. Others are full blown custom handguns. They are from the Action Works or Novak's Gun Shop. A pistol that will group the very accurate Black Hills 230-gr. JHP into two inches at 25 yards is accurate. (I have recorded a group as small as 15/16 inch at 25 yards with this load, but that is not the average.) The same pistol might do four and one-half inches with the Russian Wolf 230-gr. bullet. It will still save your life at 10 yards where either cuts a single ragged hole in the paper for eight rounds.

By the same token some loads will prove more accurate in one handgun than the others. You could take three loads from Black Hills, CorBon and Hornady and fire them in a Kimber, a Para and a Springfield and the ratings may spread all over with one or the other being tops in the three pistols but all loads giving a credible showing. But it is unlikely that generic ball ammunition will prove more accurate than a premium loading in any pistol. It is all relative. Don't cry if your GI pistol groups USA white box ball into four inches at 25 yards, but if the TRP will not group into three inches with the Winchester Bonded Core load, something is wrong with the pistol or the shooter.

Measuring Groups

We fired five-shot groups for accuracy. Groups were measured from the inside of the furthest spaced bullet hole to the other. The end result is recorded. Often, three shots might fall into an inch and a half and the final group would measure three inches. But that is the name of the game and consistency our goal. We fired three five-round groups and measured the average for record. Some of the pistols we have covered in previous chapters, but we gave a shot at them again, with different loads and shooters under different conditions.

10-Yard Group

In this test, we fired two five-rounds strings at 10 yards. The goal was to test control and combat accuracy potential. We began with the sights on target and our finger beside the trigger guard. There was no measurement of time, but we fired as quickly as we could recover from recoil. The group was measured in the same manner as the 25-yard groups. Since we fired in two strings, consistency was also a factor.

30-Round Combat Course

We fired this demanding course in five round strings, as follows:

Five rounds, five yards, one hand point, reload, five rounds, seven yards, one hand shoulder point, rapid fire.

Five rounds, seven yards, two hands, reload, five rounds, two hands, 10 yards.

Five rounds from standing, 15 yards, reload, engage 15 yard target, five rounds.

This 30-round combat course is a good gauge of the overall combat ability of a handgun. We did not score for X ring hits but dealt with each pistol subjectively. At the end I asked our raters to rate the pistol on a scale of one to 10, with 10 being the highest score. Our shooters were of varying skill levels but knew their way around the 1911. Many, however, were new to the courses. As I write these words my son is in South Korea, my stepdaughter has moved to another state and a nice new home, and my young associate Lee Berry is in advanced training at Fort Lee, Virginia. (My long-time helpers, friend and family, are progressing well without me!) New shooters are the lifeblood of the game and I relied upon quite a few and I feel that the ratings were credible. While part objective and part subjective, if we experienced an unqualified malfunction, the pistol did not receive a favorable rating. We rated on the basis of what the pistol was. A good GI pistol could rate a 10, while a poor professional grade pistol would rate a seven. It was all a matter of perspective. The pistols tested are for the most part the newest type, all commercially available. We tested some of the classics as well, including the Argentine 1927 .45 and the Series 70 Commander, for perspective. We also tested the Commander-size pistols and compacts. I think the results are valid and interesting.

Here are the handguns tested:

Argentine Modelo 1927	High Standard Crusader	SIG GSR
Modified Caspian Custom/BarSto Barrel	Kimber Tactical Compact	Smith and Wesson SW 1911 PD
Bear Coat/Rocky Mountain/Unertl	Kimber Custom II	Smith and Wesson SW 1911
Colt WWII Service Pistol	Kimber Pro Carry	Springfield Ultra Carry 9mm
Colt 1991A1 Magna-port	Kimber Eclipse	Springfield Long Slide
Colt Gold Cup Trophy	Kimber CDP	Springfield Stainless GI
Colt 1918 Retro	Kimber Gold Combat	Springfield GI
Original Colt Series 70	Les Baer Monolith	Springfield Champion
Colt Combat Commander	Para SSP	Springfield LWLM
Colt Series 80 Commander	Para Sterling Model	Springfield Loaded Model
Colt Series 80 .38 Super	Para Wart Hog	Springfield Loaded Model Target
1930-Era .38 Super Colt	Randall	Springfield LW Operator
Colt Defender	Rock Island Tactical	Springfield Novak 1911
Colt Delta Elite 10mm	Rock Island 1911	Springfield TRP
Colt Double Eagle 10mm	Rock Island 4-inch	Springfield Super Tuned Champion
Firestorm DLX	Rock Island 3.5-inch	Taurus PT 1911
High Standard 1911	Rock Island .38 Super	
High Standard G Man	Rock River Arms	

Argentine Modelo 1927

This old soldier has often been compared to the Colt. The 1927 was an attractive alternative to the military 1911 when prices were reasonable, but the internal parts are not of the same quality as the Colt. They are more difficult to tune and the metal seems denser. The Argentine pistol usually weighs an ounce more than the Colt. While well made of good material and comparable to a GI 1911, they are not quite there in quality. This example sports King's Hardballer sights and Ed Brown internals. It is a very nice pistol overall, a good example of the work we once performed on GI 1911 pistols. With the rising price of '27s, the Springfield GI is a much better choice. This pistol has been modified to consensus gun status.

The Argentine Modelo 1927 is a grand old pistol in many regards, but not quite up to the Colt of the same era.

10-yard group,
Black Hills 230-gr. ball .... 4.6 inches
25-yard group,
Fiocchi 230-gr. ball .... 5.65 inches

Combat Course
20 rounds of Fiocchi 230-gr. ball,
10 rounds of Fiocchi 230-gr. JHP:
Overall rating 7.0
Malfunctions 0

Caspian Custom/BarSto

This is an interesting pistol. It was one of the author's first project guns and took several years to finish. The frame and slide are Caspian and the barrel is from BarSto. We used a rather plain GI frame with the highly customized slide. The Caspian low mount tactical adjustable sight is a pure joy to use. Ahrends grips completed the package. This is an example of what may be done with time and patience.

10-yard group
Fiocchi 230-gr. ball .... 3.0 inches
25-yard group
CorBon Performance Match.................... 2.0 inches

Combat Course
10 rounds CorBon Performance Match:
10 rounds CorBon 200-gr. JHP
10 rounds CorBon 185-gr. JHP
Overall Rating 8.0
Malfunctions:.................................. 2 failure to feed
with 185-gr. JHP

Bear Coat/Rocky Mountain Arms/Unertl

This pistol is sometimes referred to as the Bear Coat .45 around the shooting range. It is simply a Rock Island Armory pistol with improvements. The pistol is finished in Bear Coat by Rocky Mountain Arms. As such it is highly impervious to the elements and self-lubricating. The pistol features Gator grips from CZ grips, a Smith and Alexander magazine guide, and Unertl night sights. These sights are as good an investment as any in 24-hour sighting systems. You may ask, why spend all this time on a RIA pistol? The RIA was available and we wished to see how it would hold up. It would not be very interesting to fire 5,000 rounds in a GI pistol. We threw away the Philippine internals and added Ed Brown parts, including every action part and the extractor. The pistol sailed through 5,000 rounds of ammunition over a period of four years, without a single failure to feed, chamber, fire or eject. Interestingly, the pistol came out of the box firing and was proofed to 500 rounds but demanded a break-in period after returning with the two-tone Bear Coat finish. We fired about 50 rounds and the pistol seated in. Accuracy and handling are all we can ask. At a later date, we added a BarSto barrel because the pistol deserved it. Results are listed both prior to the addition of the match grade barrel and after. This is a worthwhile pistol that shows thatthe Philippine frames and slides will stand hard use.

10-yard group
Fiocchi 230-gr. ball .... 4.0 inches
25-yard group
CorBon 200-gr. JHP .... 3.5 inches

After fitting BarSto barrel
10-yard group
Wolf 230-gr. ball .... 3.75 inches
25-yard group
CorBon 200-gr. JHP .... 1.9 inches

Combat Course
10 rounds Wolf 230-gr. ball
20 rounds of CorBon 200-gr. JHP
Rating 9.0
Malfunctions 0

Colt WWII Service Pistol/1911A1

It is always interesting to see how the original 1911A1 performed. Unfortunately finding a piece of this vintage in new condition that anyone would let us fire was out of the question. The pistol tested was true to the 1911A1 family tradition: it would not feed hollowpoint ammunition and rattled when shook. The small sights were not only difficult to use well, but the front sight was considerably worn! Just the same by our estimation the pistol would save your life if need be. Remember, this is a seventy year old pistol.

10-yard group
Winchester 230-gr. USA.......................... 5.6 inches
25-yard group
Winchester 230-gr. SXT .... 6.0 inches

Combat Course
20 rounds of Fiocchi 230-grain ball
10 rounds of Winchester 230-grain SXT
Rating 6.0
Malfunctions.................................... 2 with the SXT
hollow point

Colt 1991 A1 Magna Port

This pistol is the inexpensive 1991A1, bone stock save for two particulars. The slide and barrel feature Magna Port custom ports. These ports affect velocity very little but increase control. The difference may not be noticeable with ball loads but this pistol is especially set up for +P loads, with a heavy Wolff gun spring and specially sprung Metalform magazine. The Herrett's oval stocks also give an advantage. This is an excellent all-around pistol for those who prefer heavy loads.

10-yard group
CorBon 185-gr. JHP .... 3.0 inches
25-yard group
CorBon 230-gr. JHP .... 3.25 inches

30-round Combat Course
20 rounds of CorBon 185-grain JHP
10 rounds of CorBon 230-gr. Performance Match*
Rating..9.0
Malfunctions...0

*to confirm reliability with standard loads

There is no question the Colt is well made of good material, but the supplied grips were on the cheap side.

Gold Cup or Kimber Eclipse? Other than price, performance is pretty close. We are glad to have both.

Colt Gold Cup Trophy

The Gold Cup is still a premier target pistol. This example came out of the box with a crisp 4-pound trigger, complete reliability, and excellent accuracy. The three-point pedestal lockup of the barrel is outstanding. This pistol shows that Colt can get it right. We were disappointed by the grips as they were a poor imitation of the Pachmayr that may have saved Colt a few cents. Shame on them for that, but the pistol gave excellent results. We have used the Wilson Combat spring caddy in testing lighter target loads with excellent results. This is an overlooked excellent all-around Colt pistol.

10-yard group
Black Hills 200 gr. SWC .... 3.5 inches
20-yard group
Black Hills 200 gr. SWC .... 1.9 inches

Combat Course
20 rounds 180-gr. Oregon Trail SWC/850 fps/\
10 rounds Fiocchi 230 gr. JHP
Rating..10
Malfunctions..0

Colt 1918 Retro

This pistol is more true to the ideal than true to the 1911 format. It is more of a cut-down 1911A1. There are no finger grooves in the frame, the pistol sports a long trigger and a flat mainspring, and the sights are true to the WWI "Black Army," a relatively rare Colt that featured a different finish from other wartime Colt pistols. My friend at the gun shop chastised me for my intent to fire this Colt, but I could not wait to work it out. The barrel fit is equal to the Gold Cup in my estimation and the trigger is superb at 3.5 pounds. The pistol is a ball to use and fire, and I was glad to break it out and use it again for this work. I would recommend a pistol with better sights and more usable controls for personal defense but then this is the type of pistol that won two world wars. However, this one is far more accurate than the GI pistols and it feeds hollowpoints.

10-yard group
Fiocchi 230-gr. JHP .... 2.9 inches
20-yard group
Fiocchi 230-gr. XTP .... 2.5 inches

Combat Course
20 rounds, Wolf 230-gr. FMJ
10 rounds, Federal 230-gr. Hydra Shock
Rating 10
Malfunctions 0

Original Colt Series 70 .45 Government Model

The Series 70 has a reputation as a well-made pistol. We feel that its quality, fit, and performance are superior to the previous commercial pistols and also the GI pistol. However, at the risk of being run out of town by a tar and feathering party, we do not feel that the Series 70 offers anything that modern production does not. The Series 70 was a great pistol in its day. Today there are better choices. Just the same, I would not hesitate to use a Series 70 given new springs and proper proof. The sights are no better than the GI pistol but then here is a well made Colt that is something of an icon.

10-yard group
Winchester 230-gr. USA ball .... 5.25 inches
25-yard group
Fiocchi 230-gr. JHP .... 4.10 inches

Combat Course
20 rounds of Black Hills 200-grain SWC
10 rounds Black Hills 230-gr. FMJ
Rating...7
Malfunctions 0

Colt Combat Commander

This is a 1970s version of the Colt Commander. This Series 70 is among the first steel frame Commanders. The pistol is finished in the once popular satin nickel finish and has all of the original internal parts including the extractor, but is right at 10,000 rounds give or take a few hundred. The pistol now sports a BarSto barrel, but we fired the pistol with both barrels in the accuracy test portion in order to give the reader an idea of the accuracy potential of these pistols. While the Series 70 Commander is a great pistol I would not pay a premium for an original, but I would purchase a modern pistol with more features. Just the same, this pistol has never failed and is fast handling and well balanced.

10-yard group
Black Hills 230-gr. ball .... 4.0 inches
25-yard group Hornady 185 XTP .... 4.5 inches

**With BarSto barrel
(barrel required slight fitting)**
25-yard group
Hornady 185 gr. XTP .... 2.9 inches

Combat Course
10 rounds Zero FMJ reloads
20 rounds Black Hills 230-gr. RNL
Rating 7.5
Malfunctions ....0 (No malfunctions, ever)

Colt Series 80 Commander

This pistol has many advantages over the previously tested Combat Commander. The sighs are better, the ejection port is lowered, there is a positive firing pin block and the action is smoother. The pistol feeds any type of hollowpoint, although the old Colt did also after the BarSto barrel was fitted. The Series 80 also introduced the advantage of stainless steel consecution. This is a simple but durable pistol that will solve 99% of your personal defines problems.

10-yard group
Wolf 230-gr. ball .... 5.0 inches
25-yard group
Winchester 230 gr. SXT .... 3.6 inches

Combat Course
30 rounds Wolf 230-gr. ball
Rating...8.0
Malfunctions...0

Colt Series 80 Government Model .38 ACP Super

This is the pistol I took to my NRA instructor's course and one of my favorite teaching pistols. This is a stainless steel pistol with all of the advantages of the Series 80. Accuracy has been outstanding; in fact this is the most accurate unmodified Government Model .38 Super I have ever fired and tested. The piece is a plea-sure to fire and use and has given many young shooters their first taste of a centerfire pistol and a 1911.

10-yard group
Fiocchi 129-grain ball .... 2.5 inches
25-yard group CorBon 147-grain
Performance Match .... 2.0 inches

Combat Course
20 rounds Winchester 130-grain ball
10 rounds CorBon 115-gr. JHP

Colt 1920s Era .38 Super

This pistol is mechanically very tight. However, it has been refinished and any collector value is gone. The previous owner kept it in his dash and laid a hash sandwich on it one day. The finish was ruined and the new blue is not that great. I added Herrett's checkered grips to the pistol, laid in a few Metalform magazines, and generally enjoyed the piece. There were drawbacks. While pleasant to fire and use, the pistol was never accurate. A six-inch group at 25 yards with the Winchester Silvertip was considered a good day. I eventually added a BarSto barrel and the pistol began turning in four-inch groups. With a bit of load developed using the Nosler 115-grain JHP, Starline Brass, and Winchester 231 powder, I managed a 3.5-inch group. Nothing to brag about but useable and better than the majority of .38 Super Colts.

10-yard group Handload/Nosler
115-gr. JHP/1300 fps............................. 4.5 inches
25-yard group
Winchester 130-gr. FMJ .... 3.8 inches

**Combat Course,
Winchester 130-gr. FMJ**
Rating...7
Malfunctions ....0 (in the life of the gun)

Colt Defender

The Colt Defender is a tremendous little 1911 and in my opinion the most underappreciated Colt. There are more expensive compacts with more features that also run well, but the Defender seems troublefree and enjoys an excellent reputation for reliability. I prefer to carry a LW 4-inch pistol when possible, but at times the Defender and a Milt Sparks Summer Special holster are on my belt. I have fired well over 2000 rounds in this pistol. I added Ahrends checkered custom grips and discarded the factory synthetic model and I use Metalform six round magazines. The Defender .45 is a very important part of my defensive arsenal. In one of these worst-case scenarios we spend too much time worrying about, the Defender would be one of my only guns if I could own but two.

10-yard group Winchester
230-gr. USA ball .... 5.0 inches
25-yard group Winchester
230-gr. Bonded Core JHP .... 4.6 inches

Combat Course
30 rounds Fiocchi 230-gr. ball
Rating..10
Malfunctions........................0 (in the life of the gun)

Colt Delta Elite 10mm

The Delta Elite caused quite a stir when introduced. Without beating a dead horse we will note that the original recoil guide assembly was poorly conceived. The

The author has carried the Delta Elite professionally in a Secret Squirrel IWB holster, along with the CRKT First Strike knife.

Note the bright fiber optic sights on this Colt Delta Elite—a good shooter.

If you purchase a Colt Delta Elite, get the one with the frame relief, as seen in this late model. You will not be sorry.

Many of the bench rest groups were fired off a solid standing rest, with excellent results.

10mm pistol's reputation for accuracy suffered largely because the pistol was not correctly sprung for the heavy recoiling 10mm round. This pistol uses a Wilson Combat recoil rod assembly and works just fine, along with Metalform magazines. The Winchester Silvertip loads has proven brilliantly accurate. If your Delta Elite does not shoot this well, look to your recoil springs and ammunition.

10-yard group Winchester
175-grain Silvertip .... 4.5 inches
25-yard group Winchester
175-grain Silvertip .... 3.6 inches

Combat Course
CCI Blazer 180-grain
Rating...7.5
Malfunctions ......1 (failure to close the slide/Blazer)

Colt Double Eagle

The Double Eagle is not a true 1911 to my way of thinking but some regard it as a modified 1911. According to most reports, they were not very reliable. Just the same, my experience with two examples and several hundred rounds of ammunition seems to indicate good reliability. I regard the Double Eagle as a curiosity. The 10-yard group was fired with the first shot double action.

10-yard group
CCI Blazer 180-gr. FMJ........................... 6.5 inches
25-yard group
Double Tap 155-gr. JHP .... 3.9 inches

Combat Course
Twenty Double Tap 155-gr. JHP
10 CCI Blazer 180-gr. FMJ
Rating 3
Malfunctions .... 2 (Failure to feed/Blazer)

Firestorm DLX

This is another Philippine maker, named Metro. The DLX is a loaded type pistol, featuring good Novak type sights and an extended slide lock safety and beavertail safety. The DLX seemed well made of good material, but the sights are an odd departure from the Novak, reducing the sight radius for no reason I can imagine. The pistol demonstrated an odd tendency. It failed to lock on the last shot, but would immediately drop the slide when a loaded magazine was inserted. Finally, upon detailed inspection, the barrel link pin fell out of the barrel – it was that loose. The pistol has the potential to be as reliable as the RIA guns but attention to detail is needed. The slide stop, an outdated extended design, was to blame for the earlier problems. The link pin was peened as a cure. The pistol is a contradiction. It is a bargain pistol, presumably for the beginner, but demands experience with the 1911 to rectify its faults. I hope current production is a better pistol.

10-yard group
Fiocchi 230-gr. FMJ .... 4.0 inches
25-yard group
Fiocchi 230 gr. JHP .... 3.8 inches

Combat Course
Handload: Oregon Trail 230 gr. RNL,
WW 231 powder, 807 fps
Rating 5
Malfunctions 0
(E.g., failures to feed, chamber fire or eject –
but a major problem with the slide lock; see above)

High Standard 1911

This is another Philippine-made pistol. It is practically identical to the RIA guns, simply a Rock Island with a different finish. Overall the High Standard seems to offer the superior finish, perhaps because the importer demanded more quality. There are rough spots on the High Standard and of course the frame is cast as well as the slide. But the pistol works well enough and it is quite inexpensive. The High Standard is pure GI as the ejection port is scalloped. I experienced no malfunctions with modern JHP loads with the High Standard, only handful of feed failures with a handloaded SWC bullet. I liked the pistol so much I fitted Trijicon self luminous iron sights and used the pistol as a just-in-case piece or truck gun.

10-yard group
Hornady 200-grain XTP .... 4.0 inches
25-yard group
Horandy 200-grain XTP .... 3.8 inches

Combat Course
10 rounds 230-gr. Sierra JHP/Titegroup/830 fps
10 rounds Zero 230-gr. JHP
10 rounds Double Tap 165-gr. JHP

The High Standard Crusader demanded getting used to but overall its reliability cannot faulted.

Grade 7
Malfunctions 6
failures to feed handloaded SWC during the course of 700 total rounds

High Standard Crusader

This is an Officers Model size compact 1911. This pistol is about $100 more expensive than the GI but the features include a set of Novak sights, although they are not high quality as the steel Novak sights are. The slide lock safety is ambidextrous and the beavertail safety is an improvement over the GI pistol. Finish is good and the supplied checkered wooden grips are nice. There was one complaint. While some shooters like a light trigger, the Crusader was too light for an entry-level gun. The trigger action broke at just over three

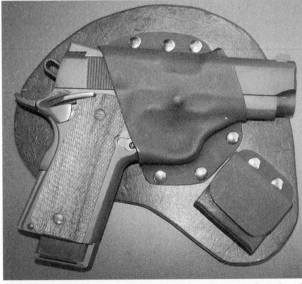

One of our raters still carries the Crusader .45 in this CrossBreed holster. Good kit.

pounds. While manageable by a trained shooter, this is not a good idea in a compact pistol. I managed good shooting with this pistol but when firing with my less proficient non-dominant hand I doubled a few rounds unintentionally. I bent the sear spring forward to increase the trigger action but this is not ideal. Otherwise the Crusader seemed a good value.

10-yard group
Hornady 200 gr. XTP............................ 4.65 inches
25-yard group
Mastercast 230-gr. JHP.......................... 4.4 inches

Combat Course
Twenty Mastercast 200-grain JHP
Ten Zero 230-gr. FMJ
Rating 7
Malfunctions 0
Approximately 550 rounds total

High Standard G Man

This is an American produced pistol that we understand is no longer being produced. Naturally, "G Man" is a play on the TRP and Professional Model. The G Man does not suffer in comparison. This was once the most expensive and accurate pistol I owned, and it has gotten me through several books and a hundred or so articles. The pistol wore out its first finish, the slide was refinished, I did not like the refinish, and I finally had the pistol finished in NP3. This is ideal. The original night sights served well over 10,000 rounds and then the front insert flew out. I had the set replaced with a set of Wilson Combat night eyes. The grips are from Alumagrips and the piece sports a Wilson Combat magazine guide. This pistol was fitted with an Cylinder and Slide Shop "Safety Fast Shooting" action. The original trigger action was 3.5 pounds. After over 20,000 rounds the pistol now sports a 2.5-pound action. I have blown the pistol up once with a handloaded round. The slide lock was blown out, the ejector was knocked loose, and my face was peppered with metal fragments. The magazine was blown out of the pistol and destroyed. I put the pistol back together and kept shooting. This is a great pistol. If you have a chance to purchase one, do so. All High Standard pistols including the .22s have demonstrated extraordinary quality and craftsmanship.

10-yard group
Black Hills 230-gr. ball .... 2.0 inches
20-yard group
Black Hills 230-gr. JHP +P .... 1.5 inches

Combat Course
30 rounds Black Hills 200-grain SWC
Rating 10
Malfunctions....................................0 (None, ever)

Kimber Tactical Pistol

The Tactical pistol tested is a 3-inch-barrel variant.

The combination of excellent night sights, a checkered front strap, and conservative magazine guide along with excellent grips that give good adhesion are a great advantage in such a light pistol. I often note that a compact pistol really needs these features more so than a full-size pistol. The compacts are more difficult to use well, the sight radius is shorter, and there are overall more issues. The Kimber Tactical version is a first class light combat pistol well worth of your attention. Our example is among the relatively few produced with an external extractor. What can we say, other than it ran well?

10-yard group
CorBon 165-grain PowRBall .... 3.5 inches
25-yard group
Black Hills 185 grain JHP .... 3.25 inches

Combat Course
10 rounds Winchester 230-gr. Ball
10 rounds CCI Blazer 200-grain JHP
10 rounds Zero 230-gr. JHP
Rating..10
Malfunctions 0

Kimber Custom II

The Custom II is the original Kimber pistol and remains an excellent all-around choice. The Custom II's combination of good sights, extended safety and controls and other features sent the competition scrambling when the pistol was first introduced. But what I think that many commentators missed is not the fact that the Kimber introduced a combination of features at a relative bargain but that they introduced consistent quality control. The Kimber pistols are as consistently well made and reliable as the European standard. This long-serving Custom II isn't an extraordinary pistol, it is simply representative of the breed.

10-yard group
Wolf 230-gr. ball .... 3.0 inches
20-yard group
Winchester 230-gr. SXT 2.75

If there is an honest best buy .45 in the world, the Kimber Custom II is that pistol.

175

Combat Course

20 rounds Winchester 230-gr. USA ball
10 rounds Federal 230-gr. Hydra Shock
Rating...10
Malfunctions 0
(over the course of almost 10,000 rounds.)

Kimber Pro Carry

The Pro Carry tested is a 4-inch-barrel aluminum frame or LW version. The Pro Carry is a good basic short barrel 1911. The four inch 1911is a relatively new idiom that many find gives an excellent balance of speed and handling. I admit less experience with the Pro Carry than perhaps any other type, but I have fired several blue and stainless versions with excellent results. The example tested, taken in context of its size and weight class, gave good results. The Pro Carry is nearly ideal as a carry gun and rates a solid best buy in any honest evaluation.

10-yard group
Fiocchi 230-gr. ball .... 4.0 inches
25-yard group
Winchester 230 gr. SXT .... 3.6 inches

Combat Course

10 rounds Extreme Shock Air Defense
10 rounds 185-gr. Nolser JHP/WW231/1050 fps
10 rounds 200-gr. Oregon Trail/WWW 231/980 fps
Rating...10
Malfunctions 0
(in over 300 rounds)

Kimber Eclipse

The Eclipse features the famous and much copied stainless and black finish. Our example sports Kimber's first-class adjustable sights, making it one of our most used sport shooting pistols. The pistol's combination of well checkered grip panels and a checkered front strap make for excellent adhesion. Kimber attention to detail is more evident in this pistol that perhaps any other we have tested. This pistol is more accurate than

the Gold Combat and is among our most impressive performers. This is a keeper that has been in service with my family for some time. The adjustable sights have a tritium insert.

10-yard group
Fiocchi 230-gr. ball 2.9
25-yard group
CorBon Performance Match................................1.9

Combat Course

20 rounds Fiocchi 230-gr. ball
10 rounds CorBon 200-grain JHP
Rating...10
Malfunctions ....0 (in 3,500 rounds)

Kimber CDP

The Kimber Custom Defense Pistol is perhaps the best all-around package for personal defense ever available from the factory. The pistol tested features a 4-inch belled barrel, tritium insert high visibility sights, an ambidextrous safety, a well developed beavertail safety, a full length guide rod, custom grade checkered grips, a crisp 5-pound trigger action, and a two-tone stainless over blue Kimpro finish. The pistol is supplied with two flush-fit magazines that are nicely engraved with the Kimber name in the floor plate. This is a striking pistol but also a very effective one. The CDP's efficient use of heavy duty premium gun springs results in excellent control of slide velocity. The pistol is simply well thought-out with nothing left to chance. Here is a modern pistol that is ready for anything, and with a trained operator arguably gives the finest performance, ounce for ounce, of any modern 1911. The purpose of this pistol is specific, not ambiguous, and the features reflect that. This is a pistol with which you can take control of a situation and save your life.

I realize I may be seeped in my own perceptions of what a combat pistol must be but I have fired them all and nothing in the size and weight category comes

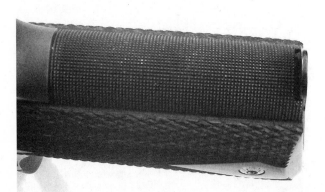

The front frame stippling of the Kimber Eclipse is well done. Many raters found it the best of the breed.

Perhaps the most impressive pistol ounce for ounce was the Kimber CDP.

close to the CDP. No non-1911 in the full-size service grade format can touch this pistol for performance. The pistol features a thumb safety that is definitely in the speed safety category but none too large and unobtrusive. You have to be careful with the beavertail safety. Some renditions are too large, resulting in a high-riding grip that gives the shooter less leverage. The CDP is well-designed. The beavertail safety releases the trigger on the first third of travel, ideal for my use. The trigger compression of my personal CDP is ideal at four pounds, clean, with no creep or backlash. The CDP is an ideal carry gun well worth your earnest attention.

10-yard group
Black Hills 230-gr. RNL .... 4.25 inches
25-yard group
Hornady 200-grain XTP .... 3.0 inches

Combat Course
Thirty rounds CCI/Speer Blazer 230-gr. FMJ
Rating 10
Malfunctions ....0 (in 2,500 rounds)

Kimber Gold Combat

The Gold Combat is Kimber's top of the line combat pistol, the Warrior aside. The Gold Combat is a well appointed Government Model pistol that handles well on the range, carries well, and gives excellent performance. The Gold Combat is bedecked with high visibility sights with tritium inserts, forward cocking serrations, a lowered ejection port, an ambidextrous speed safety, a well designed seeped bump grip safety, front strap checkering, a magazine guide, and in the newest versions well designed micarta grip panels. My personal Gold Combat

Kimber, DesBiens leather and Black Hills ammunition. Now, that is a good combination!

The Kimber Gold Combat remains the author's primary Government Model-length sidearm for alarms and excursion. Performance is faultless.

is among the last to be fitted with rosewood grip panels. I will not be changing these out any time soon. The Kimpro finish is a bit worn, and no apology. This pistol has been used hard. I have lost count of the rounds on this pistol. It is closer to 10,000 than 5000. There has never been a malfunction or a time when the pistol did not give good performance with any load. The CDP may be my favorite carry pistol from Kimber, and the Eclipse my favorite for pure target shooting, but the Gold Combat is my favorite combat pistol from Kimber. There is really nothing that outperforms the Gold Combat in a meaningful manner, although there are a few that give the piece a run for its money. I would consider the value and quality control in the Gold Combat before pursuing any other high-end 1911.

10-round group
Winchester 230-gr. ball........................... 3.0 inches
20-yard group
Black Hills 185 grain JHP .... 2.75 inches

Combat Course
20 Winchester 230-gr. ball
Ten Black Hills 200-grain SWC
Rating 10
Malfunctions 0

Les Baer Monolith

The Monolith is not a pistol made by a committee. This is one man's dream. Les Baer is a well known custom pistolsmith. He once made his living welding and modifying 1911 handguns. His standards were so high that they were practically unattainable with anything then available, at least on an economical basis. Baer elected to manufacture his own slides and frame to his demanding standards. Match grade barrels, internal parts, and controls are all manufactured in his own shop. The end result is a legendary pistol with many good features but the primary feature is quality of manufacture. Baer's products are not the result of a hub and spoke infrastructure but rather they are the product of a man's idea spoken from the mountaintop. Baer's handguns are the result of vigor and enthusiasm.

My personal Baer is a Monolith. This is an expensive handgun, and few of us are likely to own more than one Baer. This is my only example. The Monolith features an extended dust cover. It is not legal for many types of competition as a result. It will not fit the IDPA box and holster makers seldom service this pistol. (Rusty Sherrick makes custom leather and the Uncle Mike's paddle is a good fit.) The pistol features vault-tough sights that are reminiscent of the classic Bomar, but they are even tougher if that is possible. I like the Monolith. It lives up to its name. The fit is tight, very tight, but the pistol is reliable. I have to state for the record that some of the concerns on tight fit and reliability are overstated. The pistol did demand a break-in period but it runs with a wide range of loads and delivers gilt edged accuracy as promised. I would recommend cleaning the pistol every 300 rounds, it is that tight. Prior knowledge of the pistols attributes are an aid in mastering the piece. The balance is good, bring the pistol to eye level and in a flash you are focused.

10-yard accuracy
Mastercast 230-gr. JHP .... 2.25 inches
25-yard accuracy
Custom Reloads of Dallas 230-gr. XTP ...... 1.0 inch

Combat Course
20 rounds Mastercast 230-gr. JHP
10 rounds Hornady 200-grain XTP
Rating...10
Malfunctions 0

Para SSP

Para made their name with the original high capacity 1911 frame. Later, they introduced the Light Double Action trigger and today they have the PXT extractor. The PXT or Power Extractor features 50% more gripping surface than the original extractor. A big factor in the popularity of the Para pistols is the standard ramped barrel. With the double column frame, the ramped barrel was essential. It simply made sense to use the ramped barrel in the single stack pistol. Two of the pistols tested are single stack 1911s and other than firing for familiarization in the chapter on alternate trigger

This young Marine is a fine shot who finds the Para SSP a good shooter.

actions, I have not heavily tested the LDA. I find their single stack pistols attractive and operational. The Single Stack Pistol is finished in matte black and is overall a decent piece for the money. The sights are not as large as some of the competing pistol, but they are reasonably effective.

10-yard group
Fiocchi 230-gr. JHP .... 4.5 inches
20-yard group
Winchester 230-gr. Bonded Core .... 3.5 inches

Combat Course
10 rounds Fiocchi 200 grain JHP
10 rounds Fiocchi 230-gr. JHP
10 rounds Winchester 230-gr. USA ball
Rating 8
Malfunctions 0

Para Sterling 7.45

This is my favorite Para. The single stack 7.45 series is offered in a Sterling edition. The stainless finish really looks like sterling silver and the flat black flats give good contrast. The trigger is smooth enough, the pistol is positive in operation, and the white dot sights are good examples of the breed. The pistol does not sport forward cocking serrations, which gives it a more traditional appearance. The magazines were a bit tightly sprung. When the slide is locked to the rear on an empty magazine, you cannot release the slide. This may lead to peening of the slide lock indent. We simply used Wilson Combat magazines for the majority of the firing session. The Para magazines were perfectly reliable and the problem – if it is a problem – was minor.

10-yard group
Wolf 230-gr. ball .... 4.25 inches
25-yard group
Black Hills 230-gr. JHP .... 3.0 inches

Combat Course
10 rounds CorBon 165-gr. JHP
10 rounds Hornady 230-gr. XTP +P
10 rounds Oregon Trail 200 grain
SWC/Titegroup/850 fps
Rating 9
Malfunctions 0

Para Warthog

This is an unequivocal instrument, a very short and light pistol with a double column magazine. While regarded as an advance by some, this is the single most difficult to handle 1911 handgun I have ever operated. Any load hotter than 230-gr. ball threatened to cause the piece to leap from the hand. This made practice difficult. The Warthog functioned perfectly with a series of light loads I made up just for familiarization and practice. The pistol never malfunctioned or short cycled, a wonderful report for such a radical pistol. If you really

The Para Wart Hog is an interesting design that has recoil enough to confound the toughest 1911 shooters.

need a hideout 1911 with a double stack magazine this is the one, but at this size we are reaching a state of diminishing returns.

10-yard group 180-gr. Oregon Trail
SWC/WW 231/750 fps .... 6 inches
25-yard group
Hornady 185-grain XTP .... 6.5 inches

Combat group
10 rounds Hornady 185-grain XTP
20 rounds 180-grain Oregon Trail
SWC/WW231/750 fps
Rating 7
Malfunctions 0

The Randall

The Randall is included as a point of historical interest. With a relative handful produced, the Randall is becoming increasingly rare. This was the original stainless steel 1911 .45. The Randall featured improved sights, an improved slide lock safety, a full length guide rod as standard, and overall gave the impression of a

The Randall was a hot shot stainless .45 in 1983 and still commands respect.

durable fighting pistol. I have heard of mixed results with the Randall, but our pistol is at least as reliable and useful as any other 1983-vintage pistol I have used. It is somewhere between the GI .45 and the later Springfield in utility, but it is an interesting pistol. Use a modern pistol for personal defense but respect the Randall as the harbinger it was.

10-yard group
Black Hills 230-gr. RNL .... 5.0 inches
25-yard group
Black Hills 230-gr. FMJ.......................... 4.25 inches

Combat Course
20 rounds Wolf 230-gr. FMJ
10 rounds Zero 230-gr. FMJ
Rating...5
Malfunctions .... 0 (with ball ammunition. The Randall would not feed hollow point ammunition)

Special Section: Testing the Philippine Rock Island Armory (RIA) Pistols

The 1911 is no longer exclusively an American icon. Labor costs are high and ever-rising. Foreign produced clones are able to undercut American models in price. I remember the Spanish ironmongery such as the sometimes-unusable Llama and I do not believe American shooters will accept such a pistol today. The Armscor pistols most often give good results. The popular press has largely ignored these pistols but they have proven commercially successful. Practically every 1911 fan has one or more in use. They are a basic GI pistol in appearance, save that the later versions feature a lowered ejection port. Improvements over the GI pistol include a smooth trigger action and the ability to feed open mouth hollow point ammunition. I have dealt with a number of problem examples, but a minimum of tuning, including adjusting the extractor, has been all that was called for. The majority are serviceable as issued.

There are variations among the type. These include Commander-size pistols, a 4-inch barrel version with a standard size frame, a compact version with 3.5-inch barrel and compact (six-shot) frame and a Tactical Version. There is also a .38 Super version. It is interesting to note that I have encountered two types of Supers, one with a ramped barrel and one without. I think that the ramped barrel version is the more desirable. It seems that a distributor with sufficient pull can order a run of handguns to his liking.

A reflection of the quality of these cast frame and cast slide handguns is the number that are modified to suit the owner. I have added Wilson Combat night sights to a ramped barrel .38 Super and fitted a Nowlin custom barrel to another with sensational results. A mid-level custom piece was built on a Rock Island frame with good results. History repeats itself and we are able to enjoy much the same light modifications we enjoyed before the original number of GI pistols dried up from circulation. The pistols covered in the following pages are more or less ideal for different needs for those on a budget. Let me stress that the trick in personal defense is not to get killed if you want to enjoy the benefit package. You should use the best pistol you can afford. By the same token, the Rock Island Armory pistols are usually reliable and they are true to the 1911 template.

1911 GI Pistol

This is the archetypical GI .45. Our example is parkerized and supplied with plain wooden grips. The trigger is decent and the piece feeds hollowpoints. This is the most likely format to prove completely reliable in a RIA pistol.

10-yard group
Fiocchi 230-gr. ball .... 5.4 inches
25-yard group
Fiocchi 230-gr. JHP .... 4.25 inches

Combat Course
Thirty rounds Oregon Trail 230-gr.
RNL/WW 231/820 fps
Rating 7
Malfunctions 0

Our raters universally found the GI .45s friendly and easy to use well at close range. The RIA 3.5-inch .45 was a favorite.

RIA 4-Inch-Barrel Pistol

This is a brilliantly fast pistol from concealed carry. We often carried this pistol in a Sideguard holster, and it was quite comfortable. Notably, unlike a more expensive 4-inch pistol tested at the same time, the slide lock safety did not rub off during concealed carry. The 4-inch bull barrel is ideal for general use as a personal defense and home defense pistol. Although the GI sights are small, they are accurate once lined up properly.

10-yard group
Winchester 185-grain Silvertip .... 4.0 inches
25-yard group
Zero 230-gr. JHP .... 3.9 inches

Combat Course
10 rounds Winchester 185-gr. Silvertip
10 rounds Zero 230-gr. JHP
10 rounds Ultramax 230-gr. FMJ
Rating 7
Malfunctions .... 0 (1,000+ rounds total)

RIA 3.5-Inch Pistol

This is the shorter, Officer's Model pistol with the abbreviated six-shot grip frame. We fitted Wilson Combat tactical grips and used the new Wilson Combat eight round magazine for the Officer's Model. This pistol actually proved more accurate than the 4-inch pistol, although it was more difficult to control.

10-yard group
Black Hills 230-gr. RNL .... 5.0 inches
25-yard group
Zero 230-gr. JHP..................................... 3.5 inches

Combat Course
230-gr. Montana Gold/HP 38/740 fps
Rating...8
Malfunctions...0

The RIA Tactical pistol's ambidextrous safety rides on an extended sear pin. This works just fine.

The RIA Tactical is a best buy when it comes to features, and more than accurate enough for personal defense.

RIA Tactical

This is the best of the group. I prefer a 5-inch Government Model and this pistol is an improved Government Model. The differences are addressed from top to bottom. The pistol features the usual lowered ejection port. The pistol sports Novak type sights, front and rear. These sights do not trap shadows and offer an ideal sight picture. The front sight is dovetailed in place but not blended as nicely as other handguns that use this type of sight. The hammer is a lightened version of the modern hammer. Slide to frame fit is good and so is barrel to slide and barrel to barrel bushing fit. The right hand safety of the ambidextrous safety unit rests on an extended sear pin. The arrangement works just fine. The hard wood grips do not quite fit the frame properly; they are smallish, almost as if they have shrunken in place. The trigger was heavier than some at 5-3/4 pounds. The pistol's FLGR is okay as far as it goes but complicates field stripping. The pistol gave good service and remains a relatively bargain. We have found these handguns priced as only $100 more than a GI pistol. That is value.

```
10-yard group
Hornady 200-gr. XTP ........................... 4.35 inches
25-yard group
Speer 200-grain Gold Dot ...................... 3.9 inches
```

Combat Course
```
30 rounds CCI 200-gr. TMJ Blazer
Rating.......................................................8
Malfunctions...........................................0
```

RIA .38 Super

I have experience with several .38 Super pistols from RIA. One was fitted with Wilson Combat night sights and Wilson Combat slim line grips. Spitting a CorBon PowRBall bullet out at 1500 fps, this is a remarkable defensive handgun at a modest price. However, the .38

Once we fitted these GunGrips.net grips to the RIA .38 Super, hand-fit was back in the normal 1911 range, but the pistol had several problems.

One of our popular range holsters, used with two dozen pistols, was the Blackhawk Serpa. We found the large grips and nickel sights of the RIA .38 Super less than user friendly.

Super I covered for this book is another matter. I obtained a nickel plated Super with faux pearl grips. It was so loud in appearance it was almost a joke. The pistol refused to function out of the box, even though I used the reliable Fiocchi 129-grain load. Winchester 130-grain ball did no better. The pistol failed to fully chamber and often failed to extract. Work with both the extractor and the ejector was called for. Plus, the nickel plated sights were so bright in sunlight that good shooting was almost impossible. I replaced the too thick grips with a set from Gungrips.net. In the end I had a pistol suitable for informal shooting and a reliable handgun, but it was not a shooter out of the box.

```
10-yard group
Fiocchi 129-grain ball ........................... 4.75 inches
20-yard group
Winchester 130-grain ball .................... 4.25 inches
```

Combat Course
```
Oregon Trail 125-grain RNL/WW 231/ 1050 fps
Rating ...................................................5
Malfunctions............................ Before modification,
approximately 25% of alls round fired. 25 of first 100.
```

Rock River Arms 1911

This is a cheater of sorts, as it was actually assembled by the Action Works, of Chino Valley, Arizona. The Rock River handguns are famed for good fit, reliability, and excellent performance. This handgun is no different. I elected to obtain the Rock River version with Bomar adjustable sights in stainless steel. A great advantage of the Rock River type is that the frame is slightly thickened in the dust cover. I have cracked two 1911 frames in my lifetime, and while the 1911 is long-lived and the cracks did not impede function, the subtle design change is praiseworthy. The real advantage of the pistol is its close

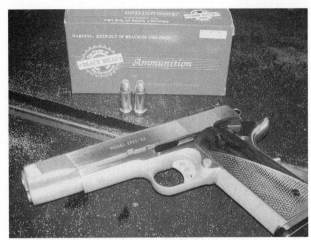

The Rock River Arms 1911 .45 is a rugged, serviceable pistol with much to recommend it. Black Hills ammunition found the sweet spot on this pistol.

tolerances and attention to detail. The checkering on the frame and the forward cocking serrations is exceptionally well done. This pistol also features a Smith and Alexander beavertail safety and a Smith and Alexander magazine guide. As I said, nothing has been spared to make this pistol first class. I mentally debated including this pistol as Rock River no long manufactures 1911 handguns. Just the same, with the 1911, purchasing an out of production pistol is seldom a great drawback. If the piece is of quality construction in the first place, then it can be kept running for many years with standard 1911 parts. It is not like purchasing a Mauser M2 pistol or a French MAB or something of that sort. The Rock River is a genuine hard-use 1911.

10-yard group
Black Hills 230-gr. FMJ............................ 3.0 inches
20-yard group
CorBon Performance Match.................... 1.5 inches

Combat Course
20 rounds Black Hills 230-gr. FMJ
10 rounds CorBon 165-grain JHP
Rating 10
Malfunctions .... 0 (4,500+ rounds)

SIG Granite Series Rail

The Granite Series Rail is named for the state of New Hampshire, where SIGARMS is located. The SIG GSR illustrated was put together in the custom shop by skilled shooters. The pistol uses a veritable Who's Who of custom parts. The original pistol used a slide mounted "manhole" cover for the Series 80 style firing pin block. There have been reports of problems with this firing pin block, and sure enough we experienced one at about 7,500 rounds. The firing pin block fell out of the slide enough to impede forward motion. The newer pistols use a different design, but there are many of the originals out there. Not all have suffered this problem but it

must be reported. The GSR, by virtue of the stabilizing extra weight from the light rail, is among the lightest recoiling 1911 handguns we have ever fired.

10-yard group
Fiocchi 230-gr. ball .... 2.5 inches
25-yard group
Hornady 200-gr. XTP .... 2.65 inches

Combat Course
Wolf 230-gr. ball
Rating...7
Malfunctions 0
(during firing course, 1 big one during hard use)

SW1911

This is Smith and Wesson's entry into the 1911 market. The SW1911 is comparable to the Kimber Custom II or the Springfield Loaded Model. This version served for many months as a teaching gun and frankly as a good example of a shootable, accurate 1911 for training of new shooters interested in the type. The SW1911 gets a clean bill of health.

10-yard group
Mastercast 230-gr. JHP............................ 4.0 inches
25-yard group
CorBon 200-grain JHP ....
2.8 inches

Combat Course
10 rounds CorBon 230-gr. JHP
20 rounds Mastercast 230-gr. JHP
Rating 8
Malfunctions 0

Smith and Wesson SW 1911PD

This is the LW frame version of the SW1911. Unlike many short pistols this is a true 4.25-inch Commander length, with the standard barrel bushing. This is a longtime carry pistol I wore enough to instigate corrosion

The Smith and Wesson SW 1911 PD has traveled more miles with the author than any other handgun, from Washington to California and through the Western states.

on the frame. The SW1911 features a modern external extractor and well-designed controls. This pistol has the distinction of traveling more miles, coast to coast, with the author than any other 1911.

10-yard group
Winchester 230-gr. ball............................ 4.5 inches
20-yard group
Hornady 185-grain FTX .... 3.0 inches

Combat Course
10 rounds Wolf 230-gr. ball
10 rounds Black Hills 230-gr. JHP +P
10 rounds Zero 230-gr. JHP
Rating...8
Malfunctions .... 0 (7,500+ rounds)

Springfield Ultra Compact 9mm

A 9mm 1911 – blasphemy! Just the same, the genre is quite popular and this is a great shooting little pistol. One advantage is that the pistol is capable of digesting great amounts of 9mm +P or +P+ ammunition without complaint. Due to the low bore axis and well designed beavertail grip safety, the pistol is comfortable to fire with practically any loading. The factory supplied Hogue grips are ideal for most uses, but would probably be changed in a dedicated defensive handgun. This is a handgun without issues. The compact size, Novak sights, good trigger compression and light recoil make it a joy to use and fire.

I try to be open to other cultures and maintain a cosmopolitan outlook. The 9mm Luger cartridge is very popular and the 9mm 1911 is a byproduct of commerce. Some favor the 9mm perhaps from a sense of romantic idealism while others look as if they have swallowed a lemon at the sight of a 9mm pistol. I will state the matter rather plainly. I have usually kept a Browning High Power 9mm or two around the house for various rea-

sons. The Springfield 9mm is better suited to personal defense or recreational shooting due to the superior trigger compression and general fit. With Metalform magazines, the pistol offers 10 rounds. The Buffalo Bore loads in 9mm offers a degree of authority in a small bore cartridge. While I prefer a big bore, a 124-grain bullet at 1250 fps (1300 fps from a 5-inch gun) is nothing to sneeze at. Building a relationship with your pistol has much value in survival, and the Springfield 9mm is an easy pistol to get to know and a likeable one at that.

10-yard group
Fiocchi 124-grain XTP............................ 2.5 inches
25-yard group
Buffalo Bore 124-grain .... 2.65 inches

Combat Course
20 rounds Fiocchi 124-grain XTP
10 rounds Buffalo Bore 124-grain JHP
Rating...10
Malfunctions................................. 0 (1500+ rounds)

Springfield Long Slide

This is a friendly enough pistol, long, heavy and accurate. The long slide is simply a 1911 with a 6-inch barrel and slide. This extra inch considerably enhances the balance and handling of the 1911 when it comes to long range pursuits. If you have never handled a long slide 1911, you have really missed something. The long slide is not something you will wish to carry concealed but as a hunting pistol or home defense handgun it has much to recommend it. The pistol does not leap into your hands as a Commander pistol will but it offers a stable firing platform. I thought it odd that the pistol features a very good Springfield adjustable rear sight but the front sight is a simple staked-on post. It worked okay for most shooting chores, but I would have preferred a taller front sight.

The level of accuracy demonstrated by this pistol has been more or less in the high grade 1911 arena, nothing startling. However, on one occasion I fired the single best group I have ever fired in my life at long range

The Springfield Ultra Compact is a fine pistol if a 9mm is your cup of tea.

The Springfield Long Slide may not be the most practical handgun but it is a very interesting 1911 variant.

with a 1911 pistol. On a lark I took aim at a 100 yard silhouette. I had had the long slide less than a week, and had fired fewer than 200 rounds in the piece. I was sighting in a .308 rifle at the time. I laid the Springfield across the shooting bench, took a solid rest, and fired three rounds. I have never been more relaxed as I was not firing for record. To top it off, the ammunition was Wolf 230-gr. ball. Wolf is reliable ammunition but not match-grade by any means. When I walked to the target, the three bullets had struck about twelve inches low and three to the right. They were in a pyramid pattern, with one at the top and the others forming almost a perfect base. The bullets measured less than four inches apart. I have never duplicated this group or even come close, but it happened. The Springfield long slide may not be the most practical .45 but it an interesting piece.

10-yard group
Hornady 230-gr. XTP +P .... 4.1 inches
25-yard group
Hornady 200-gr. XTP .... 1.75 inches

Combat Course
10 rounds Double Tap 200-grain JHP
10 rounds Wolf 230-gr. FMJ
10 rounds Winchester SXT
Rating 8
Malfunctions 0

Note: There is always interest in the approximate velocity gained with a 6-inch barrel. I carefully recorded the differences in velocity, using the 6-inch-barrel Springfield, a 5-inch-barrel Smith and Wesson SW 1911, and a 4.25-inch-barrel Smith and Wesson 1911PD. The results were interesting. It appears the Springfield long slide gets the last foot per second from a given loading.

| Velocity | | | |
Load	Springfield 6-Inch	SW1911 5-Inch	SW 1911PD 4.25-Inch
CorBon 165-gr. JHP	1309	1223	1112
Federal 185-gr. HS+P	1140	1101	1058
Double Tap 200-gr. JHP	1100	1054	1004
Wilson Combat 200-gr. JHP	925	–	875
Mastercast 200-gr. JHP	1020	948	908
Black Hills 230 gr. JHP	880	855	815
Winchester SXT +P	960	945	914

Springfield GI Pistols

The Springfield GI was the original "Springer" and the one that changed the 1911 world. This is a no-frills GI pistol in appearance, but do not let its appearance fool you. The pistol has superior manufacturing beneath that plain vanilla exterior. The pistol will feed modern hollowpoint ammunition. The trigger action is often smooth and crisp. The firing pin is a lightweight type with a strong return spring for added safety. The pistol features the original GI slide window in deference to GI .45 fans. We tested both a plain working gun (a parkerized GI pistol) and a rather nice stainless steel Springfield GI pistol. The stainless GI pistol should be a good working pistol but we ran into a snag. The trigger action was heavier than the parkerized pistol, which we can live with, but the stainless pistol suffered several break-in malfunctions. That is okay, too, but we seldom see break-in malfunctions these days. Just the same, either is a good serviceable pistol well worth the price.

Parkerized Springfield

Ten round group
Fiocchi 230-gr. FMJ.............................. 4.75 inches
25-yard group
CorBon 185-grain JHP .... 4.0 inches

Combat Course
10 rounds Fiocchi 230-gr. JHP
10 rounds CorBon 200 grain JHP
10 rounds CorBon 185 grain JHP
Rating...10
Malfunctions 0

Stainless Steel GI pistol

10-yard group
Black Hills 230-gr. RNL .... 5.1 inches
25-yard group
Hornady 230-gr. XTP+P .... 4.6 inches

Combat Course
Black Hills 230-gr. RNL
Hornady 230-gr. XTP
Hornady 185-grain XTP
Rating...7
Malfunctions ....9 break-in malfunctions, all failures to fully close the slide

Springfield Champion

The Champion is a 4-inch-barrel variant of the 1911, with a full length 7-round grip frame. The barrel features the proven bull barrel lockup common to 1911 pistols with barrels shorter than 5 inches. This variant features Novak sights, a speed safety, and a well-designed beavertail grip safety. While the pistol proved quite reliable and never stuttered, there were a couple of disappointments. I attempted to carry the piece in a favored Sideguard holster in which other 4-inch variants had resided quite well. The over-large speed safety of the Champion tended to rub to the off position in the holster. This is the type of safety used on the long slide but not the same one used with the Loaded Model. A second complaint was that the pistol was not as accurate as we would have liked. Four-inch groups at 25 yards will save your life, but from Springfield a four-inch group is pedestrian. These complaints are as significant as you care to make them. The pistol is fast from the holster, controllable, and lifesavingly reliable.

10-yard group Magnus 200-gr.
SWC/Unique/780 fps............................. 3.5 inches
25-yard group
Federal 230-gr. HST .... 4.1 inches

Combat Course
10 Federal American Eagle 230-gr. ball
10 Magnus 200-gr. SWC handload
Ten Hornady 185-grain XTP
Rating 7
Malfunctions...0

Springfield Lightweight Loaded Model

This is one of my personal carry guns. The pistol features a long sight radius coupled with a lightweight aluminum frame, a startlingly effective combination. This pistol has digested perhaps 8,500 rounds of ammunition and continues to remain completely reliable. That is all we can ask. The pistol has the standard features of the Loaded Model, but has more flash due to the two tone treatment. After a day's work at the range you may be rubbing your wrists as the pistol is lighter than a steel frame pistol but the performance cannot be faulted.

The Springfield LW .45 has done yeoman service for several years.

The author often carries his LW Springfield Loaded Model in this DGL holster. This is a good combination, proofed and tested.

10-yard group
Hornady 185-gr. XTP .... 3.65 inches
25-yard group
Hornady 200-gr. XTP .... 3.5 inches

Combat Course
20 rounds CorBon 185-gr. JHP
10 rounds Horandy 185-gr. XTP
Rating..10
Malfunctions 0

Springfield Loaded Model

The Springfield Loaded Model was largely an answer to Kimber's introduction of a pistol loaded with features. Some of the first loaded models were fitted with Novak rear sights but not dovetail front sights. They were often GI guns with a few features added. We deserved more, and today the Loaded Model is often recommended as a best buy by sage shooters. The pistol is fitted a bit tighter than the GI pistol and usually is capable of greater intrinsic accuracy.

When you begin to look to acquire a good 1911 of the better type, the Loaded Model should never be overlooked. The pistol is readily available. It has a good warranty and an excellent service record. Let's look at the Loaded Model's performance. The Loaded Model is well worthy of use as a personal defense handgun. There are many Loaded Models in use and I recommend the type without hesitation.

10-yard group
Federal 230-gr. American Eagle.............. 3.5 inches
20-yard group
CorBon 230-gr. Performance Match 3.0

Combat Course
20 rounds Wolf 230-gr. FMJ
10 rounds CorBon 165-grain JHP
Rating..9
Malfunctions 0

A target grade .45 and Federal ammunition is a dream come true for those who pursue accuracy.

Springfield Loaded Model Target

This is simply a target sighted version of the Loaded Model. Our pistol showed remarkable fit and it is also tighter than any previous Loaded Model we have tested. The pistol demanded a modest break-in period, but that is SOP for such a tight pistol. Accuracy was excellent and in the end so was reliability. Does Springfield fit the target sighted pistols more tightly? Perhaps.

10-yard group
Hornady 185-grain XTP .... 2.8 inches
25-yard group
Hornady 200-grain XTP .... 2.15 inches

Combat Course
20 rounds Fiocchi 230-gr. ball
10 rounds Mastercast 230-gr. JHP
Rating...9
Malfunctions........................11 (all break-in related)

The plastic holsters provided with the target grade Loaded Model are not ideal for service but they serve as range holsters.

Springfield LW Operator

The LW Operator is simply an Operator type built on the Champion LW aluminum frame. This pistol displayed safety and beavertail grip safety fit equal to that of any handgun tested including the high-end pistols. Trigger compression is a smooth, tight 4.25 pounds. The sights were properly regulated for 230-gr. loads. This pistol proved especially accurate with the Hornady 200-gr. XTP. The XTP breaks 900 fps from the Springfield's 4-inch barrel. Considering the light weight of this .45, a lighter bullet that delivers a good balance of expansion and penetration is ideal. This is a formidable service pistol, especially when compared to polymer frame pistols of the same size and weight.

10-round group
Hornady 230-gr. XTP +P .... 4.5 inches
25-yard group
Hornady 200-grain XTP .... 3.25 inches

Combat Course
10 rounds Winchester 230-gr. FMJ
20 rounds handload using Nosler
185-grain JHP at 900 fps
Rating 10
Malfunctions..0

Springfield Novak Custom 1911

This pistol started life as a Springfield GI pistol and it is still a GI pistol, but it has been improved with high visibility, capable handgun sights. Novak's also tuned the extractor and generally checked out the entire upper unit for function. The end result is a classic that will stand the test of time. The pistol does all a combat pistol is supposed to do.

10-round group
Black Hills 230-gr. FMJ .... 4.0 inches
25-round group
 Black Hills 185-gr. JHP .... 2.9 inches

Combat Course
20 rounds Black Hills 230-gr. FMJ
10 rounds Black Hills 185-gr. JHP
Rating 10
Malfunctions..0

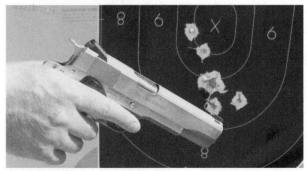

This is a rapid fire group with the Novak .45. Good performance from a legendary shop.

Springfield TRP

One of the more interesting developments during the course of writing this book was the Springfield Tactical Response Pistol. Let me quash a couple of myths concerning the TRP right off the bat. Since the TRP was intended as an affordable version of the Professional, some view the TRP as a "cheaper Pro." I fail to see how a pistol presently commanding over $1500 is a cheap pistol. Second, the pistol is sometimes referred to as a highly developed Loaded Model. While that would not be a bad thing, the truth is the TRP is much more like the legendary Professional than the Loaded Model.

The TRP is a remarkable combat pistol. Forward cocking serrations, a Smith and Alexander magazine guide, Novak sights with tritium inserts, and a match grade barrel all add up to excellent performance. But the pistol also features excellent fit and finish. The pistol is tight, so tight it invited a handloading program just to see what the pistol will do. And it will do very well. There are those who say beauty is only skin deep. If beauty is deep down as others state, you need a pile driver to find the beauty in a 1911. But this pistol is a beautiful shooter in both combat course and on the target range. The totality of features adds up to one great pistol.

There are drawbacks. One of my raters and close acquaintances is a salty old dog who speaks an archaic form of English not so familiar to younger readers. He readily commands invectives to make a sailor wilt and blush. He found the sharply checkered front strap the author found laudable a serious drawback. He holds his pistols in a death grip and cannot be convinced to lighten up, and in fact he shoots well. My only suggestion is that he wear gloves when firing my TRP. Accuracy deteriatates rapidly in low light and the pistol has tritium night sights to combat a fear of the dark. When moving quickly against multiple targets, you must have good grip adhesion. The pistol has that. This is not the pistol for beginners but rather a pistol that will challenge any shooter. If you find yourself limited by the TRP and need the Professional, you must be a hell of a shooter and I will find you a sponsor.

10-yard group
Mastercast 230-gr. JHP .... 2.6 inches
25-yard group
CorBon 185-gr. DPX .... 1.75 inches

Combat Course

10 rounds Mastercast 200-gr. JHP
10 rounds Mastercast 230-gr. JHP
10 rounds CorBon 185-gr. DPX
Rating 10
Malfunctions .... 0 (7,500+ rounds)

Note: We did experience a problem with a balky magazine, isolated the magazine, and deemed it unfit for service.

The Springfield TRP impressed this military intelligence officer so much he had to have one for himself. His personal sidearm is a Springfield/Novak custom.

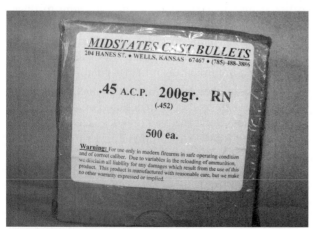

We have used many cast bullets in testing handguns. If a handgun is not accurate with cast bullets, then it will not be economical for practice.

Springfield Super Tuned Champion

This is not an old pistol by 1911 standards but a product of the Springfield Custom Shop about a decade ago. This is a very well turned-out pistol. The front strap shows hand checkering and the pistol was ordered with Heinie three dot tritium sights. The trigger action is as good as anything we have ever compressed on a 1911. Quite simply the custom shop got it right and this is a great shooting pistol and an excellent carry gun. There is something nice about a slide that says Super Tuned.

This is the most accurate four inch barrel .45 we have tested.

10-yard group
Black Hills 185-grain JHP .... 3.5 inches
25-yard group
Hornady 200-grain XTP .... 2.0 inches

Combat Course

10 rounds Zero 230-gr. JHP
10 rounds Wolf 230-gr. FMJ
10 rounds CorBon 200-grain JHP+P
Rating...10
Malfunctions 0

The Taurus PT 1911 has served well and while Taurus may be overly optimistic concerning a military contract we could do worse – and we have done worse!

Taurus PT 1911

Taurus of Brazil has introduced double action revolvers, self loaders, and single action revolvers into the American market. While generally regarded as bargain-grade handguns these clones have prospered enjoy a good reputation. Taurus has also introduced a number of original designs including the commercially successful 24/7 line of handguns. On introducing their own 1911 Taurus did not take the track of obtaining parts from other makers but makes every piece in house, including the magazines. The Taurus sports an impressive list of features, including

- *A full length guide rod*
- *High visibility sights*
- *Forward cocking serrations*
- *Thirty line per inch checkering, front strap, trigger guard and rear strap.*
- *Ambidextrous safety*
- *Beavertail type safety with memory bump*
- *Target hammer*
- *Lightweight trigger*
- *Lowered ejection port*

There are a lot of features, and the PT 1911 is destined to compete against the Kimber Custom II and the Springfield Loaded Model. In reality the reputation of these two makes the PT 1911 more of an entry-level pistol that will compete against the less expensive imports. The Taurus has shown reliability in our testing and has won acclaim as a good affordable 1911. It isn't fair to compare the pistol against a piece costing twice as much, but you must understand what you are getting or you will be disappointed. The forward cocking serrations are not as well defined as some pistols. They are rather broad with wide lands in between the flats. That's

okay, but again understand you are not getting a Rock River style slide serration. For the money, the Taurus works and works well. The pistol features a forged frame and slide which puts it head and shoulders above many of the rest in my opinion.

10-yard group
Fiocchi 230-gr. FMJ................................. 6.0 inches
25-yard group
Black Hills 230-gr. JHP............................ 3.5 inches

Combat Course
10 rounds Fiocchi 230-gr. JHP
10 rounds Hornady 230-gr. XTP +P
10 rounds Black Hills 185-gr. JHP
Rating...7
Malfunctions...0

The .22 Conversions

We mentioned the caliber conversions in the chapter on handgun calibers. There are several months separating this chapter and the other, and these conversions have been put to the test. I think that the results are worth publishing.

The Ciener performed as expected, with good reliability and a need for maintenance every 300 rounds. Clean the unit and lubricate it as required and you have a fine recreational shooter. Average accuracy depends on the frame it is wedded to. Some have better fit than others and the trigger action plays a part in practical accuracy. I have used the Wolf 40-grain solid in great quantities with good results and an average group of three inches or a little more at 25 yards. With the Winchester Dyna Point, the groups are a little less. This means little in practical practice.

The Wilson Combat unit is my second, and it is giving good results. The first unit featured either Wilson tactical sights or a close copy. The unit I am currently using features adjustable sights. It is very similar to the Ciener. Performance is similar as well, although the Wilson Combat unit seems to shade the Ciener slightly in the accuracy department. I am not going to fidget over a group of 2.75 inches versus 3.1 inches and swap the conversions about on a half dozen frames and test a dozen types of ammunition, unless the editor gives me a definitive assignment. Accuracy is good.

The Tactical Solutions conversion has given excellent service. Due to its construction, you can easily go far above and beyond the recommended cleaning schedule, although I do not recommend it. I simply tested it and found it reliable at over 300 rounds. Function was sluggish at 450 rounds. This type of sludge may actually damage a pistol so beware. The Tactical Solutions conversion unit occasionally produces a one-inch 25-yard group, but you have to work for it.

THE 1911 IS FOR EVERYONE

Chapter 26:

Over the years I have read many articles and heard many more comments, opinions and dissertations concerning the 1911 pistol. A common thread is the opinion that the 1911 is a more complicated handgun than most and that the type needs an extraordinary amount of diligent practice to master.

Respectfully, I feel that what is being expressed by such remarks is a preconceived notion rather than a learned fact. I agree that competency is gained by making brass. You have to know how far to push. I have kept students on the range longer than expected on occasion only when their exuberance called for it. Others take more time overall but less time in each training session. (The NRA recommends no more than 50 minutes followed by a break, and I agree.) Training time isn't something administrators appreciate. Military cadres agree when it comes to personal defense weapons

Whether for sport or for the challenge of testing your own marksmanship, there is not better handgun than the 1911. A dedicated shooter is tested and the novice will be challenged.

Having a run at the steel plates is exhilarating for its own sake. The 1911 is a fine recreational pistol.

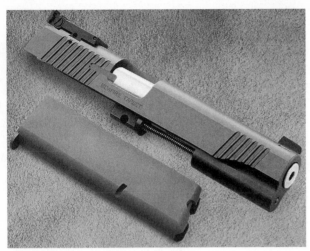

The Kimber .22 conversion is an essential element in the 1911 story. The 1911 may rightly be viewed as a system as well as a single handgun.

they view as less than essential. The military adopted a double action first shot pistol with a slide mounted decocker. As a trainer, I find this pistol a difficult pistol to train a shooter to a high level of proficiency with. Still, I train all shooters to the best of my ability and do not undermine their choice of handguns. They must build confidence in the duty weapon.

The primary advantage of the 1911 is its single action trigger. The 1911 system is superior by dint of its straight to the rear trigger compression. The trigger is easier to manage than any other for a trained shooter. The other primary advantage of the 1911 is hand fit. The pistol's trigger reach, grip span and grip circumference are ideal for most hand sizes. True proficiency at arms is more inspirational than operational with the other action types. There are good slowfire shots with every action type but in a demanding combat course, the 1911 will bring home the gold. The 1911 is more likely to produce good results on any course stressing speed, control and accuracy of repeat shots.

There are two competing types I will mention to prove I am not a doctrinaire but a realist. The Glock trigger system demands concentration whereas the double action first shot demands coordination; but the Glock has a superior trigger system to any double action first shot pis-

tol. The Glock's trigger press is short and light enough. The Glock has a lower bore axis than most pistols. The main criticisms of the Glock revolve around the lack of a manual safety, an unsupported chamber, and the girth of the grip in the big bore (.45 and 10mm) versions. Most modern pistols are a triumph of the technical over the tactical but the Glock has tactical merit. It is a second-rate pistol only when compared to a good 1911.

The only handgun I am willing to admit is as fast to an accurate first shot as the 1911 is the Browning High Power. A common thread among experienced shooters is that the 1911 is the single most reliable of handguns except for perhaps a carefully maintained Browning Hi-Power. I cannot disprove the point and will not argue, although I believe the High Power is less robust than the 1911 in long-term use. The Hi-Power is thinner than the 1911 and holsters well. Almost two decades ago when limited to the 9mm service pistol, I carried a Browning Hi-Power. I did not feel poorly armed except for the caliber. The bottom line, however, is that the Hi-Power is a small bore. The 1911 is a big bore. We keep coming back to the combination of the 1911 and the .45 caliber cartridge.

When I say the 1911 is for everyone I am making a bold statement. But I have collected my argument carefully. My contention is not without evidence. I believe that with a minimum of training a solider is better armed with the 1911 than with any other handgun. I believe that a soldier who has studied computers and missiles can be brought up to speed on the 1911 quickly, and I have done so with many, including a 17-year-old female reservist. Most shooters realize they may be in a critical situation. They quickly grasp the fundamentals of the pistol with diligence.

I strongly recommend that every handgun shooter take the NRA basic handgun class. That being said, if you are going to learn the single action there are trade offs and considerations. You must learn trigger discipline and the manual of arms. For casually interested shooters, the 1911 may not be the best choice. But I cannot imagine anyone who is only casually interested in saving his or her life. Just the same, I suppose they do exist. Don't be one of them.

Embrace the 1911. You life will be the better for it.

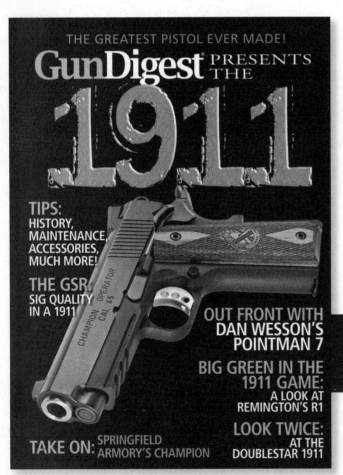